THIS FAR BY FAITH

"This historical reflection doubles as a primer for growing a church that reaches out to its neighbors, develops leadership from a variety of ethnic groups, and is built to last in a constantly changing culture."

Rudy Carrasco, US regional facilitator,
Partners Worldwide

"*This Far by Faith* is a must-read for congregational leaders who are seeking to build and sustain healthy multicultural ministry and desire to balance power and privilege in ways that empower People of Color."

Emmett A. Harrison Sr., lead pastor,
Oakdale Park Christian
Reformed Church

"Madison's unfinished story is about utilizing the gifts of women and men alike, addressing racism in the pursuit of diversity, and seeking community restoration in its neighborhood and world. It's a journey from which all can learn."

Steve Timmermans, executive director,
Christian Reformed Church
in North America

100+ Centennial Logo Designed by Tim Jen

THIS FAR BY FAITH

THE UNFINISHED STORY OF MADISON SQUARE CHURCH

The Editorial Team
Alfred E. (Al) Mulder and Jackie Venegas, editors
Don Bryant, Victoria Gibbs, and William A. Wiarda

Madison Square Church
1441 Madison Ave. SE
Grand Rapids, MI 49507

Chapbook Press
Schuler Books
2660 28th Street SE
Grand Rapids MI 49512
(616) 942-7330
www.schulerbooks.com

ISBN: 978-1-943359-63-9

LCCN: 2017937844

1. Congregational Mission 2. Christian Reformed Church History
3. Christian Worship 4. Church Leadership 5. Women in Church Leadership
6. Racial Reconciliation 7. Multiracial Church 8. Multisite Church

Cover design courtesy of Ed Van Poolen; front cover photo courtesy of Alfield Reeves.

Unless otherwise acknowledged, all other photos and illustrations are courtesy of former or current members or are property of Madison Square Church.

Thank you,
Madison volunteers!

This Far by Faith is dedicated to the thousands of Madison volunteers who, for more than one hundred years, have served God and His mission in His world. With dedication and faithfulness, your generous service has greatly blessed the members and friends of Madison Square Church and the people of the surrounding community in a myriad of ways.

This service that you perform is not only supplying the needs of the Lord's people but is also overflowing in many expressions of thanks to God. Because of the service by which you have proved yourselves, others will praise God for the obedience that accompanies your confession of the Gospel of Christ, and for your generosity in sharing with them and with everyone else.

2 Corinthians 9:12–13

Contents

1

Welcome to Our Story

BY AL MULDER

> Jesus prayed: "Now this is eternal life: that they know you,
> the only true God, and Jesus Christ, whom you have sent. . . .
> As you sent me into the world, I have sent them into the world."
>
> John 17:3, 18

A reluctant Moses, the great apostle Paul, an African American abolitionist, and a Dutch immigrant pastor had one thing in common: *They were all on a mission!*

God sent Moses on a mission to lead the Jews out of Egypt. Paul was commissioned to share the Good News of Jesus with Gentiles. Harriet Tubman, a former slave, made it her life's mission to abolish slavery. In 1913, the year Tubman died, the Rev. William P. Van Wyk published his rationale for starting a mission among his non-Dutch neighbors in the Madison Square area of Grand Rapids, Michigan.

Van Wyk was pastor of the Dutch-speaking Oakdale Park Christian Reformed Church (CRC), and his Dutch immigrant parishioners practiced what he preached. The fruit of their mission was Madison Square Church. Madison, now a centenarian, was the first Christian Reformed *mission* to be launched within the greater Grand Rapids area.[1]

One hundred years ago, all established Christian Reformed churches in the Grand Rapids area had been started and were populated by people of Dutch origin, the majority of whom still preferred the Dutch language in their homes and churches. In fact, the prevailing opinion was that the *church* was "for us," folks who spoke "our" language; and the *mission* was "for them," folks who didn't speak "our" language. Granted, there was the practical problem of language differences. Yet for many in that era, a separate mission was also a way for some CRC folks to maintain distance from those whom they considered spiritually and culturally inferior.

1. J. Vande Water, "The Story of Twenty Years of Home Evangelism in the Christian Reformed Church," *The Banner* (November 4, 1932), 952.

Al Mulder

In sharp contrast to such thinking and practice, Madison was the first continuing Grand Rapids area ministry started by a Christian Reformed congregation for the expressed purpose of helping others—the non-Dutch, if you will—come to know and love Jesus as their Savior and Lord.

Celebrating a Centennial

Early in 2013, Senior Pastor David Beelen convened a small working group to plan and prepare for a major celebration in 2014, the one hundredth anniversary of Madison's beginnings. Surprise, surprise! Not too far into its work, this Centennial Committee learned that Madison's mother church, Oakdale Park, actually had started Sunday School classes in the Madison Square area as early as 1912. Oops! Was the celebration going to be two years too late?

As more information was gleaned, the 1914 date seemed correct after all. Yes, Oakdale Park volunteers had started classes in 1912. Then, in 1914, Oakdale Park hired Elizabeth Smitter as its first worker for the mission. What's more, the first official meeting space for the mission was secured in 1914. So it's official: *Madison was conceived in 1912 and born in 1914.*

The Centennial Committee's first expectation was to plan a celebration worthy of one hundred years of God's favor. Co-chaired by Victoria

Don Huizinga, Centennial Committee Co-Chair

Her Name Is Madison

Our church's story has a wackiness to it—sometimes funny, sometimes painful, but always purposeful. God is knitting together in the womb of a 149-year-old Dutch mother a laughably impossible child; her name is Madison. God isn't finished yet, but she's destined for greatness.

By Don Huizinga*

*Don Huizinga, *Madison Creation Story* (New Members Class Notes, 2006), 1. In 2006, the 149 years was calculated in relation to the founding of the Christian Reformed denomination in 1857.

Gibbs and Don Huizinga, the committee planned and scheduled the bulk of its centennial festivities for August 2014. Former preachers came back to preach. Former pianists returned to play. Former choir directors were invited to direct. Stories were told in words and pictures. Young and old eagerly participated in the festivities, thanking God and enjoying one another in the celebration of this milestone anniversary (also see appendix B).

Victoria Gibbs, Centennial Committee Co-Chair

Victoria Proctor Gibbs attended Buckley Chapel and First CRC in her early years. She was the first African American to graduate from Oakdale Christian School and the second to graduate from Grand Rapids Central Christian High School. In 2008 she was among the first women to be delegated to the CRC Synod. In 2013 Gibbs was hired as Madison's Reaching In co-director. Five people call her Mom and thirteen call her Nana.

Some Kind of Booklet

As noted in the Centennial Committee's March 2013 minutes, "Pastor Dave would like to get pictures put together in some kind of booklet." Thus, alongside the planning of centennial events, work also began on a commemorative booklet. Archives were searched. A number of histories were gathered. Boxes of pictures were collected. Several writers were recruited. Outlines were drafted. As more time passed and more ideas flowed in, the booklet began morphing into a book. Specifically, co-chair Victoria Gibbs was inspired by a copy of *Fifty Years of Grace*, an attractively bound history of her childhood church, Buckley Chapel, now Grace CRC.[2] Yet, one year after Pastor Dave had proposed "some kind of booklet," there still was no clear flight plan, no designated pilot, and no lift-off.

It was then that Gibbs asked Rev. Al Mulder to consider piloting the project. They had teamed together previously as council co-chairs at Madison and in other ministry settings. Mulder, a thirty-year Madison member, had his name on a few books and was officially retired. He was still active in other ministry roles; but he agreed to move into the pilot's seat with the assurance

2. Roger Van Harn, et al., *Fifty Years of Grace* (Grace Christian Reformed Church, 2012).

A Path That Was Laid Out

Jayber Crow is a fictional creation of author Wendell Berry.* An orphan, Jayber had an early life that seemed to consist of blind corners and dead ends. Years later, working as a small town barber, grave digger, and church janitor, Jayber testifies to God's leading in his life. "I can remember those early years when it seemed to me I was cut completely adrift, and times when, looking back at earlier times, it seemed I had been wandering. . . . But now it looks to me as though I was following a path that was laid out for me, unbroken, and maybe even as straight as possible, from one end to the other, and I have this feeling, which never leaves me anymore, that I have been led."

This mirrors the unfinished story of Madison with its own times of trial and error, turbulence, and uncertainty. Yet, when recounting Madison's journey in retrospect, there is this clarity about God's good purposes and guiding hand, giving the sense of "A path that was laid out."

*Wendell Berry, *Jayber Crow* (Washington, DC: Counterpoint, 2000), 66.

that Gibbs and other able crew members were already on board to help bring the project to completion. That was in March 2014.

The Committee agreed that the crew needed a clear flight plan. Mulder and Gibbs, with the expert assistance of Madison member Ann Spangler, were tasked with developing a proposal for telling the Madison story in book form. The first guiding principle was that the story be *less* about Madison's centennial and *more* about God's faithfulness. A second guiding principle was to place *less* emphasis on an exhaustive history with people, places, and dates and *more* emphasis on unique ministry themes within God's Madison story.

With a draft flight plan in place, no one imagined that it would take another two and a half years to get this bird to fly.

Between the Covers

This chapter, chapter 1, serves as an introduction by recounting the occasion for creating *This Far by Faith*, and meets several other purposes. It provides a succinct summary of the nature and content of each chapter, defines specific vocabulary you will encounter in your reading, and introduces you to the editorial team.

Chapter 2, written by Senior Pastor David Beelen, whets the appetite by lifting up seven characteristics of the church he has served since 1982, with his first twenty-two years as one of Madison's co-pastors. Each characteristic adds to Madison's unique feel and flavor, and each provides a window into Beelen's personal passion for this particular church over more than three decades.

Chapters 3 through 5 are primarily chronological. Chapter 3 celebrates the missionary vision of Oakdale Park's Dutch immigrant pastor W. P. Van Wyk. It spans four decades of following the Spirit's leading among unchurched neighbors in the Madison area, a mission spearheaded by three lay leaders and one blind ordained minister. Chapter 4 picks up with the impact of White flight and northern migration in the fifties and sixties. This presented multiple challenges of continuing to minister in the same neighborhood but with different neighbors. The chapter concludes with a painful leadership transition. Chapter 5 is a firsthand account of the unfolding Madison story from 1968 to 1978. This decade includes strong pastoral leadership, official recognition as a CRC church, racial breakthroughs, a series of setbacks, and the beginning of a second wind.

Chapter 6 is both chronological and thematic, describing Madison's co-pastor era from 1978 to 2004. For twenty-six years, Madison's pastoral leadership consisted of a succession of three Black-and-White co-pastor teams, a highly unique arrangement for what proved to be a highly significant period in the Madison story.

Chapters 7 through 11 are also chronological and thematic, starting out in the late 1970s and then continuing all the way to the present. Chapter 7 recounts the transition to multicultural worship with a Black Gospel flavor, the introduction of Tabernacle Progression, and the expanded use of the arts in worship. It concludes with an overview of Madison's prayer ministry journey—from prayer teams to spiritual warfare to healing prayer. Chapter 8 highlights Madison's long-time intentionality around developing gift-based leadership by profiling a parade of persons who matured as leaders and as multipliers of leaders. Some bloomed right here at Madison; others were called to lead and multiply leaders elsewhere.

Chapter 9 documents the journey of affirming the role of women in leadership. Already emboldened by the precedent of female evangelists in its early days, in the 1970s and 1980s Madison became a CRC pioneer in ordaining women for the full use of their gifts—both in the council room and behind the pulpit. Chapter 10 offers insight into People of Color joining a still predominantly White church. It also traces the demanding work of White leaders and Leaders of Color learning together to navigate and mitigate the destructive turbulence of institutional and cultural racism, even in the church. Chapter 11 provides an updated portrait of Madison's original 1914 vision for loving its neighbors. This newer portrait begins with Madison adopting Christian Community Development principles; the portrait's frame is then enlarged to include expanded facilities, church planting initiatives, and transitioning to a multisite church.

The epilogue was authored by Darrell Delaney, campus pastor for the Madison Square congregation since 2014. Under the familiar and faith-affirming phrase, "leaning on the Lord," Pastor Darrell challenges the people of God to face the future prayerfully, humbly "trusting in his holy Word," in the confidence that "He's never failed us yet."[3] Other special features provide additional information on such topics as a summary timeline, quotes and stories of longtime members, Madison missionaries, the August 2014 Centennial celebration, references, and website resources.

About the writers: photos and brief biographies of the writers appear in their respective chapters, but additional words of explanation and appreciation are in order. First, all writers made their contributions as volunteers, as labors of love, *pro bono*. Second, early drafts of several chapters overlapped considerably with other chapters in both time and content, prompting some "exchanges" from one chapter to another. Third, the writers—to a person—were totally gracious about some of their best lines being attributed to others.

Regrettably, *This Far by Faith* is unable to recount all of the many dimensions of Madison's ministry that deserve to be recounted. There are no summary stories about ministry to children, the discipleship pathway, Madison's governance structures and policies, the Christlike work of the deacons and pastoral caregivers, the neighborhood prayer team, the church's finance teams, Madison's Care Group ministry, and more. Sincere apologies to those dozens of committed servant leaders and hundreds of passionate volunteers whose contributions have been—and are—so vital to Madison's overall ministry impact. Readers who are interested in obtaining more information about any of these ministry areas are invited to contact Madison Square Church.

A Shared Language

Over time, congregations generally develop a language or vocabulary that works for their time and context. This was true for Madison also, especially when it came to language around race and culture. A number of key terms took on shared meaning in antiracism conversations at Madison. Generally speaking, these language choices were informed and affirmed by respected journalistic and academic sources.[4]

3. "We've Come This Far by Faith," *Psalter Hymnal* (CRC Publications, 1987), 567.

4. Xavier University Office of Diversity and Inclusion, "Glossary of Terminology," accessed November 4, 2016, http://www.xavier.edu/diversity/Glossary-of-Diversity-Terminology.cfm.

- *AFRICAN AMERICAN* or *BLACK*. The term African American refers especially to persons whose ancestors were brought to America as slaves. Increasingly, the terms African American and Black are used interchangeably for all persons who trace their origin to Black racial groups of Africa. This book follows the pattern of those diversity and inclusion leaders who, as a show of respect, capitalize the word Black. This is the same as with Asian, Hispanic, Latino, Pacific Islander, and other people groups.[5]
- *CULTURE*. This term includes ideas, values, beliefs, language, behaviors, and treasures. Because a church as an institution tends to reflect the dominant culture of which it is a part, an authentic multicultural church seeks to reflect a variety of cultural expressions which regularly brings itself into conflict with the dominant culture.
- *ETHNIC*. This word is derived from the Greek word *ethnee* and refers to national or tribal people groups with a shared language, history, and geography. Ethnicity is not to be confused with race. For example, Hispanic and Latino are ethnic terms that refer to people from many national backgrounds, even though their shared *ethnicity* includes more than one *racial* identity.
- *PEOPLE OF COLOR*. The terms People of Color and Leaders of Color mostly apply to a self-naming and inclusive grouping of Asian, Black, Latino, Pacific Islander, and indigenous people groups in North America. In Madison's antiracism work, People of Color is the term of choice when referring to all people groups who do not self-identify as White. After the destruction of the Twin Towers in NYC on September 11, 2001, people from Middle Eastern countries also tend to be identified, and self-identify, as People of Color.
- *RACE*. This entire construct is a faulty and discredited scientific attempt by Europeans, especially in the nineteenth century, to assign superior worth and status to Europeans and inferior worth and status to everyone else, based on superficial differences such as skin color and head size. From an antiracism

5. Luke Visconti, "Why the 'B' in 'Black' Is Capitalized at Diversity Inc," *Ask the White Guy*, August 10, 2009, http://www.diversityinc.com/ask-the-white-guy/why-the-b-in-black-is-capitalized-at-diversityinc.

perspective, *racism* is more than personal prejudice. It is defined as race prejudice *plus* the misuse of cultural, systemic, and institutional power to enforce such prejudice.[6]

- *WHITE*. This racial term refers to all persons who do not identify as Persons of Color. Although White, Anglo, and Caucasian are used interchangeably in casual conversation, Madison antiracism leaders prefer the term White. At the nation's founding, Whiteness was a standard for citizenship. White supremacy has long been dominant in American history, and White privilege is real in American society today. The decision to capitalize Black and White, while controversial, was made to affirm equality and encourage mutual respect as image bearers of God.[7]

In addition to vocabulary around race, the reader will come across a number of terms peculiar to the Reformed tradition or unique to the era in which they occur. For those who may be unfamiliar with these terms, effort was made to define them when they first occur.

The reader also will note that pronouns for God, the Father, Jesus, and the Holy Spirit are all capitalized. This has been a long preference of the editorial team, both for clarity and out of respect for the Divine. Therefore, with the exception of references to God in quotations from the Bible or other sources, the reader will see You, Your, He, and His.

The Editorial Team

In the course of creating *This Far by Faith*, this writer was privileged to log hundreds of hours in volunteer flight time, many of those in collaboration with other crew members. With regularity we checked the instructions; once in a while we flew in circles; on occasion we hit turbulence; now and again we had to stop and refuel; and here and there we took on a new crew member or made changes in assignments. With grit and with grace, "We've come this far by faith, leaning on the Lord."

Personally, I am very grateful to God for the passionate and persistent labor of love that graced each member of the editorial crew throughout this journey.

6. *Understanding Racism Workshop: CORR Participant's Manual*, June 16–18, 2016. These formulations are attributed to Dr. Maulana Karenga, as adapted by Barbara Major and Michael Washington of the People's Institute for Survival and Beyond.

7. For additional reflection see Merrill Perlman, "Black and White: Why Capitalization Matters," *Columbia Journalism Review* (June 23, 2015), http://www.cjr.org/analysis/language_corner_1.php.

- ***William Wiarda*** initially gathered and guided staff and volunteers for beginning the work of researching and writing Madison's history. He drew on his communication skills to help writers be more coherent and better understood. In 2016, his focus shifted from editing to photo selection.

William A. Wiarda

William Wiarda became a staff member at Madison in 2002. As Director of Church Communications, he experienced fourteen years of Madison history firsthand and was exposed to many stories from prior decades. He has been blessed with a wonderful and beautiful wife, Jeannie, and four miraculous children: Moses, Josiah, Hannah, and Levi. William sees God at work in his life even as he seeks to give life to his family and others around him.

Don Bryant

Don Bryant grew up attending the First Evangelical Covenant Church in Grand Rapids, where he and Mindy married in 1976. Serving on Madison's staff since 2010 as Information Technology Manager, he coordinates the technical aspects of worship and the sound and projection volunteer teams. He is a graduate of Cornerstone University with a bachelor's degree in business management. The Bryant family includes daughter Breanne and Matt Zalewski, son Jacob and Staci with their son Liam, and daughter Britni.

- ***Don Bryant*** has a passion for family and local history, which attracted him to the idea of a centennial book project. In 2013 and 2014 he researched and amassed historical materials both for the centennial celebration and subsequently for informing and helping the writers in their work. Don rejoined the editorial team in 2016 to give critical and timely assistance with photos and other visuals.

Jackie Venegas

The Venegas family—Pastor Dante, Jackie, Andrea, Michele (Shelly)—followed God's calling in 1978 to leave New York City for Grand Rapids and Madison Square Church. Over the years at Madison, Jackie took on many volunteer roles including Sunday School superintendent, musician, heading the visual arts team, designing special worship services, serving on the worship committee, and bringing big pots of Puerto Rican rice to church potlucks. The family left Madison in 1996; Pastor Dante went to be with the Lord in 2007. Jackie has six wonderful grandchildren.

- ***Victoria Proctor Gibbs***, as noted earlier, presented a bold vision for the creation of this book and contributed to its clear storyline sensibilities. She eagerly encouraged the project while she was on staff and continued her involvement as a volunteer.
- ***Jackie Venegas*** joined the editorial team in 2015 and reinvigorated the project as it was appearing to stall in midair. Her knowledge and skill with words and grammar improved every writer's clarity and accuracy, and her experience as a pastor's wife provided deeper insight into the joy and pain of those who lived the story. The hundreds of volunteer hours she invested in this project were priceless! As a team, we thank God for Jackie's key role in helping shepherd this book to completion.
- I ***(Al Mulder)*** provided volunteer leadership and support to the editorial team from early 2014 forward, copiloting the home stretch in collaboration with Jackie Venegas. It was my privilege to see and experience these hundred-plus years up close through the stories told and retold by the writers and their sources. It also was my privilege to serve as the primary writer for chapters 1, 8, 10, and 11. I accept responsibility for the content of this book and am willing to provide further explanation as feasible upon request.

This Far by Faith

We've Come This Far by Faith is the title and first line of a well-known Gospel hymn. The lyrics and music were written by Albert A. Goodson

"We've Come This Far by Faith"

(1933–2003), a prominent figure in the development of African American Gospel music.

> In a manner similar to many of the Old Testament lament psalms, this text affirms God's saving power in the past; God's compassion and providential care for his people throughout history give us hope for the future. Thus the text becomes a milestone on life's journey: "We've come this far by faith, leaning on the Lord" (1 Sam. 7:12, "Thus far has the Lord helped us"). With confidence in the Lord's help, we can go forward and face "burdens . . . misery and strife."[8]

Made indelible for Madison by Pastor Dante Venegas, with his wife Jackie at the piano, *We've Come This Far by Faith* has stood out as one of Madison's favorites ever since the late 1970s. Its hopeful words and upbeat rhythm are a special encouragement to Christians of every race and culture. As *This Far by Faith*

8. "We've Come This Far by Faith," © 1965, 1995 Manna Music, Inc., admin. ClearBox Rights, LLC, http://www.hymnary.org/hymn/LUYH2013/341.

traces God's often surprising grace at work through always imperfect people, God's people are encouraged by how faithfully and creatively the Lord provides. Madison dares to face the future confidently, also in the spirit of this song's second line: "Leaning on the Lord." On behalf of the editorial team—Victoria, William, Don, Jackie, and myself—we are delighted to present this unfinished story to all past, present, and future family members and friends of Madison Square Church. As you read and reflect on *This Far by Faith,* may Jesus, the Head of the Church, inspire you to a clearer, bolder world-and-life witness for Him.

Welcome to our story!

Al Mulder
October 2016

About the Writer

After pastoring CRC churches in Kansas, Utah, and New Mexico from 1960 to 1983, Al served as church planting director for the CRC from 1984 to 2003. At Madison he has filled a variety of leadership roles from 1984 to the present. He has authored two study books on the Christian faith and a CRC case study: *Learning to Count to One*. Al and his wife Darlene have four daughters (the youngest in heaven), ten grandchildren, and fifteen great-grandchildren.

2

We've Come This Far by Faith

BY DAVID BEELEN

> "The Spirit of the Sovereign LORD is on me,
> because the Lord has anointed me
> to proclaim good news to the poor.
> He has sent me to bind up the brokenhearted,
> to proclaim freedom for the captives
> and release from darkness for the prisoners."
>
> Isaiah 61:1

As I entered the sanctuary, I began to weep. I did not expect this. I felt something that just overwhelmed me. I came back again. That was it. I was home."

Words something like these have been spoken over and over again by people who stumble into the sanctuary of Madison Square Church. There is nothing obvious to explain such a reaction—except the Holy Spirit. Certainly it is not the beauty of the building itself. It is unpretentious. Although one of the largest buildings in the neighborhood, it is a rather plain building inside and out. But once the people come in and the worship team begins to sing, they sense something. Something divine. Something of the Spirit.

A Spirit-Dependent Community

This is what happened to Melanie and me when we began attending Madison years ago, when it was still in the small chapel building on Lafayette. We were just married and looking for a church home; we found ourselves in tears again and again. As we worshiped with this small and diverse family, we were immediately and warmly welcomed into their circle. Our faith began to grow.

And we were challenged. We stopped worshiping mostly from our heads and included our whole bodies and our emotions. We were humbled again and again to see brothers and sisters in Christ with little means and little influence yet demonstrating a deep and large faith.

Senior Pastor David Beelen

David and Melanie Beelen were married in 1976. He was a seminary student and mentee of Pastor David Sieplinga and Pastor Dante Venegas from 1979 to 1982. He considers it a great privilege to have served Madison Square from 1982 to the present, as co-pastor for twenty-two years and as senior pastor since 2005. Kendra, Jackson, and Acacia, the Beelens' adopted children, were all baptized and made profession of faith at Madison. Grandsons Javion and Benjamin were also baptized at Madison.

When the church began to grow in the late 1970s, our New Testament theme text was Luke 4:18–19: "The Spirit of the Lord is on me, because he has anointed me to proclaim good news to the poor. He has sent me to proclaim freedom for the prisoners and recovery of sight for the blind, to set the oppressed free, to proclaim the year of the Lord's favor."

The members of Madison would wear leather strap necklaces with a small clay medallion resembling the image of a dove hovering over an urban landscape. Pastor Dave Sieplinga and Pastor Dante Venegas would often tell us, after some amazing answer to prayer, that "The Spirit is on the move at the Square." He was and is.

Part of what God has wired into our DNA is a Holy Spirit dependence. I regularly ask our congregation to "Listen for and obey the promptings of the Spirit." The Spirit is still on the move at Madison. God's power is evident in the simple journey of our history. Yes, *we've come this far by faith!*

Yet this history of leaning on the Holy Spirit and being open to His person and work was not all smooth sailing. Part of our history includes the resignation of Pastor Virgil Patterson, our first African American pastor, in part over his

Holy Spirit clay medallion

Madison Square Church

frustration with our church family's slow response to the Spirit's leading. Our history is full of both Spirit-empowerment and human failings.

has brought over the years. Ministry in the Madison neighborhood was initiated by the Rev. William P. Van Wyk, whose "real job" was

A Diverse Community

To help us celebrate our differences, I often say, somewhat in jest, that Madison resembles a group of mixed nuts. God has gathered together a remarkable variety of radically broken and wonderfully restored Jesus followers. While people often express appreciation for engaging worship and meaningful preaching, many also are attracted to check us out and hang around because of this remarkable diversity.

This diverse make-up has grown in part because of the leaders God

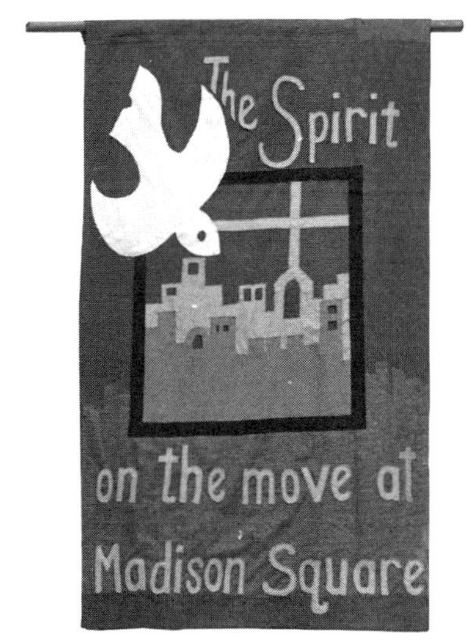

The Spirit on the Move

Mixed Nuts is a playful portrayal of Madison's diverse congregations and their leaders. The above visual is a playful portrayal of Pastor Dave and other ministry leaders, created by Madison's own graphic artist, Tim Jen.

Ministry Partners. For fourteen years, I was privileged to partner with an anointed and uniquely gifted man, Pastor Dante Venegas. "Dante was the straw that stirred the drink of multiculturalism in our church. . . . He drew racial patience into the church."*

*Chris Meehan and Jackie Venegas, *Dante's Dance* (Grand Rapids: Chapbook Press, 2011), 114.

pastoring the nearby Oakdale Park CRC, a large, established, Dutch-speaking congregation. Pastor Van Wyk felt called—simultaneously—to serve as an evangelist to English-speaking people from the hill country of Kentucky and Tennessee who had come to work in northern factories prior to World War I.

For its first fifty years, the Madison Square Mission was sustained primarily by ministry leaders who would not have been accepted in established churches: Bible college–trained but unordained evangelists and teachers—two females and two males. For around ten of those fifty years, the mission was also sustained largely by college students and volunteers. The lone exception to lay leadership throughout this fifty-year period was a fourteen-year stint (1948–1962) by a blind ordained minister whose opportunities were limited mostly by the shortsightedness of others.

From 1968 forward, ordained pastors became the norm. Madison's pastoral ranks included the first CRC African American pastor in Grand Rapids who was trained and ordained in other traditions, a Puerto Rican pastor from New York City (NYC) whose early training was in a penitentiary, and a Princeton Seminary–trained pastor from Liberia, West Africa—plus three CRC-trained White male ministers.

More recently, when Madison transitioned to become a multisite church, the first three pastors to launch new sites were an African American man from Alabama, a Puerto Rican man from New Jersey, and a Dutch American woman from Minnesota. With educational backgrounds ranging from some college work to a MSW degree to a PhD in immunology, all of them were prepared for ordination as commissioned pastors with the assistance of pastoral mentoring and independent study. Through these three leaders, along with the supervision and support of a White CRC-trained male minister, yours truly, God provided diverse leadership for a diverse multisite church.

In large part, Madison's mixed nuts character has simply reflected the rich diversity of the people God gathers. Early outreach to people from "the other side of the tracks" became a permanent part of our DNA. To this day, Madison continues to attract people whom some would describe as "other side of the tracks" people. This includes large numbers of people in recovery, prompting some to refer to our weekly worship services as "weekly recovery meetings." Recently someone suggested to me that our tagline ought to be "Looking for square pegs who don't fit in round holes." At the same time, particularly from the 1970s forward, Madison has consistently attracted an interesting mix of college-trained professionals with a passion for ministry in the surrounding community.

Over the years, Madison also has attracted racially diverse households. Recently we counted sixty-six couples in our congregation who are in a mixed-race marriage. In addition, Madison has enfolded same-race husbands and wives who have adopted children from other nationalities. These families, too, have chosen our church because their multiracial make-up as families

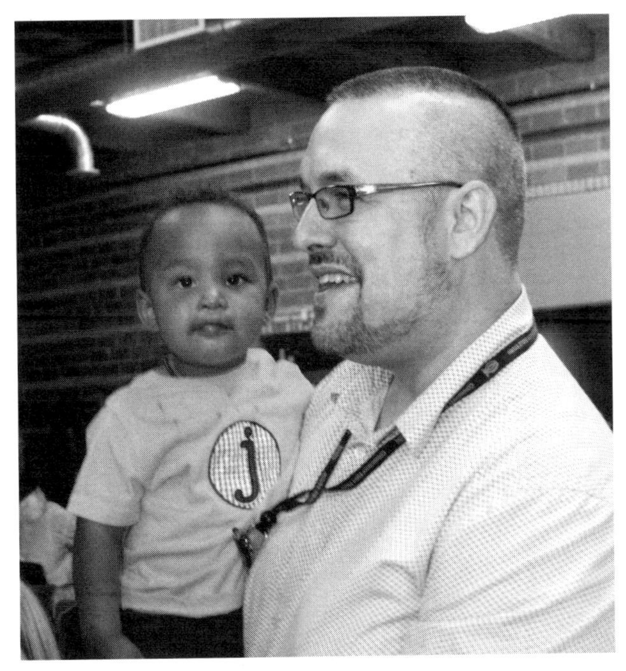

Jeannie and William Wiarda have one biological child and three adopted biracial children. Josiah is pictured here with his adoptive dad.

Diversity in Worship

makes it feel like home. They can be part of a church family where their mixed racial heritage is commonly shared and deeply loved.

This is an important part of Madison's DNA: Consistently seeking to break down racial and cultural barriers, bringing God's children together to celebrate both our similarities and our differences. One of our longtime ministry leaders, Laura Pritchard, recently married a man from Liberia. Other members of the African diaspora are finding a home in our church as well. On any given Sunday morning, our worship leaders will lead us through a medley of music ranging from Black Gospel to a traditional hymn to a contemporary Christian chorus in English or Spanish to a West African song.

A Healing Community

Another feature of Madison's unique DNA is that God has used our church to be a healing community. God seems to have given Madison this special assignment to heal broken lives, to bring mending to broken relationships, and to be a home for persons recovering from substance abuse. We are a church for "the bird with the broken wing." One of our former members, Tony Buschini, made a carving of a large bird with a broken wing nestled in the hand of the Father as a symbol of what God had done in people's lives through the ministry of Madison. The Spirit of the Lord continues to use Madison to bring recovery and healing.

When I first came to Madison, I observed the elders laying hands on people as they prayed for them after the worship service, sometimes also anointing them with oil. I even heard of the pastors praying for people to be released from the bondage of Satan's power. Now, decades later, we sponsor healing services for our people every third Sunday evening of the month. God is a healer and we have become, by God's grace, a healing community. Most often the need for healing is prompted by pain. We are far from a perfect church. As a church family, our dysfunction shows up regularly. Too often we need to be healed from the consequences of our sins, as I can readily demonstrate from examples of God's healing in my own life.

In the early 2000s, our son went into recovery, and we soon learned that our whole family needed intervention, counseling, and change. Melanie and I will never forget the outpouring of love, support, and grace that came to us day after day. Our care group, especially, surrounded us with their love. In our helplessness and need, we learned to become receivers when we were accustomed to being on the giving end. We were humbled by our need for community and acceptance. Our need and love for our church grew deeper, as did my compassion toward families struggling with addictions. God used this experience to help me become a better person and a better pastor.

The Bird with the Broken Wing

God's healing hand in my life is a work still in progress. God continues to use Madison Church to heal me of prayerlessness and self-righteousness, of overreliance on my intellect and my position, and of taking for granted my privileged childhood and home life. God has a way of appropriately humbling us when we rub shoulders with persons in recovery. If we're paying attention to God's Spirit, we soon learn we are all in recovery.

A Persevering Community

In the CRC denomination, which started in 1857, centenarian

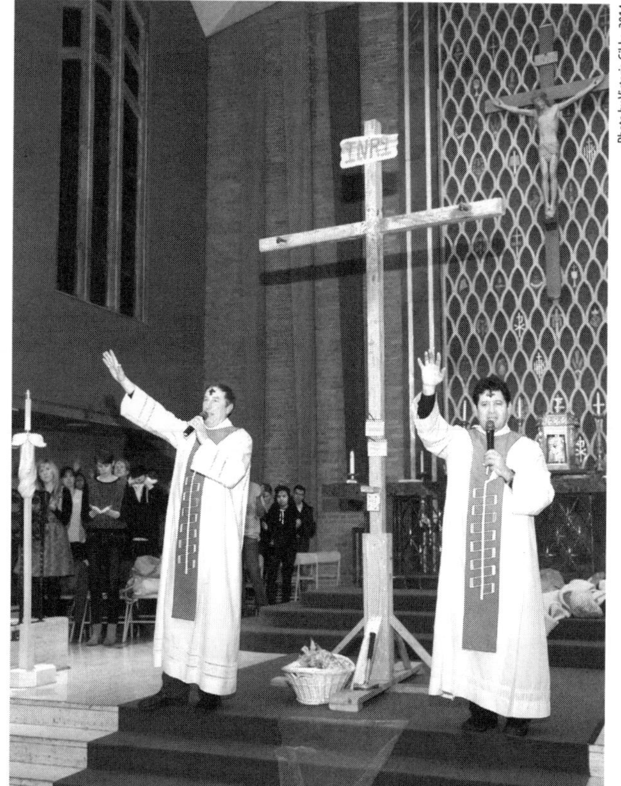

Photo by Victoria Gibbs, 2014

Pastor Beelen and Father Quintana, both clothed in traditional Roman Catholic robes, co-led the 2014 Ash Wednesday service at St. Francis Xavier.

A Centennial Surprise

As we approached our 2014 Centennial, God gave us a surprise! Saint Francis Church, a Roman Catholic Church just a few blocks south and west of us, likewise had been planted by a Northern European (Irish) ethnic group. They too began in 1914. They too stayed in the city all these years. They too, by God's grace, became multiethnic. They too are open to the working of the Holy Spirit. In February 2014, Father Jose Luis Quintana preached at Madison Square and Pastor David Beelen preached at Saint Francis. In March, the two congregations celebrated Ash Wednesday together at Saint Francis. We also celebrated Ash Wednesday together in 2015 and 2016. (For more information about the 2014 Centennial Celebration, see appendix B.)

churches are not all that unusual. What is unusual—and this is another feature of Madison's DNA—is our staying power in the Madison Square community. God has called us to remain right here and has empowered us to bloom where we were planted. Notwithstanding the radical social and economic changes in this community for generations, it is only by God's grace that we celebrated our centennial in the very same neighborhood in which our ministry was started more than one hundred years ago. Some Sundays the sanctuary rocks with the song "I Shall Not Be Moved." Indeed, we have not been moved.

There was one time in particular when Madison's "planted-ness" was at risk. In 1975, when Pastor Virgil Patterson resigned because of what he called entrenched racism in the denomination, and because of perceived resistance to the person of the Holy Spirit in our congregation, we were at a very low point. After he resigned, people started trickling away. The few remaining were discouraged. But God provided a women's prayer group that called us back to our roots in Holy Spirit stability. We stayed. We persevered. God kept us planted here.

Soon afterward, Madison called David Sieplinga as pastor, even though the congregation had no idea how it would meet a pastor's salary or other ministry expenses. Older members have told of the deacons visiting them on Sunday nights in their homes, asking for another check to cover the expenses in the coming week. Madison almost gave up more than once, but God never gives up.

I remember congregational meetings in which we struggled with having almost no off-street parking, our worship space full to overflowing, and long lines forming outside to get in. Yet when someone suggested that we consider moving out of the neighborhood for more space, the idea didn't even come up for a vote. No one wanted to think about moving. Even now, when Madison starts new congregations in other locations, our pattern has been to worship in neighborhood schools so that we can reach out to our city. We were planted in the urban landscape. God has called us to the city and we are staying put in the city.

Our staying power is rooted in the DNA of our Reformed theology. One of its teachings is the Perseverance of the Saints. Oh, how we need this biblical doctrine, which assures us that those whom God calls, God keeps. If you are a true believer, God will empower you to persevere in faith and obedience (not perfection) to the end and be saved. God will see to it.

Jesus said in John 10:27–28 that God holds us securely in His hands, and He does! "My sheep listen to my voice; I know them, and they follow me. I give them eternal life, and they shall never perish; no one will snatch them out of my hand." And Paul wrote in Philippians 1:6 that when God starts something, He sees it through. And He will! "Being confident of this, that he who began a good work in you will carry it on to completion until the day of Christ Jesus."

Calling

The word *calling* has two special meanings in the Christian tradition. The first meaning is personal and spiritual. God by His Word and Spirit *calls* people to believe in Him, to live for Him. The second usage has a particular meaning for a church. People drawn to Christian ministry speak of being *called*. A person prepares for ministry with the goal of receiving a *call* to serve the church. Churches recruit a specific pastor by issuing a *Letter of Call*. In turn, the pastor-elect acknowledges the *call* with a formal acceptance or decline of the *call*.

A Uniting Community

God's purpose for His saints is to live in racial harmony! The age-old animosity between Jews and Greeks revolved around nationality and religion. Today's world is estranged over similar divisions plus the real hostilities around racial differences. The fact that the road to unity is long and hard should not deter us. God does not abandon His purposes, and His saints may not abandon His purposes either. The Gospels and Epistles alike are filled with the exhortation to love one another (Matt. 22:39; John 13:34) and the expectation of being one new people in union with Christ (2 Cor. 5:17; Eph. 2:15). God never

"Racism Is a Goliath." Artist Jonathan Quist painted this image of Pastor Alton Hardy, prompted by a sermon in which he compared the sin of racism to the giant Goliath.

lets up on calling His saints—Blacks, Whites, Asians, Latinos, Natives, and others—to persevere in breaking down the walls of hostility.

We would like to think that two thousand years after Christ walked the earth, all sinful human hostilities would have gone away. Not so. Sin, including the sin of racial division, is not vanquished. It will keep on raising its ugly head until Jesus comes back. At the same time, we praise God for a welcoming church community that works hard at transcending cultural and racial divisions. The very fact that God sustains Madison's multiracial membership and leadership is a testimony to the Spirit's persevering work.

With thanks to God for not giving up on us, what are we learning from our struggles to persevere in this calling to unity in Christ? *First*, we need to keep on grappling with the effects of sin and pride in our lives. Along with acknowledging our shameful national history, we need to keep on learning about our own racialized hearts. Even in my role as a White pastor of a multiracial church, too often I have been tempted to take personal pride in what I am doing rather than being humbly grateful for the work God is doing in and through us.

Second, we need each other! Every time any one of us—whether a White person or a Person of Color—divorces ourselves from this calling of God to build a multiracial community of faith, it tatters the ties that bind us together. Just as enduring commitments within marriage and other relationships inspire the young and the faint of heart, abandoning commitments to one another as members of God's diverse family—for whatever reason—discourages all of us and makes the hard work of reconciliation only that much harder.

Third, how desperately we need a Savior! Only in Christ can we persevere. Racism is the Goliath that taunts the children of God to concede that racism is too strong an adversary to overcome. God chose his servant David to stand up to the historical giant and assert God's sovereignty. God also is sovereign over the Goliath of racism. How can we give a more eloquent testimony to the power of Christ and his cross than to persevere in standing up against racism, in the confidence that Christ perseveres for us?

A Sending Community

Being sent and sending also are an important part of our DNA. We were sent out as a mission from Oakdale Park CRC, and we have kept on sending people out from our congregation. Madison seems to be missional by nature. We grow leaders and then send them away. At first, this sending seemed to be almost accidental. We were not growing leaders on purpose; they just moved on. Sometimes their leaving was painful. We especially struggled with growing and then having to release Leaders of Color. To this day we continue trying to learn how to best prepare leaders with biblical grounding and the know-how to lead in complex, multicultural settings.

Pastor Dante taught us a lot about growing leaders, something that was instinctual with him. He taught me, his ministry partner and co-pastor, how to serve in a multicultural church. He was a natural disciple-maker. He would take seminary students and others along with him for hospital visits, prison worship services, and door-to-door evangelism. It didn't seem like he was intentionally investing in young leaders' lives; Pastor Dante just did what he did. He loved people and asked them to come along. Those who knew Pastor Dante don't have to dig very far into their memories to see the real deal: an unpretentious but very effective disciple-maker.

Shortly after moving into our present sanctuary, Madison also decided to plant churches. After a false start in 1992, we committed to a second start in 1995. We sent off around a dozen church-planting families to help start the Centre-Pointe Church.

Ten years later, Madison sent off my ministry partner, Pastor Sam Reeves, who felt led to return to Liberia. This time, rather than call another co-pastor to serve with me, Madison decided to raise up leaders from within, also as part of a plan to develop a multisite ministry. Our vision was to fulfill our mission by combining our passion for developing leaders and our commitment to planting churches in a way to expand our church's ministry to other parts of the city (see chapter 11 for more information about Madison's church plant and multisite initiatives).

God has graciously guided us into our new identity as a multisite church. And God is blessing us with even more leaders in the pipeline as we are increasingly intentional about developing leaders from within and also pursuing His calling to be a sending church.

A Redemptive Community

Madison was officially started in 1914 as a mission of a neighboring CRC congregation. For more than fifty years this tender plant, with the support of Oakdale Park CRC and later also Fuller Avenue CRC, moved from one nearby place to another like a tabernacle in the wilderness. Eventually we were planted, as providence would arrange, at the intersection of Madison and Oakdale.

Since then, history has begun to repeat itself. From these humble beginnings, God brought together this unique family and impressed on them His call to serve the city. In the providence of God, this mixed nuts family has not only survived but has also thrived. By the grace of God the originating congregation, now called Madison Church: Square Campus, continues to flourish in the same general area where it was started more than a century ago. It has been augmented by a second congregation serving six blocks to the north at the Madison and Franklin intersection, Madison at Ford, and by a third congregation serving several miles from the Square at Kent Hills Elementary School in North Grand Rapids, Madison North.

I am humbled by God's call to give most of my adult life to pastoring this beautifully diverse community of faith. I am overwhelmed with thankfulness over our Triune God's love for His Madison church family. Our history is redemptive: an unlikely combination of Jesus followers, determined to serve God in this part of the city for more than a century. We also anticipate a redemptive future: God continuing to put together surprising combinations and continuing to open up new pathways for serving Him and our neighbors.

Through the ministry of this church I have learned to weep in worship, to love those from other backgrounds, to be open to the Spirit, and to love God with my whole being.

We have come this far by faith. God has been faithful to us. And I am deeply grateful.

As you read this book, may God deepen your love and gratitude for Him, for His church, and for His people everywhere!

3

Reaching Across the Tracks

BY RICHARD ROCKWOOD

> "But you will receive power
> when the Holy Spirit comes on you;
> and you will be my witnesses in Jerusalem,
> and in all Judea and Samaria,
> and to the ends of the earth."
>
> Acts 1:8

An Adoptive Immigrant Parent

During the last half of the 1800s, thousands of people emigrated from the Netherlands to the western part of Michigan's Lower Peninsula, generally having endured ocean trips of a month or more. They moved because of economic hardship and also tension within the Dutch Reformed Church, which many of them believed had become too liberal.

Leaving the homeland could be heartbreaking.

> I left Hellevoet on June 9, 1856 at 4:00 a.m., when a steamboat took us to the North Sea. The island of Walcheren was the last bit of the Netherlands I could see, and when I lost sight of it, my heart nearly broke." *Jan George Zahn* (1856).[1]

1. As quoted in *Origins* vol. 8 no. 1 (Grand Rapids: Calvin College and Seminary, 1990): 6.

To ease the cultural and psychological shock of leaving their homeland, newly arriving immigrants tended to hold on to familiar practices such as their language, food, ways of doing things, and perspectives on life. For this Dutch-immigrant community, it was their shared culture and their own (*onze*) beliefs and worship style that held them together. They especially found unity in their faith because they "shared a deep inner piety and a familiarity with Reformed theology."[2]

The Oakdale Park neighborhood where they settled, nicknamed "Dutch Town," consisted mainly of immigrants from the northern

2. Linda Samuelson, Andrew Schrier, et al., *Heart and Soul, the Story of Grand Rapids Neighborhoods* (Grand Rapids: Eerdmans, 2003), 63.

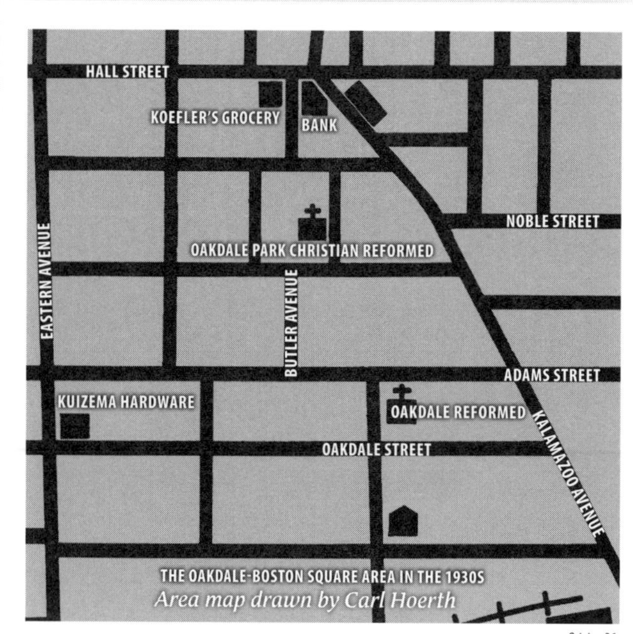

The Oakdale Park Neighborhood

Richard Rockwood

province of Groningen in the Netherlands. The neighborhood developed over a period of decades and was incorporated into the city of Grand Rapids in 1901. Like many other neighborhoods populated by immigrants, it was a walking neighborhood. "People lived, shopped, worked, worshiped, and played within a short walking distance of their homes."[3]

It was in this vibrant neighborhood that Oakdale Park CRC was established in 1890 as an offshoot of Eastern Avenue CRC. While inner piety and commitment to Reformed theology ran deep among these immigrants, for some their love of the Dutch language and culture ran even deeper. In March 1897 the Oakdale Park consistory, the church's governing board, refused a request for one of their Sunday School classes to be taught in English on the grounds that something important might be lost in the translation.[4] But by 1913, some immigrants had begun throwing off their "Dutchness" by shunning many practices such as "eating Leiden (sic) or Gouda cheese" or speaking "the abominable, lowly Dutch language."[5] Nevertheless, valuing the Dutch heritage and resisting change were still prevalent when this immigrant congregation began focusing its mission sights on the area known as Madison Square.

Moving Beyond the Boat

In 1914, some Dutch immigrants from a Dutch-speaking congregation in a Dutch-immigrant

3. Ibid., 57.

4. *Oakdale Park Christian Reformed Church 25th Anniversary* (self-published booklet, 1915), 7.

5. *Origins* vol. 8 no. 1 (Grand Rapids: Calvin College and Seminary, 1990): 36.

neighborhood in southeast Grand Rapids were observed offering afternoon Sunday School about a mile away, across the railroad tracks, to English-speaking migrants from Kentucky and Tennessee. How unusual was this?

For recent Dutch immigrants to reach out beyond their culturally insulated community into a neighborhood that was very different from their own must have been uncomfortable at best and perhaps even threatening at worst.

Yet this is precisely what Jesus said the Holy Spirit would do! Just as the Spirit empowered early Christians to overcome geographic and cultural barriers to carry the Good News of Jesus from Jerusalem to Samaria, so the Holy Spirit emboldened these Dutch-speaking folks from the thriving Oakdale Park CRC to share the Gospel with people living in the "poverty hollow" area of the Madison Square community.

Oakdale Park CRC

A Minister for Uncertain Times

Twenty-one years and five ministers after its founding, Oakdale Park called Rev. Willem (William) Van Wyk to serve as its pastor. Van Wyk proved to be a "new breed" of minister. Born in 1874 in Haarlemmermeer, the Netherlands, Van Wyk immigrated to the United States in 1893 with the goal of becoming an architect. However, when he ended up in Pella, Iowa, his vocational ambitions changed after becoming a Christian under the ministry of Rev. J. Manni. Van Wyk sensed a call to the ministry, trained at Calvin Theological Seminary, and was ordained in 1902. He served congregations in South Dakota and Iowa prior to accepting the call to Oakdale Park.

Rev. William P. Van Wyk

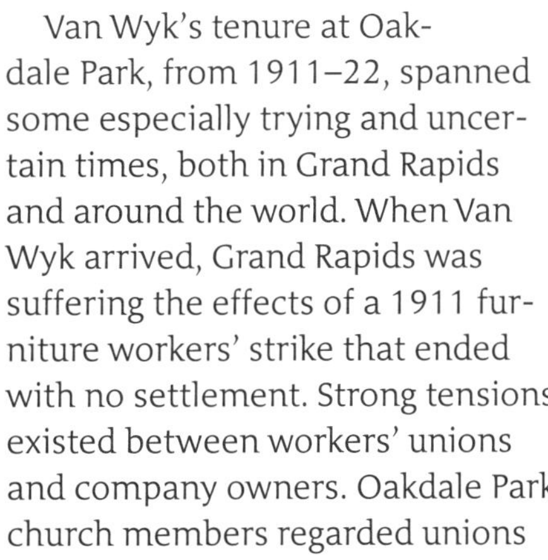

Van Wyk's tenure at Oakdale Park, from 1911–22, spanned some especially trying and uncertain times, both in Grand Rapids and around the world. When Van Wyk arrived, Grand Rapids was suffering the effects of a 1911 furniture workers' strike that ended with no settlement. Strong tensions existed between workers' unions and company owners. Oakdale Park church members regarded unions as secret societies and therefore opposed membership in them. Also, some company owners and supervisors were not above price fixing and other questionable business practices.[6]

In 1914, the official birth year of the Madison Square Mission, an April issue of the *Grand Rapids Herald*, the predecessor of the *Grand Rapids Press*, informed locals about the civil war unfolding in Mexico as the US Navy assumed a combat posture with the Mexican military at the port of Vera Cruz, a port the Navy held for five months. That same year, major European powers went to war with each other over the assassination in Sarajevo of Archduke Franz Ferdinand of Austria. World War I, later called "the war to end all wars," caused untold damage and the loss of millions of lives around the world.

In other parts of the world, discontent was spreading among the working classes and the poor. Vladimir Lenin, a Russian activist who was temporarily living in Switzerland, was agitating for a worldwide workers' revolution. Only a few years later, a massive Russian revolt would see the unimaginable overthrow of their czar and the establishment of communism in that vast country. Many Christians were convinced that Bible prophecies were being fulfilled and that the end of the world was at hand!

"The Church of the Lord Must Awaken!"

In retrospect, it is apparent that God had been preparing Rev. Van Wyk for such a time as this and had already brought him to the conviction that the work of evangelism in larger cities was just as important as supporting missionaries overseas. It was within this climate of urban restlessness and burgeoning global uncertainty that Van Wyk issued his groundbreaking pamphlet entitled *Stads-evangelisate, Waarom and Hoe* (*City Evangelism, Why and How*).[7] The timely, powerful, and challenging words of the pamphlet's introduction follow:

> We are living in a serious time. The powers of unbelief are rising up with more and more boldness. Only for those with a limited view, the battle between those who are for or against Christ has taken on the form of guerrilla warfare. He who looks further and starts to

6. Samuelson and Schrier, *Heart and Soul*, p. 81.

7. William P. Van Wyk, *City Evangelism, Why and How*, translated from Dutch to English by H. VanReenen (self-published booklet, 1913).

Photo credit, Grand Rapids History & Special Collections, Archives, Grand Rapids Public Library, Grand Rapids, Michigan

Madison Avenue Street Scene, Early 1900s

see the background of life discovers the seriousness of the spiritual battle among the developed nations. The forces of the enemy are growing by the day. Its ranks are closing tightly. At strategic points the enemy is concentrating in places where it sees a chance to gain the battle and remove the spoil.

It is clear that in the larger cities, which influence the world in every field, Satan establishes his strongholds. What can we do in these difficult times? This, that we deliberately follow the victorious King. That we as Christian warriors feel rising in our souls the will to fight. . . . When we hear the King's music, we must close our ranks. The church of the Lord must awaken to fiercer battles. . . . She is to go out in the larger cities in order to get engaged with the power of the enemy. She is to go into battle accompanied with the word of God as her banner. And even in the slums, where Satan has unlimited dominion, the Gospel must there be introduced.[8]

A number of pioneering Dutch-immigrant congregants from Oakdale Park had already started Bible classes in the area of Madison and Hall in 1912. However, the release of Van Wyk's pamphlet in 1913 leaves no doubt that these pioneer evangelists not only had his informal support but also experienced his formal blessing when their work coalesced and was officially recognized as a mission in 1914.

City Evangelism, Why and How articulated Reformed belief in the sovereignty of God and the Great Commission of Jesus with boldness and clarity. Van Wyk's writing

8. Ibid., 1.

William P. Van Wyk, the Man (1874–1941)

Although there is no record of Van Wyk having preached in English at Oakdale Park, he advocated consistently for reaching out to English-speaking neighbors by way of the Madison Square Mission. He also supported the 1915 founding of nearby Neland Avenue CRC as an English-speaking congregation.

An Oakdale Park member reflected on Van Wyk's preaching, "His sermons were so logically constructed and to the point that his expositions were easily remembered."* An appreciative Eastern Avenue CRC congregant wrote, "Because of his rugged personality and close association with the Men's Federation, he became a man's man. His wisdom and leadership were especially vested when he served Eastern Avenue after its devastating schism of 1924. . . . Van Wyk's healing presence caused 'the joy of angels to invade the consistory room on many occasions.'"†

**Oakdale Park CRC 75th Anniversary Book* (self-published, 1965).

†John Knight, *Echoes of Mercy, Whispers of Love, a Century of Common Outreach by the Christian Reformed Church* (self-published by Grand Rapids Area Ministries, 1989), 4.

Elizabeth Smitter

exuded Holy Spirit–empowerment not unlike Pentecost. Suddenly, sharing the Gospel with one's American neighbors was more important than preserving one's heritage or surrendering to fears.

Van Wyk's evangelistic leadership was practical and grounded. He "believed that the entire congregation should be involved in evangelism. He maintained that evangelism consisted of three emphases: Family visitation, Gospel meetings, and Sunday School. He also recommended that monthly evangelism meetings be held to arouse the congregation to the task."[9]

Practicing what he preached, Van Wyk wrote a pamphlet that was a trumpet call for Christians—at Oakdale Park and beyond—to rise out of their isolation and enter a new posture of embracing the challenge to share the Gospel. God was calling His church to embrace people everywhere with the love of Jesus, not just people who were thousands of miles overseas but also people who were right next door.

9. John Algera, *The Neland Avenue CRC* (course paper, Calvin College, 1974), 4.

On the Move . . .

In September 1914, Oakdale Park secured its **first** rental space for its mission, a storefront at 340 Hall Street, which was just west of Madison Avenue. Also in 1914, Elizabeth (Lizzie) Smitter was hired as the mission's first employee. Born in Grand Rapids in 1874, Smitter was forty years of age when she began working for the mission.

"At this time the immediate area of the intersection of Hall and Madison was noted for its fine businesses and shopping facilities. It was a thriving community, mostly

Urban Appalachians

Appalachians by the thousands came to the cities seeking work and a better life for their families. Concentrations of low-cost housing became temporary "ports of entry" for some families and long-term homes for others. . . . Some family networks were weakened or virtually destroyed by the moves from farm to coal camp to metropolitan areas. These weakened families became the concern of social agencies and church-sponsored outreach ministries.*

*"Urban Appalachians," *Wikipedia*, accessed December 14, 2015, https://en.wikipedia.org/wiki/Urban_Appalachians.

middle to upper class persons of the white race."[10] The mission workers had decided to *not* target the immediate and more prosperous area of Madison Square proper. Instead, they began reaching south along Madison Ave., across the railroad tracks, to an area occupied primarily by poor Whites from Appalachia. "There was . . . very literally [on] the 'other side of the tracks,' south of Madison, [an area] known as 'poverty hollow.' In this area lived a lower working class of whites. It was this group which was the primary target of what came to be known as the 'Madison Square Mission.'"[11]

This rented space at 340 Hall Street provided a stable meeting place for Sunday and weekday Bible classes for children in the surrounding neighborhood. Smitter, who only had an eighth-grade education, began mobilizing volunteer workers, organized afternoon Bible studies called "cottage meetings" for neighborhood women, led evening adult Bible classes, and was the principal speaker at the Sunday evening Gospel meetings.[12] She also visited many homes, especially the sick and shut-ins. One can only imagine the occasional awkward or humorous misunderstanding between mission workers with heavy Dutch accents

Madison Square Gospel Mission

10. Douglas Vander Schaaf, *Square Roots: The Story of a Changing Church in a Changing Community* (course paper, Calvin College, 1978), 2.

11. Ibid.

12. Vander Schaaf, *Square Roots*, 3.

A Second Parent

In 1925, thirty-nine members from Oakdale Park CRC started Fuller Avenue CRC. The administration and oversight of the Madison Square Mission then fell under the jurisdiction of a supervisory committee with representatives from both churches.

Fuller Avenue CRC

and the children of factory workers with Appalachian accents.

From 1918–29, the mission functioned from its **second** location, which was on the second floor of the Stiles' Hall at 1209½ Madison, just south of Hall.[13] The mission was recognized as growing roots and was reported in the CRC's 1918 Yearbook as follows: "Oakdale Park Missions—Madison Square Mission, Miss E. Smitter in charge, Stiles' Hall, Madison Ave. near Hall S.E." During the 1920s, the Madison Square shopping area provided various forms of public entertainment in vacant lots and on street corners, including clowns, acrobats, and street musicians. The mission also appealed to the public in this manner by holding outdoor meetings at various locations during the summer months. They made use of a portable pump organ, clarinet, and accordion for singing hymns and special music. People passing by could stop and listen or participate as they chose.

During the 1930s, outside meetings were held near Cottage Grove Street, again as a means of attracting more people to the mission. The mission also conducted vacation Bible schools lasting three weeks in length, with more than sixty children attending from the local neighborhoods. Throughout this decade (1929–40), the Mission was at its **third** location, a Lodge Hall at 1164 Madison.

During the twenty years that Elizabeth Smitter worked with the Madison Square Mission, many people responded positively to the Gospel. As Smitter reflected in 1932, "Our first meeting consisted of five teachers and eight scholars—after a great deal of canvassing. Undaunted, we opened the doors again the following Sunday and the attendance increased." She also reported that throughout the years, "We have an average enrollment of about 100—sometimes a few more, at others a few less."[14]

13. Ibid., 2–3.

14. Elizabeth Smitter, "The Story of Twenty Years of Home Evangelism in the Christian

Photo courtesy of Mary Boes

Madison Square Mission Sunday School Picnic, 1917

Smitter concluded on a note of faith, hope, and praise:

> We cannot estimate what the results of the street preaching, cottage and mission hall meetings, Sunday school, and personal work are in souls saved for eternity; but we believe we may look forward to meeting many among the redeemed who came to the knowledge of themselves and the way of salvation through the work at Madison Square. . . . What a precious blessing it is to know that God has chosen human beings to bring the name of Jesus to a sin stricken world and that the Holy Spirit sanctifies their poor efforts to the glory of the Triune God.[15]

Reformed Church," *The Banner* (November 4, 1932), 952.

15. Ibid.

Under New Management

After Smitter's departure in 1933, the work was continued by volunteers from the Oakdale Park and Fuller Avenue churches, assisted by students from Calvin College. In the early 1940s, congregational volunteers were assisted by students from the Reformed Bible Institute (now Kuyper College). In 1941, the mission moved to its **fourth** location which was on the second floor of a Lodge Hall at 1163 Madison, across the street from the previous location.[16]

In 1942, the supervising churches hired Tielus (Tom) Afman from Denver, Colorado, as the mission's first full-time lay evangelist. Afman was born in the Netherlands in April 1892, the first of five children. He immigrated to Kalamazoo,

16. Vander Schaaf, *Square Roots*, 4–5.

Photo courtesy of Wilma Lotterman

Tom and Freda Afman

Michigan, with his family in 1911 and married Fredrica (Freda) Van Dam in 1915. The entire Afman family soon relocated to Denver, where Tom's father and one brother died of tuberculosis. They were members of First CRC in Denver, and Afman worked part-time as a salesman and part-time with the Champa Mission there. Gifted in leadership, evangelism, and visitation, Afman coordinated the work of the Madison Square Mission.

David Taylor, a Madison member in the 1990s and 2000s, knew Afman personally. The Taylor family attended the mission during the Afman years, and young David experienced him as someone who looked out for kids in the neighborhood. Taylor recalled how he earned his first income—50 cents a week—as a young janitor at the mission. Afman kept track of this young helper, teaching him how to clean well and even helping him start a savings account. Taylor looks back at his relationship with Afman as foundational to his long life of faith.[17]

Afman submitted regular monthly reports to the supervising board regarding his evangelistic work and the mission's progress. He served the Madison Square Mission from 1942–48.

One year after Afman had begun working with Madison, the sponsoring churches hired a second staff worker, Gertrude Holkeboer, a native of Holland, Michigan. Although Afman was the Mission's superintendent and Holkeboer was the full-time assistant, her responsibilities were also ministerial in nature:

Betty Lotterman, a daughter of Tom and Freda Afman, was sixteen when she moved to Grand Rapids with her family. Betty, with her parents and her younger sister Sylvia, lived in an upstairs apartment near Eastern and Alexander. Betty recalled teaching Sunday School and attending worship services in the mission's storefront location at Madison near Crawford. Betty also remembered when Virginia Tummill (later Timmer), a local teenager, confessed her faith in Jesus under her father's ministry.

Now living in Raybrook Estates in Grand Rapids, Betty spoke of her father with admiration. She described him as a very enthusiastic, pleasant, kind, and loving man. After Madison, Afman served as the evangelist with Grace Chapel in Bellflower, California. He died unexpectedly in 1953, at age sixty-one, while serving in a similar position at Beacon Light Chapel in Racine, Wisconsin.*

*Betty Lotterman, personal interview with Al Mulder, May 20, 2016.

17. David Taylor, personal interview with Bob Schuyler, April 2015.

shepherding people on a personal basis, being active in calling, conducting Bible classes, and leading Gospel services.

In 1945, with both Afman and Holkeboer on staff, the Mission moved to yet a **fifth** location, which was a storefront at 1230 Madison, one block south of Hall Street on the corner of Madison and Crawford.

The 1947 CRC Yearbook listed Afman as superintendent of Madison Square Mission; in 1948 he moved to a mission in California. Meanwhile, Holkeboer continued working with Madison as solo-staff for a period of time, and then worked with the Rev. Walter Dubois for eleven years—the majority of those years as a volunteer. Given the traditional limitations on the role of women in the 1940s and 1950s, it is remarkable that Holkeboer not only led Gospel services but also was known to preach. The issue of her "preaching of the Word" was raised and discussed by the supervising board, but no restrictive or contrary action was taken.[18]

Photo credit, Grand Rapids History & Special Collections, Archives, Grand Rapids Public Library, Grand Rapids, Michigan

A new street light is installed in front of the Madison Square Gospel Center on the corner of Madison and Crawford.

We Came to Jesus: Now What?

New believers were God's answer to many prayers. Yet in the mission's early decades, these new believers also raised an interesting practical problem: Where did they go from here? Madison pastor Walter Dubois later explained this period in Madison's history this way:

> The goal of the Mission was to bring people to Christ, but the Mission was ill-equipped to offer opportunities for continued and extensive growth in the faith. It was difficult for these new Christians to attend Oakdale Park because the services were still conducted in the Dutch language. There were also individuals from the sponsoring church who did not appreciate the presence of the Mission's new converts. The result

Gertrude Holkeboer

18. "Oakdale Park CRC Council Minutes," January1948.

Getting Organized

Organized and *organization* are terms commonly used to describe congregations when they are officially recognized as member churches in the CRC. A *mission chapel* functions under the supervision of a neighboring church or churches. By contrast, an *organized church* has its own council, consisting of elders, deacons, and one or more ministers. And this newly-formed council is primarily responsible for its own governance, ministry, and financial support.

was that these converts were encouraged to become members in churches of other denominations in the area[19]

This placed the mission in the crosshairs of a debate over its specific role and function in the overall ministry of the church. The original intent for the mission was to "stick to their knitting," that is, to lead unchurched people to Christ. When people came to faith, they were required to profess their faith before the elders of the sponsoring church and then expected to become members there. Initially, as Dubois explained, the Dutch language was a barrier to membership. But even as the language barrier diminished, the expectation of new believers leaving the mission to join the sponsoring church was met with resistance—both by the mission and by the new believers. These new believers were vital to the life and ministry of the growing mission.

Eventually, as Madison and other CRC-sponsored missions and chapels in the city began to demonstrate their ability to look and act like "real" churches, they were encouraged by their sponsoring churches to request permission to organize and be officially recognized as Christian Reformed churches.[20]

Looks and Acts Like a Church, but . . .

In December 1947, the oversight committee of the Madison Square Mission made two important decisions. First, it went on record declaring that the "ideal of the Mission was to eventually become an organized church."[21] Second, they decided that the next mission supervisor/coordinator needed to be an ordained minister.

Although it is not known if these decisions led to Afman's leaving, within months of his departure the supervising churches called the Rev. Walter Dubois as Madison's new pastor. Born in Hilversum, the Netherlands in 1912, Dubois immigrated to America with his family in 1914. He had lived in the Madison Square area and was familiar with the mission and its work in the community. In fact, as a young man he had been active in door-to-door calling for the mission. In the 1930 census he listed his work as a meat

19. Vander Schaaf, *Square Roots*, 3.

20. Al Mulder provided this analysis of the CRC's developing missiology.

21. Paul James, *Madison Square on the Move: The Saga of a Little Church with a Big Vision* (course paper, Calvin College, 1982), 3.

cutter; in the 1940 census he was listed as a "house-to-house salesman of literature." Dubois graduated from Calvin Seminary in 1944 and served one other pastorate before coming to Madison in 1948.

Although Dubois had suffered the loss of his sight in 1936, thanks to his wife who was his constant companion and guide, he was able to carry on *all* his duties with the mission. He was a soft-spoken and gentle man whose sermons were delivered in a conversational style. Because he was ordained, the mission also could conduct baptisms, weddings, and funerals, which more fully met the needs of the surrounding community.

This increase in church activities and functions prompted a growing discontentment about the temporary nature of their rented facilities; it even prompted discussion between Dubois and attendees about how a facility of their own would be beneficial for the mission. Worshiping in rented facilities was restricting because there were always limits to what they could do.

Dubois did not like the storefront; he felt it looked too much like a rescue mission. He, and the people with him, wanted something that looked more like a church and would be suitable for weddings and funerals. Dubois wrote up these sentiments and recommended a

Photo courtesy of Lori Dubois Banaszak

Alice and Rev. Walter Dubois, with his father Anthony in the center

new building that would resemble a traditional church building. Disliking the name "Mission," he also recommended that the name Madison Square Mission be changed to Madison Square Chapel.[22] A location was purchased at 1164 Lafayette Avenue, just north of Hall Street. At last, the wandering mission was to have its own home.

Plans were finally in the works for building a chapel that would look more like a church. Three years had passed since the supervising committee affirmed "the ideal" that the chapel would become an organized church. In early 1951 therefore, right on cue, Dubois also recommended to the committee that the chapel take steps toward becoming an organized church.

22. Vander Schaaf, *Square Roots*, 5–6.

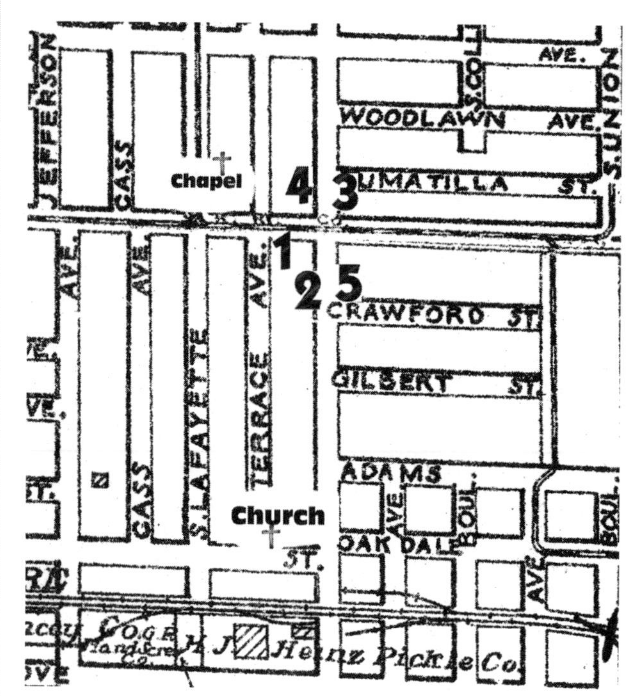

Madison's Mission, Chapel, and Church Locations: 1. 340 Hall St; 2. 1209½ Madison Ave; 3. 1164 Madison Ave; 4. 1163 Madison Ave; 5. 1230 Madison Ave; Chapel, 1164 Lafayette; Church, 1441 Madison Ave.*

*Ogle, Geo. A. "Outline Street Map of the City of Grand Rapids." Standard Atlas of Kent County, Michigan. Chicago, Geo. A. Ogle & Co., 1907. Annotated by Don Bryant.

However, contradicting its "ideal" decision of four years earlier, the committee adopted a more cautious "statement of policy" that recommended slowing the process toward organization.

The statement read, in part:

> We go on record as believing that we must be very slow in our work at Madison Square in moving away from the idea of a neighborhood Gospel center in the direction of an organized church or a so-called branch church, that the primary function of our Gospel center shall continue to reach out to the unconverted, that the administration of the sacraments at the Gospel center shall for the present be done in order to conserve and consolidate the results of our work, always with the idea that when it is warranted the converts may be organized into a church of their own and that this shall not take place until such a time as the members at our Gospel center will be of such a number and character as to be able to sustain such organization.[23]

While this response no doubt frustrated Dubois and others, it was not inconsistent with other prevalent viewpoints about the nature and purpose of mission chapels: "The mission is not a church; it is a channel through which people are brought into the church."[24]

The new Madison Square Chapel building was completed in 1951, but it certainly was not the only new construction in the area. The "poverty hollow" area was also changing. Several factories had been built recently or were in the process of being built. This resulted in evicting many residents who had been the focus of the chapel's ministry at that time.

23. Vander Schaaf, *Square Roots*, 7.

24. John Vande Water, *Miracles in Forgotten Streets* (Grand Rapids: Eerdmans, 1936), 2.

Madison Square Chapel at 1164 Lafayette Ave.

Most of the residents in the Madison Square area were now middle class whites, "a more contented and satisfied group of people." Because they had no pressing needs, their response to the Chapel was not as great. Dubois felt a certain amount of frustration working in an area which had been "burned out." That is, people heard the Gospel before and it seems to be falling on deaf ears. Many of the area residents were also members of (or influenced by) the Lodges in the area, or an organization known as Unity. Both of these prescribed a type of secular Christianity with an emphasis on good works.[25]

These radical changes in the target community prompted the chapel to reset and expand its outreach focus. Despite its disappointments and challenges, the chapel's outreach ministry continued to yield fruit, with a yearly rise in membership that reached its peak in 1958.[26]

In 1959, once again Dubois felt it was time to organize and recommended that the Madison Square Chapel now take the necessary steps. However, once again both supporting churches and their pastors disagreed. Without their support it would have been useless for Dubois to appeal the matter to the classis.

For the second time in a decade, decisions of the supervisory leadership made the already challenging work of chapel ministry even more challenging and complicated. With the rejection of Madison's request to organize, the chapel continued as before. Dubois also continued with the chapel as before—for three more years.

God in His ever-surprising grace continued to use the chapel's outreach to bring new converts to

A **classis** consists of a group of neighboring Christian Reformed churches whose representatives meet together periodically for official purposes. A request to become organized requires classis approval.

25. Vander Schaaf, *Square Roots*, 6–7.
26. Ibid, 7.

the faith. And the chapel faithfully educated the converts in Christian doctrine and Christian Reformed expectations. This included the expectation of converts publicly professing their faith before one of the supervising churches—not at the chapel. "In this state of affairs, public professions were typically sad, draining and frightening experiences rather than joyful, exuberant experiences as any conversion should be."[27] Despite the expectation of the supervising churches that the converts would join them, many converts chose to remain at the chapel following their public profession of faith.

Who Would Have Thought . . .

The curious course of the Madison Square Mission-Now-Chapel often seemed strange and even surprising. Who would have thought . . . a pamphlet written by a Dutch immigrant architect-wannabe-turned-preacher would shift a congregation's mission sights to its own backyard? Who would have thought . . . an immigrant congregation would reach out so unwaveringly to people so different from themselves? Who would have thought . . . God would use women to lead Madison in bringing untold numbers of people to Himself? Who would have thought . . . God would use a former meat cutter, a former door-to-door salesman, and a blind minister to lead the chapel to a position of promise?

And so it was that Madison Square Mission, begun in 1914, became Madison Square Chapel in 1951. After fourteen years of diligent missionary leadership, Rev. Dubois left for another charge in 1962. Throughout these early years, nearly five decades in all, faithful people of God continued to move ahead in humble and unconventional ways, seeking and obeying the leading of the Holy Spirit.

About the Writer

Rev. Richard Rockwood began attending Madison after two female Calvin students recommended Madison to his friend who was vacationing in Mexico. Rockwood, a retired RCA minister, joined Madison in fall 2007. He has been involved in adult Sunday School classes, writing devotionals, doing video and still photography of church activities, and attending a Tuesday evening men's community Bible study. His wife, Cindy, joined Madison in 2012, and together they have been care group leaders.

27. James, *Madison Square on the Move*, 5.

4

Radical Change and a New Direction

BY BOB SCHUYLER

"I have other sheep that are not
of this sheep pen.
I must bring them also.
They too will listen to my voice,
and there shall be one flock
and one shepherd."

John 10:16

The 1950s and 1960s brought dramatic social change throughout the United States. In the Madison area, the racial makeup was shifting dramatically from a predominantly White population of Appalachians and other groups to a growing African American population.

In the American South and elsewhere, the 1960s began with peaceful, non-violent demonstrations led by Dr. Martin Luther King Jr., protesting Jim Crow laws and resisting other forms of racial discrimination. Then came this incredible and unforgettable five-year period: President John F. Kennedy was assassinated in 1963, the Watts community in Los Angeles was decimated by riots in 1965, the destructive five-day 12th Street riot in Detroit occurred in 1967, and Dr. King and Robert Kennedy were assassinated in 1968. A movement that began with peaceful demonstrations erupted into anger, violence, and turmoil on urban fronts everywhere. The threat of racially charged bloodshed and destruction had engulfed many residential neighborhoods in the country—including Grand Rapids—with a spirit of fear and foreboding.

In this context the Spirit of God tested and strengthened Madison's staying power. God also used this period of radical social change, more than any other factor during Madison's first fifty years, to focus its vision and direction for future ministry.

Bob Schuyler

Marty and Lois Meyne

God's Design

Madison was created right from its very beginning to reach out to the neighborhood. It was never a church established to serve primarily Christians but was created to do evangelism in a specific area that was perceived as unchurched and needy. God put into Madison's DNA that we were located where we are, not by circumstances or accident, but by God's design; and along with that came the idea that we are to stay there unless God Himself tells us to move.*

Marty and Lois Meyne

*Marty and Lois Meyne, email interview, April 12, 2015

Racial Change

In the course of these two decades, the African American population in the Madison Square area swelled from 20 percent to nearly 80 percent and was still growing. Conversely, commercial activity in the area all but dried up. Whites were migrating out to new suburbs in large numbers. This, in turn, prompted many congregations to also move out of the city, to larger and newer facilities, forcing those who remained to radically revise their ways of doing ministry.

Not so with Madison Square Chapel, which had started as a cross-cultural ministry: White Dutch immigrants interacting with White Appalachian poor. Not bound to fixed traditions or a single ethnic mold, Madison's leaders and members were uniquely positioned to respond to this new wave of cultural and racial change. Over the years, and under the urging and guidance of the Holy Spirit, compassionate and flexible leaders helped develop a growing commitment to cross-cultural ministry. In small numbers initially, and ultimately in the hundreds, God moved leaders and members alike to adopt, nurture, and sustain this vital commitment.

In September 1951, on the front end of seismic social change, Madison secured its first permanent location. Under the leadership of Pastor Walter Dubois, the congregation moved into its new chapel building at 1164 Lafayette SE, near the intersection of Hall and Madison. For the decade that followed, Madison Square Chapel remained a relatively stable but also relatively small congregation, and it was still dependent on its sponsoring churches for direction and support. Along with its sponsors, the chapel was faced with two overarching questions: One, should the congregation (a) welcome, (b) tolerate, or (c) reject interaction with its Black neighbors? And two, if Madison did choose to welcome this interaction, how would it cope with the conflictive and destructive effects of the community's social displacement, economic diminishment, housing degradation, and all the other negative human effects of civil and racial injustice?

These large questions are answered, at least in part, in the last half of this chapter. Before proceeding to those answers, however, it is important to understand and appreciate the cultural context in which these critical questions were being addressed.

Black Migration, White Flight, and Redlining

During the 1950s and 1960s, in the aftermath of World War II, many cities of varied sizes went through dramatic societal changes. The post–World War II economy had shifted to peacetime rebuilding and new levels of personal prosperity. In proportions similar to the Great Migration from other continents that followed World War I, a virtual flood of African Americans left the South for employment and a better life in northern and western cities of the United States.[1] Chasing the dream, many thousands of African Americans from Georgia, Alabama, and Mississippi flocked to burgeoning industrial centers like Chicago, Detroit, and even Grand Rapids.[2]

These major moves were driven by expectation and hope, yet too often were met with frustration and despair. This was true for many who migrated north and also true for the cities that received them. African Americans and their families needed places to live. "The conditions they confronted in the North were improved but still full of hardship. Racism and prejudice abounded."[3] Real estate and lend-

1. "The Great Migration: The African American Exodus from the South," accessed May 31, 2016, http%3A://priceonomics.com/the-great-migration-the-african-american-exodus/

2. "Geography of the Great Migration," accessed May 31, 2016, http%3A://priceonomics. com/the-great-migration-the-african-american-exodus/

3. Femi Lewis, "Causes of the Great Migration: Searching for the Promised Land," accessed May 31, 2016, http://afroamhistory.about.com/od/segregation/p/Causes-Of-The-Great-Migration-Searching-For-The-Promised-Land.htm.

Redlining is the unethical practice whereby financial institutions make it extremely difficult or impossible for residents of poor inner city neighborhoods to borrow money, get approved for a mortgage, take out insurance, or access other financial services, often because of the area's history of high default rates or a perceived lack of profitability. In some cases of redlining, financial institutions would literally draw a red line on a map around neighborhoods in which they did not want to offer financial services, giving the term its name. . . . The assumptions of redlining resulted in a large increase in residential racial segregation and urban decay in the United States.*

*"Redlining," accessed May 31, 2016, http://www.investopedia.com/terms/r/redlining.asp?ad=dirN&qo=investopediaSiteSearch&qsrc=0&o=40186.

ing institutions in particular kept Blacks out of many neighborhoods through the practice of redlining. And sadly, "Christian" Grand Rapids was no more welcoming to African Americans than other northern cities.

The practice of redlining soon concentrated the growing African American population in Grand Rapids to the inner city, especially its southeast quadrant. They had few options where they could live, where their children could go to school, and where they could work, which at that point was almost exclusively maintenance and service work.

> By the mid-1950s Grand Rapids was a far less integrated city than it had been in its early history. . . . As the number of Negro Migrants increased in the city the racial composition of a few of the neighborhood schools changed . . . the Negroes were restricted to where they could live. 99.8 percent of the African-Americans lived in a tightly restricted segregated area bounded by Eastern, Grandville, Wealthy, and Franklin streets, an area of about 30 blocks.[4]

With White landlords reluctant to sell their homes at a loss, Blacks were taken on as renters in the hundreds of vacated houses left behind by White Flight. In greater Grand Rapids, as well as in other northern cities, entire inner city neighborhoods were abandoned by fearful Whites, sometimes seemingly overnight, and taken over almost as quickly by Blacks who had no other real estate options.

The Madison Square business district was not exempt from this social and economic upheaval. What had been a thriving commercial center since the turn of the century now fell on hard times as White business owners began moving to suburban sites. Basically, they were following the steadily increasing flow of White residents moving out to new homes and modern schools elsewhere. To flee the influx of unwelcome new neighbors, many White families moved out even further to the suburbs. These monumental population shifts in the 1960s radically transformed the ethnic, cultural, and economic

4. Dr. Randal Jelks, as quoted in Philip J. Bostic, "The Grand Rapids Civil Rights Movement from 1954–1969: A Sociological Study," *McNair Scholars Journal*, vol. 6 no. 1 (2002), article 4.

White Flight is a term that originated in the United States, starting in the 1950s, and applied to the large-scale migration of people of various European ancestries from racially mixed urban regions to more racially homogeneous suburban or exurban regions. As Blacks arrived in northern neighborhoods, more Whites left. By the 1960s, there were more than three White departures for every Black arrival.*

*"White Flight," accessed May 31, 2016, https://en.wikipedia.org/wiki/White_flight.

character of southeast Grand Rapids. And area churches were also profoundly impacted by these radical changes.

The Shame of Grand Rapids

A pamphlet entitled "The Shame of Grand Rapids,"[5] written in 1967, zeroed in on land as being the major tool of the dominant White population to exercise control over where incoming and up-and-coming Black people could live, go to school, and, in many ways, even where they could find work. The writer described the inner city this way: "The Ghetto is 'fenced-in' land. The Ghetto is a *land* problem, not a housing problem. The Ghetto is a Black Reservation made by White Land Power." The author saw clearly what redlining was doing and how it was imprisoning Blacks economically and socially while consolidating the economic and racial superiority of Whites. This pamphlet gives eloquent voice to the deep frustration felt by many Blacks who found themselves unable to purchase or rent housing anywhere outside of the bounds set arbitrarily by White-controlled economic interests.

Not only was land an issue but also at the heart of inner city problems was housing decay. Most available houses dated back to the 1880s, with the newest from the building boom of the 1920s. By the late 1960s, hundreds of these homes needed repairs and maintenance that absentee or uncaring landlords, poor tenants, or low-income owners could not afford or did not have the skills or the will

c.	Average Age	25 Years		30 Years		Years	
d.	Repair	Fair to poor		Fair to poor			
e.	Occupancy	96 %		95 %		%	
f.	Home ownership	50 %		50 %		%	
g.	Constructed past yr.	None		None			
h.	1929 Price range	$2 M to 4500	100%	$ 3 M to 5500	100%	$	100%
i.	1936 Price range	$ 1500 to 3 M	70.5 %	$ 2 M to 4 M	69 %	$	%
j.	1937 Price range	$ 1500 to 3 M	70.5 %	$ 2 M to 4 M	69 %	$	%
k.	Sales demand	$ Very poor		$ Very poor		$	
l.	Activity	Very poor		Very poor			
m.	1929 Rent range	$ 20 to 40	100%	$ 15 to 25 per flat	100%	$	100%
n.	1936 Rent range	$ 15 to 30	75 %	$ 10 to 15	63 %	$	%
o.	1937 Rent range	$ 15 to 30	75 %	$ 10 to 15	63 %	$	%
p.	Rental demand	$ Fair		$ Fair		$	
q.	Activity	Fair		Fair			

4. AVAILABILITY OF MORTGAGE FUNDS: a. Home purchase None ; b. Home building None

5. CLARIFYING REMARKS:
Negroes in area are of better type. They are concentrated on Sherman, Bates and Thomas between Union and Eastern Streets.

6. NAME AND LOCATION Sherman - Union SECURITY GRADE D AREA NO. 4

HOLC [D4] Sherman – Union Area Description. Retrieved Oct. 21, 2016 from www.historygrandrapids.org

See bolded remarks above. Local bankers and realtors used collected data to determine mortgage rates based on the "type of negroes" living within designated areas.

5. Benjamin F. Smith, PE, "The Shame of Grand Rapids" (pamphlet), *The Crisis XVII* (1967), 2.

South High School, ca. 1958.* In 1968, the Grand Rapids School Board closed the predominantly Black South High to "destroy the black power structure" and bused the students to predominantly white schools, thereby ensuring that "integration would become a black child's burden."†

*Photo credit, Grand Rapids History & Special Collections, Archives, Grand Rapids Public Library, Grand Rapids, Michigan
†Ibid, 128.

to undertake. These factors led to a steady degradation of external home appearances, a decline in property values, and a loss of neighborhood desirability. Fearful for both their economic and social welfare, more and more Whites chose to move to the suburbs or to other city neighborhoods.

As Todd Robinson explains in detail in *A City within a City: The Black Freedom Struggle in Grand Rapids, Michigan*,[6] the city fathers had been maintaining a semblance of peace through *managerial racism*, a White-controlled power structure that excluded Blacks from good jobs and limited their housing options to the urban core of the city. This growing separation by race throughout the greater Grand Rapids area also had a profound effect on the schools.

> As a result, segregation between municipalities in a metropolitan locale created segregation in schools. In 1952, no schools in Grand Rapids contained more than 90 percent nonwhite students. By 1961, three schools had nonwhite populations of more than 90 percent . . . . The increased concentration of minorities within the inner city, coupled with the exodus by white residents to the suburbs, strained inner-city school funding and often forced overcrowded black student populations to attend aged school facilities with limited resources. . . . Thus black inner-city dwellers were casualties of the metropolitan problem, not the cause.[7]

The appearance of tranquility in Grand Rapids would eventually give way to the expression of growing resentment over the underlying racial prejudice and social injustices inflicted on the Black residents of the Grand Rapids inner city.

6. Todd Robinson, *A City within a City: The Black Freedom Struggle in Grand Rapids, Michigan* (Temple University Press, 2013), chapters 3–4.

7. Ibid, 72.

A Question of Direction

The Madison Square community was deeply affected by these years of transition and turmoil, and so was Madison Chapel. In the earlier phases of racial change, the chapel continued to attract and serve a White majority. In the late 1950s, Rev. Dubois observed that "Some of these new worshipers were African American" and that there was a "reluctance to mix."[8] Since the African Americans were the ones checking out the chapel, obviously the reluctance was on the part of Whites.

Increasingly surrounded by a majority African American population, the chapel was uniquely positioned to reach the burgeoning population of African American neighbors. The longer the chapel hesitated to embrace its Black neighbors, the more it began feeling like a guest in the neighborhood rather than being a host. It could no longer avoid the question: How would this predominantly White congregation respond to its predominantly Black neighborhood? The sponsoring churches studied the question, and in 1959 the oversight committee made this declaration: "We should work with all people regardless of race," and, "If some of the whites do not favor integration, special arrangements may have to be made for them to attend at either Oakdale or Fuller."[9]

8. D. Huizinga, *Madison Creation Story* (new members class notes, 2006), 3.

Bill and Ann Navis

As Madison Square Chapel moved into the 1960s, once again God brought a uniquely prepared person to help the mission-now-chapel deal with the challenges of changing times. When Dubois left in 1962, the oversight committee appointed lay evangelist Bill Navis, who was then serving at Immanuel Chapel in Kalamazoo, Michigan, to become Madison Chapel's new leader. Navis had emigrated in 1948 from the Netherlands, where he had been a state policeman. After working various jobs, he felt called to the work of evangelism, and he became first a student and then a graduate of the Reformed Bible Institute (now Kuyper College).

9. Ibid.

Rev. James White

The oversight committee went by a variety of names throughout Madison's years as a mission and as a chapel: supervising or oversight committee, supervising or oversight board, and even Madison Square Board. Whatever name they went by, it is important to understand that this group was appointed and mandated by Oakdale Park, and later by Oakdale and Fuller, to supervise and support the work of the Madison Square Mission-turned-Chapel.

Navis began his work at Madison in 1962, three years after the declaration by the oversight committee that Madison was "to work with all people regardless of race." Yet either the message had not been well communicated or not everyone was on board with it; twenty years later, Navis explained that he felt restrained from working cross-racially by certain individuals from the sponsoring churches who wanted him to focus on reaching out to Whites rather than Blacks.[10]

Why would these individuals pressure Navis to deal only with Whites? What underlying elements might have been at work? In a 1982 conversation with Paul James, the Rev. James White—then a professor at Calvin College—ventured this insight:

> The problem basically was one of rural CRC attitude and orientation not knowing how to deal with the urban attitude and the orientation of the blacks. The supporting churches didn't know how to deal with the situation they found themselves in so they pressured Navis to limit his ministry to the white segment of the community.[11]

These outside restraints put Navis in a quandary, given his own eagerness to work with Blacks.

> Navis felt a sense of kinship with the blacks, himself being a member of a minority as a Dutch immigrant. He felt compassion for the souls of the unsaved greater than his sense of fear for the situation he was in, and also felt he had an advantage in being a foreigner, in that, he didn't have negative feelings toward the blacks. He saw them as equals. They were both on the outside looking in. In this aspect, his being Dutch was a help, not a hindrance.[12]

10. Paul James, *Madison Square on the Move: The Saga of a Little Church with a Big Vision* (course paper, Calvin College, 1982), 7.

11. Ibid, 6.
12. Ibid.

On the other hand, in that same 1982 interview, Navis reflected that "even with this great compelling drive to reach out to the blacks, he thought that for the time being it was better to not get them involved than to have them deal with such hostility as was in the church at that time."[13] It appears this "hostility" emanated not just from influential individuals outside of Madison but also from isolated attitudes within the chapel congregation itself: "There was a fear due to ignorance of worshiping with these people who now were a majority in the area, but as time passed the Chapel members realized their fears were unfounded."[14]

Whatever racial attitudes and undercurrents were at work, by 1965 the number of African American buyers and renters had risen so dramatically that Navis could no longer avoid reaching out to Black families. At one point, Whites were moving out so fast that "he would find blacks living in formerly white-owned homes to whose former occupants he was planning to pay a second visit."[15]

It was during these difficult and perplexing years that a number of African American families came into fellowship with the chapel congregation. In the mid-1960s, one of Navis's early contacts was John Toliver. John and his wife soon joined the catechism class and became members of the chapel. Several years later, Toliver also became Madison's first Black elder.

Around the same time, Ardie Burger dropped by with his wife and family. As Burger recalled:

> What drew me there was God Himself. My wife, Irma, and I had dressed the kids to take them to church. . . . We lived just a few houses north of the Chapel on Lafayette. . . . I was conflicted about church at the time but had prayed for guidance. Anyway, that Sunday I drove all the way to Franklin, turned right, then to Madison, turned right, then to Hall, turned right, and then back to Lafayette, where I turned right again. . . . Maybe I meant to just go back home, but we stopped in front of the Chapel and a man at the door of the church called for us

The Avalanche

The rushing ebb tide of White Flight reached its apex in southeast Grand Rapids in 1964–65. Navis aptly described this radical racial shift as "The Avalanche."*

*Vander Schaaf, *Square Roots*, 9

13. Ibid.
14. Douglas Vander Schaaf, *Square Roots: The Story of a Changing Church in a Changing Community* (course paper, Calvin College, 1982), 9.
15. James, *Madison Square on the Move*, 7.

The Burger Family, 1980
From left to right: Crystal, Robin, Ardie Jr, Ardie Sr., Irma, Pamela, Chaya, and Brian

> to come in. I wasn't dressed for it and didn't want to go in; but Irma and the kids went in and eventually I parked the car and followed. The kids really enjoyed it, but Irma had reservations. The next week we came again."[16]

Navis invited the Burgers to a weekly Bible study at his home. Within a few months, Irma's reservations were resolved and the Burgers became fully invested in Madison's congregational life.

Initially some of the White worshipers were reserved and unsure how to relate to African Americans. Yet the faithfulness, patience, and love shown by the Toliver and Burger families were ultimately embraced and reciprocated by the majority of Whites in the congregation. This, in turn, paved the way for many other Blacks to be welcomed into the fellowship.

Two other African American families were soon baptized into Madison. One of those new families

16. Ardie Burger, personal interview, October 6, 2015.

Mr. Friendly

For over fifty years, Ardie Burger has been "Mr. Friendly" at Madison, greeting people with a hug or handshake as they enter the church and its sanctuary. He has been an elected elder at Madison for more than thirty years, usually with only one year's rest between terms. He also is fondly remembered for his role in baptisms and of so liberally pouring water into the baptismal bowl that it overflows, graphically illustrating the outpouring of God's grace.

Bobbie Riley

was Bobbie Riley and her children. Bobbie's daughter, Rhoda, shared these memories:

> I was five years old when we started going to Madison in 1965. We were one of four Black families at that time. My mother stayed at Madison because she felt good going here; it was a good place for her and her family to be. We've been a part of Madison since; we never left. She didn't see color; she saw good people, so we stayed. And the Rileys are still here.[17]

With God's blessing, Navis's compassion and open heart toward the changing racial makeup of the neighborhood was a key factor in the congregation's successful welcoming of the Rileys and other Black families who began showing up for Sunday services.

The Mandate

In 1966, the chapel oversight committee decided to study whether the chapel was ready for organization. Released in January 1967, and referred to simply as "the mandate," this study observed that "Madison Square Chapel had reached a plateau. It could disband, remain on the plateau with the possibility of becoming stagnant, or call an ordained pastor and take steps toward becoming an organized church."[18]

At one of Madison's most pivotal and vulnerable moments, when its first Black families were being welcomed into the full fellowship of congregational life, chapel leaders were suddenly forced to make a difficult decision. Whether this challenge came as a result of the supporting churches' reservations about multiracial ministry cannot be determined, but the timing was significant. If Madison was to continue as a viable congregation, it was now being pressed to accept new leadership and move out on its own—as soon as possible.

To Navis, this was very bad timing, and he was not the only one who held this opinion. A special committee reported to the board in January of the year Navis left that "Madison Square Chapel is in

17. Rhoda Riley, email interview, April 23, 2015.

18. Vander Schaaf, *Square Roots*, 10.

A Mid-City Uprising

In *A City within a City*, Todd Robinson describes the following scenario:

> On the evening of July 24, 1967, a day after the Detroit rebellion, Grand Rapids experienced its own racial uprising, which lasted nearly four days. That evening, police received reports that a group of black juveniles was throwing rocks at storefront windows along South Division Avenue. . . . Police managed to squelch several scenes of unrest, but the number of fires and disturbances overwhelmed officers and fire crews. City officials contacted Governor George Romney to declare a state of emergency for Grand Rapids. . . . Romney issued a proclamation that outlawed the sale of firearms and intoxicating liquors. He also restricted the sale of gas after 6:00 P.M. Finally, Romney implemented a citywide curfew from 10:00 P.M. to 5:30 A.M. . . . After two days of unrest, the police finally managed to gain control of the streets. Almost 350 people were arrested and 44 injured, and an estimated $175,000 in property damage resulted from the racial uprising.*

*Robinson, *A City within a City*, 122.

a social community hell where sinners can be witnessed to; but an organized church cannot flourish."[19] That very summer, 1967, the rioting that erupted in Grand Rapids (described above) left a trail of fear and physical destruction that only added to the racial and economic stress of the Madison Square community. As a poignant and sobering reminder, a sign of the unrest was a burnt-out vacant lot that had been torched next to the chapel.

> Although the Grand Rapids riot did not have the massive burning and destruction of some larger cities, there was a great deal of unrest, tension, and some violent activity in the streets, including the Madison Square area. Members of the community and the Chapel were understandably afraid. Despite this, the ministry of the Chapel continued throughout this time. Navis visited the homes of those he knew were afraid to venture out. Even the Summer Backyard Bible School continued to meet during this period.[20]

The oversight committee held its ground. While seeming to have limited confidence that Madison could survive the inevitable challenges and tensions of an interracial ministry, paradoxically the committee continued pressuring the chapel congregation to move toward organization as a self-supporting and self-governing church. The mandate made clear that organizing also would require replacing Navis—a lay evangelist—with an ordained pastor.

> The response of the Chapel was an emotional and reactionary one. A signed petition was presented to Oakdale Park and Fuller Ave. requesting that Bill Navis remain at the Chapel as evangelist and that a new ordained man not be imposed on them. Navis did not discourage this action, for he also was opposed to this plan towards organization. He objected on the basis that the Chapel had not matured since it sought to organize in the 1950s (membership was in fact lower), and he felt the

19. James, *Madison Square on the Move*, 9.

20. Vander Schaaf, *Square Roots*, 10–11.

potential for immediate, strong leadership simply did not exist.[21]

Navis also suspected, as he acknowledged to Vander Schaaf in 1978, that the oversight committee's action was personal. "Navis felt strongly that the whole concept of the Mandate and process towards organization was promoted by certain individuals of the sponsoring churches who were not appreciative of his emphasis on positive interracial relationships."[22]

In brief, the chapel leadership loved and respected Navis and objected to the decision of the sponsoring churches to replace him against their will. In addition, some Madison folks also shared Navis's suspicion that certain leaders from the sponsoring churches were eager to distance themselves from the uncomfortable tensions related to racial integration and reconciliation.[23] Nevertheless, the chapel's petition went unheeded. The governing bodies of Oakdale Park and Fuller Avenue were determined that Madison—ready or not—needed to move toward organization.

On October 30, 1967 a Letter of Call was mailed to Rev. Vernon Geurkink, Pastor of Ellsworth CRC in Northern Michigan, officially calling him to become Madison's new pastor. As was the custom in that era, the Letter of Call was followed with letters from congregants expressing their prayers for a favorable decision. And despite the reaction and resistance described above, eight days after Geurkink's

Douglas Vander Schaaf

Douglas Vander Schaaf attended Calvin College and Madison Square Church in the 1970s. In 1978 he submitted a course paper for a college history course under the title *Square Roots: The Story of a Changing Church in a Changing Community*. His research and recording of the Madison story through 1978 was quoted at some length in subsequent course papers written by David Beelen and Paul James. Excerpts also found their way into class notes for new members and in the early chapters of *This Far by Faith*.

21. Ibid., 11.
22. Ibid.
23. Don Huizinga, email interview August 24, 2016.

Grand Rapids, November 7, 1967

Dear Rev. Geurkink,

The combined consistories of Oakdale Park and Fuller Ave. C.R.C. urged their congregations to write to you concerning the call you received to be the worker at The Madison Square Chapel. Regardless of this request I want to write, or come in contact with you.

Even though I love my work in the chapel and its community,I may and will not stand in your way to accept this call. I have also encouraged the members of the Chapel to come in contact with you and to pray for you.

Dear brother, may the Lord lead you to the right decision, to the furtherance of His Kingdom.

Yours in Christ,

William Navis.

William Navis,

743 Fuller Ave. S.E.
Grand Rapids, Mich.
49506

Phone: 2450046

Letter from Navis to Geurkink, November 1967

Letter of Call went in the mail, a gracious letter from Navis to Geurkink also went in the mail.

Not fully aware of local tensions surrounding his call and crediting his youthful optimism, Geurkink accepted the call enthusiastically. This was just before Thanksgiving 1967. Geurkink agreed to start as Madison's new pastor in January 1968.[24]

Shortly after Geurkink announced his acceptance, Navis announced his resignation. Ironically, Mr. and Mrs. John Toliver had become the first African American

24. Vernon Geurkink, email interview, April 14, 2015.

members of the chapel only weeks before Navis resigned. Navis referred to his last Sunday at Madison as "the saddest day of my life," and continued: "I only hoped Madison Square would become and remain a bulwark against Satan reaching an arm in . . . the hearts of unbelievers."[25]

An Enduring Legacy

Navis helped build the first bridges across the divide between Blacks and Whites at a time when Madison could easily have succumbed to fear, discouragement, and covert racial prejudice. "Madison Square did survive but it would not have been possible without the link in the chain Bill Navis provided during some of the hardest years Madison Square has known."[26] His courageous and compassionate leadership helped Madison begin to establish its identity as a congregation grounded in biblical principles, committed to Reformed theology, led by the Holy Spirit, and committed to racial reconciliation with justice.

Obviously, Navis suffered loss as a result of the changes instituted, yet the impact of his work was enduring and brought great gain to Madison Square. Even though he came and went in the span of just a few years, the things this Holy Spirit–led man initiated impacted Madison's deeply embedded core values, providing good soil and an enduring basis for spiritual growth and integrated church life and worship. Clearly, Madison's early struggle toward racial diversity was a tension that has brought blessing.

Agape love is at the core of a multiracial and multicultural church. The ministry of Jesus Christ and His example show us the importance of reconciling all peoples, tribes, and nations to God, and to one another, regardless of difficulty or cost.

A divine encounter between a fast-changing neighborhood and a uniquely positioned yet struggling congregation led Madison to courageously open itself to the ministry of reconciliation. Adopting this ministry of pursuing cross-racial reciprocal relationships is surely the work of the Holy Spirit and has been a key to Madison's staying power over the years. God has since used this ministry to win many hundreds of people from varied ethnic and racial backgrounds to be among those who have received God's love and promises, despite cultural and economic differences.

All to the glory of God!

25. James, *Madison Square On the Move*, 8.
26. Ibid., 9.

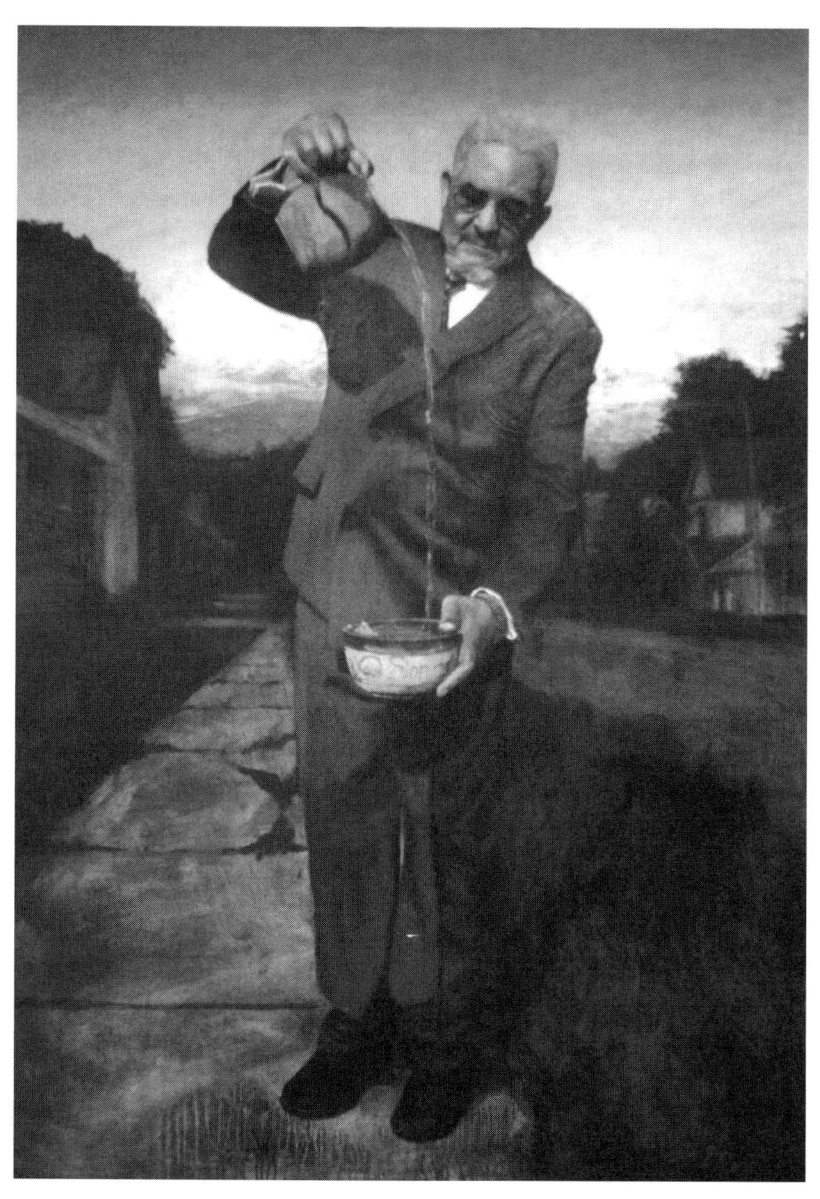

Elder Ardie Burger, 50 years after first attending Madison. Artist Jonathan Quist depicts Elder Burger's lavish pouring of baptismal water within an urban backdrop.

About the Writer

Robert R. (Bob) Schuyler was born in 1941 and raised in Erie, Pennsylvania. With master's degrees in literature and biblical studies, he has enjoyed a varied career, including college teaching, evangelism and ministry administration, home building and restoration, and overseas missions. He and his wife, Brenda, have partnered in all aspects of his work since their marriage in 1981. A member of Madison Square since 1992, he has served as a worship leader, elder and pastoral care elder. The Schuylers are the grateful parents of two sons.

Summary Timeline

1857 to 1967

Brenda Schuyler

Brenda Schuyler and husband, Bob, have been members of Madison since 1992. She has served with prayer, hospitality, and worship design ministries, and as a pastoral care elder. After she retired from Inner City Christian Federation (ICCF) in 2006, they served for three years at the Kibbuse Foundation in rural Uganda. They are blessed with two sons and daughters-in-love: Jim and Alison in Grand Rapids, Michigan, and Aaron and Melissa in Carthage, Texas.

Note: The lines in ***italics*** identify contextual events; the numbers in parentheses refer to page numbers.

1800s & early 1900s Thousands emigrate from the Netherlands to West Michigan (33)

1857 The Christian Reformed Church denomination is founded (10)

Late 1800s Many poor folks from Appalachia settle in the "Poverty Hollow" area of Grand Rapids (24, 39)

1890 Oakdale Park CRC Is established by Eastern Avenue CRC (34)

1901 Oakdale Park neighborhood is incorporated into City of Grand Rapids (34)

1911 Grand Rapids citywide furniture workers' strike (35)

1911 Rev. William P. Van Wyk becomes Oakdale Park CRC's fifth pastor (35)

1912 Oakdale Park CRC members begin Sunday School classes in Madison Square area (9, 10, 38)

1913 Van Wyk publishes *City Evangelism, Why and How* in the Dutch language (9, 36)

1914 Madison Square Gospel Mission's first rented space at **340 Hall Street SE** (38)

Miss Elizabeth (Lizzie) Smitter is hired as full-time Mission Coordinator (38)

1918 The Mission's second rented space at **1209 Madison Avenue SE** (39)

1920s Summer outdoor meetings are held, with hymn singing and Gospel preaching (40)

1925 Fuller Avenue CRC is established by Oakdale Park CRC and becomes joint supervisor (40)

1929 The Mission moved to its third rented space at **1164 Madison Avenue SE** (40)

1933 Lizzie Smitter leaves the employ of Madison Square Mission (41)

1930s The Mission is led by volunteers from Oakdale Park and Fuller Avenue and students from Calvin College and the Reformed Bible Institute (41)

1930s Miss Gertrude Door begins her forty years of service as pianist and organist (112)

1941 The Mission moves to its fourth rented space at **1163 Madison Avenue SE** (41)

Dec 7, 1941 Attack on Pearl Harbor prompts the United States to enter World War II

1942 Tom Afman is hired as Madison's first full-time lay evangelist and Mission Coordinator (41)

1943 Miss Gertrude Holkeboer is hired as the Mission's full-time staff worker (42)

1945 Madison Square Mission moves to fifth rented space at **1230 Madison Avenue SE** (43)

1945 World War II ends in Europe on May 8 and in Japan on Sept. 2

1947 Oversight Committee sets goals for the Mission to become "organized" and have an ordained leader (44)

1948 Afman leaves and Rev. Walter Dubois becomes the mission's first ordained minister (44)

Holkeboer serves for eleven years, much of it as a volunteer, and is "known to preach" (43)

1949 Madison Square Gospel Mission is re-named Madison Square Chapel (45)

1951 Dubois recommends that the Chapel organize, but the Oversight Committee declines (45, 46)

The new Chapel building at 1164 Lafayette Avenue SE is completed (46)

1950s and 1960s Millions of African Americans migrate from the American South to Western and Northern cities, including many thousands to Grand Rapids (51)

1959 Again Dubois recommends the Chapel organize, and the Oversight Committee again declines (97)

Oversight Committee declares, "We should work with all people regardless of race." (56)

1962 Dubois leaves Madison Square Chapel. (48)

William Navis is hired as the Chapel's lay evangelist (55)

Navis feels pressured by some to reach out to Whites rather than to Blacks (56)

Nov. 22, 1963 President John F. Kennedy is assassinated (49)

1964 Mr. Navis refers to Whites leaving the Madison Square area as "the Avalanche" (57)

The John Toliver and Ardie Burger families begin attending the Chapel (57, 58)

1965 The Bobbie Riley family starts attending the Chapel (59)

1965 Racial riots occur in Watts community of Los Angeles, California (49)

1966 Voting Rights Act is signed into law by Lyndon B. Johnson

1967 "The Shame of Grand Rapids" is published by Benjamin F. Smith (53)

1967 Racial riots occur in Detroit and Grand Rapids, Michigan (49, 60)

1967 Oversight Committee decides the Chapel needs to be organized with an ordained pastor (59)

Oversight Committee denies the Chapel's petition to retain Navis as lay evangelist (60)

John Toliver and family become the first African American members of the Chapel (62, 63)

Navis resigns his position effective Dec 31, 1967 to make room for the new pastor (62)

5

Organization, Setbacks, and a Second Wind

BY DON GRIFFIOEN

> Do not conform to the pattern of this world, but be transformed by the renewing of your mind. Then you will be able to test and approve what God's will is—his good, pleasing and perfect will.
>
> Romans 12:2

Madison's story began with a group of committed Christians who were determined to share their joy in the Good News of Jesus Christ with a neighboring community that, from their Dutch separatist perspective, seemed to be living without that joy. They began with a Sunday School and then with worship services. They cast their bread upon the waters, trusting that after many days it would come to fruition (Eccles. 11:1).

Sacrificing time and energy, these faithful servants from Oakdale Park CRC focused their efforts initially on poor Whites from the Appalachian Mountains who had come to Grand Rapids looking for work and were living in the Madison Square area south of the tracks. Over time, especially after World War II, the entire Madison Square community became increasingly inhabited by African Americans from the South who also had come looking for jobs and a better life.

The Changing of the Guard

In 1967, just as Grand Rapids was reaching a boiling point in racial unrest, Madison's supervising churches adopted—in essence—the same two decisions they had adopted in 1947: That it was time for Madison to get organized, and that this action required new chapel leadership. And this time, the supervising churches sought out a new pastor with diligence and determination.

Rev. Vernon (Vern) Geurkink, then serving the CRC in Ellsworth, Michigan became a person of interest. On October 26, in keeping with a joint decision of the Fuller Avenue and Oakdale Park consistories (now known as councils) to extend Geurkink a Letter of Call, the letter was signed by all twenty-six members of the Fuller Consistory. In addition, the members of all three congregations—Fuller, Oakdale, and Madison—were urged to write to Geurkink. He received thirty letters in all, including more than one masterpiece!

Don Griffioen

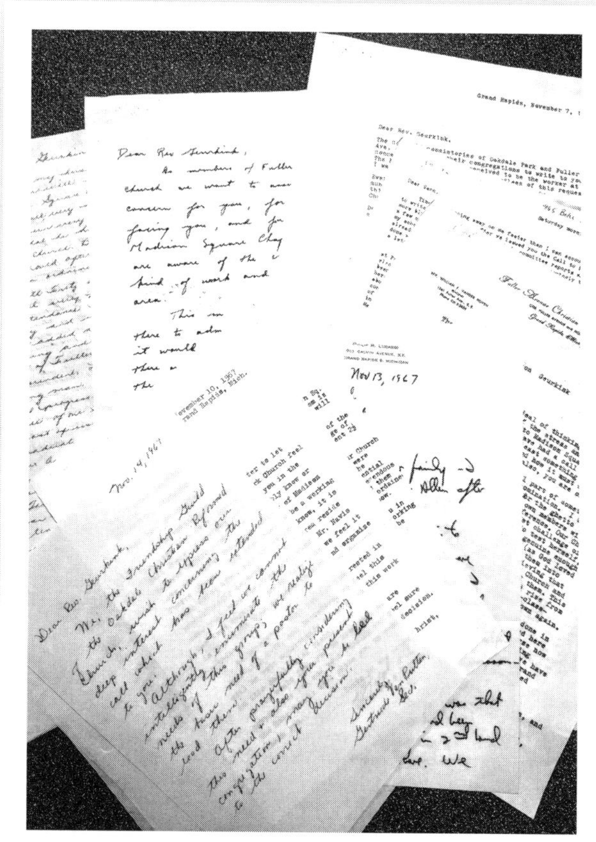

Letter Campaign to Pastor-Elect Geurkink

One such letter was from M. H. de Vroome, a member of Oakdale Park CRC:

My association with the Chapel goes back to the time when as a teenager I served as an accompanist at the Gospel Services and later as a teacher in the Sunday School. Then, in the early 1920s I assumed the duties of a treasurer—which function I am still holding. . . . Through all those years I have seen many changes at the Chapel. There have been changes of place—from upstairs halls to storefront and finally to a Chapel. There have been economic and social changes in the community, and especially in the last few years—racial changes. I believe that the Chapel stands now at a crucial point which calls for a dynamic, vigorous leadership in an inter-racial neighborhood.

A second invitation was from George Fritsma:

I and my wife are Sunday School teachers at Madison Square Church, and we felt as if we should write to urge you to come. . . . It is a sad fact that Mr. Navis through his own diligence may work himself out of a job, but the need for an ordained man of young ideas is clear, and we certainly hope that you feel called upon to take this call.

A third sampling offers insight into the humble but elegant piety of Fuller's Pastor William Vander Hoven:

If ever the C.R.C. has failed, she has failed in her Jerusalem. We owe God and this city a strong Church in Madison Square. . . . It is to people like those living on Prospect, and Cass, and Lafayette, to whom Jesus says: "Come unto me, all ye that labor and are heavy laden." I could hardly imagine a segment of society that is in more dire need of the Gospel, and of the things Christ has to offer. . . . Not all the residents in this area are unchurched, by any means. But many of them are. And I believe the Holy Spirit is working in Madison Square just now as He may not have been for several years past. . . . If the Lord leads you to Madison Square, you will have been given one of the most strategic, one of the most important, one of the most difficult but also most rewarding positions in Grand Rapids.

Geurkink accepted the call to Madison in November, Navis concluded his service with Madison Square Chapel in December, and Geurkink was installed as the chapel's new pastor on January 14, 1968.

On April 4, 1968, a mere eighty days after Geurkink's installation, Dr. Martin Luther King Jr. was assassinated. Four days later, Geurkink

A Family Affair

The de Vroome family was part of the many Oakdale Park and Fuller Ave. volunteers who offered help and encouragement to the chapel. By 1967 M. H. de Vroome had served as volunteer treasurer for the Madison Square Mission and then the Madison Square Chapel for nearly fifty years. His wife, Carolyn, was a member of an a capella women's quartet that enjoyed providing special music at the chapel once a month. Their son David served as janitor there for a number of years; their daughter Anne, now a professional violinist, also provided special music periodically with her father accompanying her at the piano.*

*Anne de Vroome, personal interview with Jackie Venegas, June 2016

One Problem

"I should bring up . . . one problem, that of the old-line psalm-singing conservatives in our churches who still can't believe there are names like Rasmus Washington on Christian Reformed rolls. You will find in some part this attitude embodied in the Madison Square Board. This is a group of elders who sit in state once a month . . . to deliberate on how to further economize. Forgive me for my sarcasm. . . . Actually our board is composed of many well-meaning men, only a few of which are progressive thinkers." (George Fritsma)

Pastor Vern Geurkink

submitted this insightful challenge to the Madison Square Oversight Board:

> The tragic events of the past week dramatically underline the extreme urgency of the need in the inner city. More important than this, we have witnessed in Grand Rapids the Black community's mature restraint and peaceful response to the violence that a White racist mentality has inflicted on its most respected Civil Rights leader. Riots have too often proved to be the only language that America will listen to, but we have also been reluctant to "reward rioters." Now we have been given an opportunity to show whether we are willing to "reward nonviolent restraint." Does the Christian Reformed community in Grand Rapids dare to ignore this opportunity by sitting on our hands in the vain confidence that we have done our job and have the situation in hand? This gesture of good faith from the Black people must be viewed as a summons to a greater commitment of ourselves and our resources to the crying needs of the neighborhood God has given us to serve[1]

Painfully aware of his newness to urban and cross-racial ministry, Geurkink had already "set about the task of trying to understand the strange, alien culture and language of this new mission field."[2] Intentionally becoming acquainted with Madison neighborhood organizations and attending seminars on urban ministry and racial reconciliation, he worked persuasively and persistently to pass on these newly acquired concepts to the congregation. "A group known as P.A.R. (People Against Racism) began to meet on a weekly basis. . . . A consciousness began to develop among the members at the chapel about the challenge and importance of the ministry in which they were involved."[3]

Geurkink also observed that early commitment was mixed. "Looking back, I sense that responses among Madison members were varied. I know that some were very much

1. Vern Geurkink, letter to Oversight Board, April 8, 1968.
2. Vern Geurkink, email interview with Bob Schuyler, April 14, 2015.
3. Vander Schaaf, *Square Roots*, 11.

in favor of the new vision that the Supervisory Board had for MSC to become a vibrant urban ministry and were eager for the new phase. I had a sense that there were some signers who were pretty well gone by the time I arrived. Yet another part of the congregation seemed to me to be taking a 'wait and see' approach and continued their level of involvement."[4]

Gertrude Door

Madison Gets Organized

As expected by the supervisory board, Geurkink led the chapel leadership through the required steps and procedures for bringing the chapel to *church* status. In 1970, two years after Geurkink's arrival, Madison was officially organized and granted full recognition as a Christian Reformed congregation. Its newly ordained elders and deacons, along with Geurkink, constituted Madison's first self-governing body, then called a consistory (or council). John Toliver also was an ordained elder of this otherwise all-White body.

A year later, in August of 1971, John Toliver and his family left Madison to join an all-Black church. Though the decision had been difficult for him and his family, he felt pressured by people in the local community who criticized him for being a Black leader in a predominantly White church. However, his main reasons for leaving were a Christian Reformed school in Cicero, Illinois denying enrollment to Black children and also the Christian Reformed Church Synod failing to strongly object to such racial prejudice.

Generous support for Madison over the years from Oakdale and Fuller was not only monetary; they also had supplied elder care, a treasurer, janitor, many other volunteers, and regular visiting worshipers. Ruth Broene faithfully led ladies' Bible classes for many years. A few others from Oakdale also stayed with the newly organized Madison Square Church. Gertrude Door was the principal organist for two services each Sunday, playing on a small electric organ. She also announced the worship services to the community by playing chimes

4. Vern Geurkink, email interview with Bob Schuyler, April 14, 2015.

Reroofing the Chapel

in the church tower. Hilda Aukeman continued on as a Sunday School teacher.

The newly organized Madison Square Church was expected to become totally self-supporting and self-sustaining as soon as possible, including the responsibility of developing and managing its own budget. That was a huge challenge for a very small church. At times there was not even enough money to pay the pastor, and by the end of Geurkink's first year the future was looking dismal. "The congregation was down to approximately 10 'families' and a number of individuals who were active and committed to the vision, augmented by a number of enthusiastic volunteers from the supporting churches and Calvin College."[5] Nevertheless, as Geurkink reflected, "In all of this I never detected any strong sentiment that the Chapel should close its doors or move out of the neighborhood. If those possibilities had been considered by the congregation or the supporting churches, I never heard about it. . . . Most of us were eager to communicate the saving Gospel of grace and highly motivated to draw Black neighbors into active fellowship."[6]

In 1972, Marty Meyne became the treasurer and vividly recalled that the total budget for that year was $20,000. The mother churches, Oakdale and Fuller, each provided $5,000 with the expectation that Madison would come up with the remaining $10,000. He also recalled how their financial challenges led to greater resourcefulness. In 1974,

5. Ibid.

6. Ibid.

A White Liberal

During one summer in the early 1970s, Geurkink received a phone call from a local "Black militant leader" who called him a "White liberal" and warned him to "get your White missionaries off the street before they get hurt," and, "You better turn off those damn chimes on Sunday mornings."*

*Vern Geurkink, email interview with Don Griffioen, June 24, 2014

the chapel building needed a new roof. With no available funds for hiring roofers, the members decided to take it on by themselves. On the appointed day, all the Madison men showed up. Despite many of them having no previous experience in this type of work, they dug right in and finished the project in one day. A good time was had by all![7]

Under Pastor Geurkink's faithful leadership and good preaching, the church grew to over thirty families. Young families from area churches, professionals, plus some students from Calvin College also began to attend. A new hymnal introduced a greater variety of hymns, and piano accompaniment was gradually used alongside the organ. Maggie Hollis organized and led a choir singing mostly Black selections. The small church building was quite full each Sunday with a mixed membership of both Black and White.

Madison also began to attract and serve kids with disabilities. The congregation was very active with Boy Scouts, a Girls' Club, and Bible studies for men and women. An active Sunday School program made use of two large vans. Around this time, the Guiding Light Mission discontinued its Sunday school to concentrate on helping adult addicts, alcoholics, and homeless people, so Madison also picked up children from Guiding Light.

To better minister to the neighborhood, Summer Workshop in Missions (SWIM) teams, mostly from New Jersey and New York, came and were a big hit with neighborhood kids in the 1970s. They provided intensive and extensive summer programs for kids—VBS, recreation, tutoring, and youth employment in summer jobs. A summer weekend neighborhood cleanup program, which was advertised by distributed flyers, recruited neighbors and volunteers to clean up yards and alleys on Madison Ave., Hall St., Jefferson Ave., and Garden St. Trucks hauled the trash to a vacant lot on the corner of Cass and Hall. The fear of someone torching it moved Grand Rapids City Commissioners to mobilize city trucks and loaders to clean it up in the wee hours of Sunday morning.

Neighborhood youth used basketball hoops in the church parking lot constantly, even on Sunday morning during church services. Madison actively brokered resources from area churches, programs, and organizations, especially

7. Marty Meyne, interview with Jackie Venegas, August 2016.

working to get kids from the church enrolled and supported in Oakdale Christian School, Grand Rapids Christian High, and Christian summer camps such as Camp Roger and Camp Tall Turf. Pastors of area urban Christian Reformed churches formed the Grand Rapids Urban Fellows Fellowship (GRUFF) for mutual support and planning.

Key 73: Evangelism Thrust

A nationwide evangelical outreach ministry named "Key 73" was adopted by the denomination's Christian Reformed Home Missions as an outreach strategy under the title of "Evangelism Thrust." Various evangelism materials were published to help churches reach out to people of non-Dutch background. These "Called to Serve" materials encouraged the churches to set specific goals to witness to their neighbors. Madison developed its own version of Key 73 called "Key Contact." Madison's key leaders—Larry Kuipers discipling Valerie Cassell and Mary Smith; Don Huizinga mentoring Mary Cancler; Martheen Griffioen tutoring Michael Traylor and becoming acquainted with his mother, Deloris; Marian Takens mentoring Betty and Stella Vaughn; and others meeting with Bobbie Riley and Cora Diepstra—gathered once a month to support each other with suggestions, prayers, and ideas for authentic cross-cultural friendships. They were trying to discover the best ways for building bridges to enfold these neighbors into the fellowship of the church. This resulted in several strong Black/White friendships. Some of their children were enrolled in Grand Rapids Christian Schools. Several of these students or their parents were able to move into better jobs or occupations as a result. A special fruition of these contacts is that the Cancler and Traylor families are still attending Madison.

The First Black CRC Pastor in Grand Rapids

In 1974, after six years as pastor, Geurkink accepted the invitation of Calvin Seminary to head up its Field Education Program. The congregation decided after his departure to take a bold step to reveal its determination to become a multiracial, multicultural congregation. In the same year, Madison called Pastor Virgil Patterson to be the first Black pastor to serve in a Grand Rapids area Christian Reformed Church and the third Black ordained pastor in the CRC. His impact on Madison was significant.

Pastor Virgil Patterson

Patterson was a graduate of Boston University School of Theology. While serving as Executive Secretary of the Association of Urban Ministries of Chicago for the United Presbyterian Church, he became acquainted with two Christian Reformed pastors in Chicago: Pastor Rich Grevengoed of Lawndale CRC and Pastor James LaGrand of Garfield CRC. Prior to coming to Madison, Patterson had been recruited by the Fuller Avenue CRC to serve as Minister of Education and Evangelism. While at Fuller Avenue, he also enrolled in a few courses at Calvin Seminary.

Patterson was welcomed by Madison with great excitement and enthusiasm. He was affirmed by the Classis as an ordained CRC minister by way of a Colloquium Doctum (Doctrinal Conversation). Under his leadership, Madison continued to grow. Several Key Contact participants and their families decided to become members of the church.

In 1975, a decision was made to hire Tom Raysor, an African American, to give leadership for youth ministry. He was a graduate of a Bible college in Denver, Colorado, and had been working for the Grand Rapids Christian Development Center. Raysor organized bike trips for the young men to ride as far away as St. Louis and Montreal, he took them on camping outings, and he coached them in basketball. In doing so, he greatly impacted the lives of these young men. He loved playing the guitar and taught the congregation to sing several Psalms and other Bible verses to new tunes. He also developed a small choir and taught them cantatas, which they performed in interested churches in West Michigan.

To employ Tom, Madison needed additional money. A request was made to the Christian Reformed Home Mission Board for a $10,000 Grant-in-Aid such as many other churches in the denomination were receiving. A grant was approved but only for one year, because Madison was told that Grand Rapids area churches had enough money to support their ministries without needing help from the denominational board. As a result of that stipulation, the Grand Rapids area churches developed their own Grant-in-Aid program. Many of the

Tom Raysor (standing, center)

inner city churches and some outlying churches were assisted with support for employing second staff persons hired to help congregations reach out and evangelize people in their neighborhoods. The impetus for developing this program came from Madison Square.

After some time, Patterson began to feel increasingly uncomfortable serving as a Black pastor in the predominantly White Christian Reformed denomination. He also became interested in the Charismatic Movement, which advocated more enthusiastic and less-structured worship services that he felt the congregation, elders, and deacons of Madison were not ready to support. He had recently experienced the "baptism of the Holy Spirit" and had brought to the church an emphasis on following the leading of the Spirit, an emphasis that sometimes created tension. Patterson also worried about the hesitancy on the part of certain White council members to follow Black leadership.

Patterson became deeply involved in the work of the Synodical Committee on Race Relations which included challenging racism at home and abroad. It was in this upper echelon of denominational work that he experienced distinct and sometimes blatant racism. He also visited the Reformed Ecumenical Synod—a consortium of Reformed Churches around the world—which was held in South Africa in 1977. South Africa declared him to be "an honorary White" so that he could participate

Tish Patterson

The Lord My Peace

By Tish Patterson, as told to Al Mulder

When Loutisha (Tish) Patterson's son was attending a Christian School in Des Plaines, Illinois, a CRC pastor told her husband, Virgil, about a ministry position with Fuller Avenue. Tish did not want to move to Grand Rapids, but she prayed for grace to accept God's will. During their visit at Fuller, the moment they stepped into the building she knew this was God's will, and she was at peace.

One year later, in 1974, her husband accepted the call to Madison Square. Tish was a busy mother and pastor's wife, taught Sunday school, and sang in the choir. She made special friends there, including Mary Cancler, who remains a prayer partner today. Tish has fond memories of Madison.

She also remembers the day in 1977 when Virgil decided to leave Madison. On Sunday mornings she would bring their children to Sunday School and he would arrive later for the service. This particular Sunday he did not come at all. She then remembered a dream in which he was preaching but she could not see him. The Lord already knew Virgil would be leaving, and she was at peace.

Only five years after leaving Madison, Virgil was diagnosed with lung cancer. Tish quit her job, gave up her car, and cared for her husband. Living close to Neland Ave. CRC, she walked there on occasion and even saw herself joining, but Virgil was not so sure. She prayed, "Lord, I want to go where you want us to go." One month before Virgil died, they became members of Neland Ave. And Tish was at peace.

in discussions with the Dutch Reformed Church in South Africa, which would not otherwise accept his inclusion. Patterson experienced firsthand the strong commitment of the Reformed Churches of South Africa to confront the official political policies of their Apartheid societal structure. He was troubled by the reluctance of the other Reformed denominations to speak out clearly in opposition against Apartheid. This reluctance, plus the deeply troubling "honorary White" experience, left him wounded.

Feeling the increasing tension with the council and congregation over a Spirit-led worship style and preaching, Patterson felt called by the Holy Spirit to resign as Madison's pastor. He then began to worship with a local charismatic church. It was a sad day of confusion and uncertainty for the congregation.

Attendance at worship services was in steep decline after Patterson's resignation in 1977; on one Sunday there were as few as thirteen worshipers. A question arose: Should they close the doors of the

James Haveman

Never Give Up

James Haveman served multiple terms as a Madison elder and council leader and, subsequently, as a nationally recognized public servant. Reflecting on these times of change and challenge, he shared these insights: "I can't remember any discussion about giving up. I think that people came to Madison for the purposes of friendliness, racial integration, progressive style of worship, social justice, social action and great preaching. We knew issues like this are challenging, but the rewards are many . . . so we kept on plodding along with the Holy Spirit leading us."*

*James Haveman, email interview with Bob Schuyler, July 13, 2015

newly organized Madison Square CRC and disband the congregation? The elders committed themselves to praying on their knees together for several Saturday mornings, praying for each member and family of the church and for guidance and wisdom. Several women of the church (Mary Cancler, Karen Coger, Maggie Hollis, and Tish Patterson) also met regularly to pray for the church. Clearly the sentiment to disband was not the mind of the majority of the congregation. The mind and heart of the congregation was to continue as a multiethnic church committed to reconciling Blacks and Whites in the city and to be a living testimony of the multiracial character and complexion of a faithful Church of Jesus Christ.

Madison could not agree with the Church Growth Movement centered in Fuller Theological Seminary in Pasadena, California, that was teaching as a cardinal principle of church growth that "people like to worship among their own kind of people." While it might have been true sociologically that people connect with people who are similar, this principle could not be defended biblically as a church growth principle. In fact, it was completely contrary to the teaching and example of Jesus reaching out to Samaritans, Romans, and Gentiles. Church growth in the book of Acts repeatedly demonstrated that the Gospel must break down ethnic and racial barriers in order to grow. And so Madison was determined that their church growth would follow that biblical and Spirit-led model.

The prayers of the people were answered. In 1977, Rev. David

No Money

Madison had no money to hire a moving company to bring the Sieplingas to Grand Rapids. So three members—Don Griffioen, Larry Kuipers, and Don Huizinga—rented a truck, drove to Omaha in a very bad snowstorm, loaded the truck, turned around, and drove straight back to Grand Rapids. There was no money for a motel either! The pattern repeated itself in 1978 with the Venegas family, this time with Sieplinga and Vince Bivins making a nonstop trip to NYC and back.

Pastor David Sieplinga, 1981

Sieplinga, a White pastor serving in Omaha, Nebraska, indicated his desire to move from a suburban congregation in Omaha to the inner city ministry of Madison Square. Sieplinga was brought up in a White urban congregation in Muskegon. As a seminary student, he served a full year's internship at Manhattan CRC in the heart of Harlem, NYC. He was strongly committed to Madison's vision to be an integrated congregation of Blacks and Whites as an authentic witness to the true character of the multiethnic church of Jesus Christ. Sieplinga came to Madison with a well-developed vision for cross-cultural ministry and was the strong leader the church needed. His leadership style also had a certain flair that generated enthusiasm.

The Madison Square community was still in cultural transition, with Whites continuing to move to neighborhoods further out and African American families continuing to move in and around the chapel area. Sieplinga—committed and creative—was well-received, and

Pastor David Sieplinga, 2013

Madison soon witnessed something unusual: nontraditional Christians and community seekers sliding into the short wooden pews of the undersized chapel. By May 1978, Sieplinga was already voicing caution that he "wanted steady and slow growth" at the chapel.[8] In July he began a sermon series on "What it means to be a truly integrated church of Christ."[9]

One month later, in August 1978, Tom Raysor submitted his resignation after only three years as Madison's youth leader. He had come to Madison believing that the church was serious about wanting to raise up young African American leaders. But somehow he concluded that his leadership was questioned. He gave three jolting reasons for his decision to resign: (1) He felt that he never really functioned as the leader of the youth; (2) He perceived a hesitancy on the part of White members to submit to his leadership; and (3) He believed his goal of developing Black leadership could best be served by operating outside of a traditionally White congregation and denomination.[10]

8. "Madison Council Minutes," May 9, 1978.

9. "Madison Council Minutes," July 8, 1978.

10. "Madison Council Minutes," August 8, 1978.

A Second Wind

Another abrupt resignation could have prompted another setback, but Raysor's decision was firm and final. Sieplinga, with an unwavering commitment to racially diverse leadership, convened an emergency session of council and obtained approval to contact his friend, Dante Venegas, a Black Puerto Rican from NYC, to ask him to consider ministering at Madison.

When Sieplinga was asked whether Madison's decision to hire racially diverse staff was important to Madison's perseverance and growth, he responded:

> Absolutely. There were some visionary leaders in the seventies who sensed the importance of having multicultural leadership if Madison ever wanted to be more authentically multicultural. I honor Don Griffioen, Jim Haveman, Don Huizinga and Rodney Mulder as being among those leaders who were *intentional* about seeking to hire Persons of Color. Even after the pain and disappointment following the resignations of Patterson and Raysor, they were not deterred.[11]

To make a long story very short, Venegas and his family were

11. David Sieplinga, email interview with Bob Schuyler, April 23, 2015.

Photo credit, Grand Rapids History and Special Collections, Archives, Grand Rapids Public Library, Grand Rapids, Michigan

Architectural drawing of the 1955 expansion of the Immanuel Presbyterian Church, also illustrating the stained glass windows in the new sanctuary.

persuaded to come to Grand Rapids, and the Sieplinga/Venegas partnership was truly a God thing—ushering in a remarkable period of learning, leadership, and growth. Lay leadership was recognized, honored, trained, and used. With a second wind blowing, the walls of the chapel building were soon bulging.

A Larger Building

When the much larger Immanuel Presbyterian Church building at the corner of Madison and Garden became available, Madison decided to take a giant step of faith and purchase that building. In Presbyterian governance, the presbytery holds the title to church buildings rather than the local congregation. Rev. John Teeuwissen, pastor of a Presbyterian church in Rockford and also president of the presbytery, met with Don Griffioen and Jim Haveman, both elders at Madison, to negotiate the sale of the building.

In August 1979, the former Immanuel Presbyterian Church building became the new home of Madison Square Christian Reformed Church.

The presbytery wanted to demonstrate its abiding commitment to inner city ministry in Grand Rapids by using the money received from the sale of the building for such a ministry. The plan was to hold in escrow the down payment and the monthly mortgage payments until there was enough money to employ a Presbyterian worker to become part of the Madison staff. This proposal was not only to continue their commitment to the inner city and cross-cultural ministry but also to work ecumenically with Madison.

After a few years, the presbytery decided it had collected enough money to place a Presbyterian staff

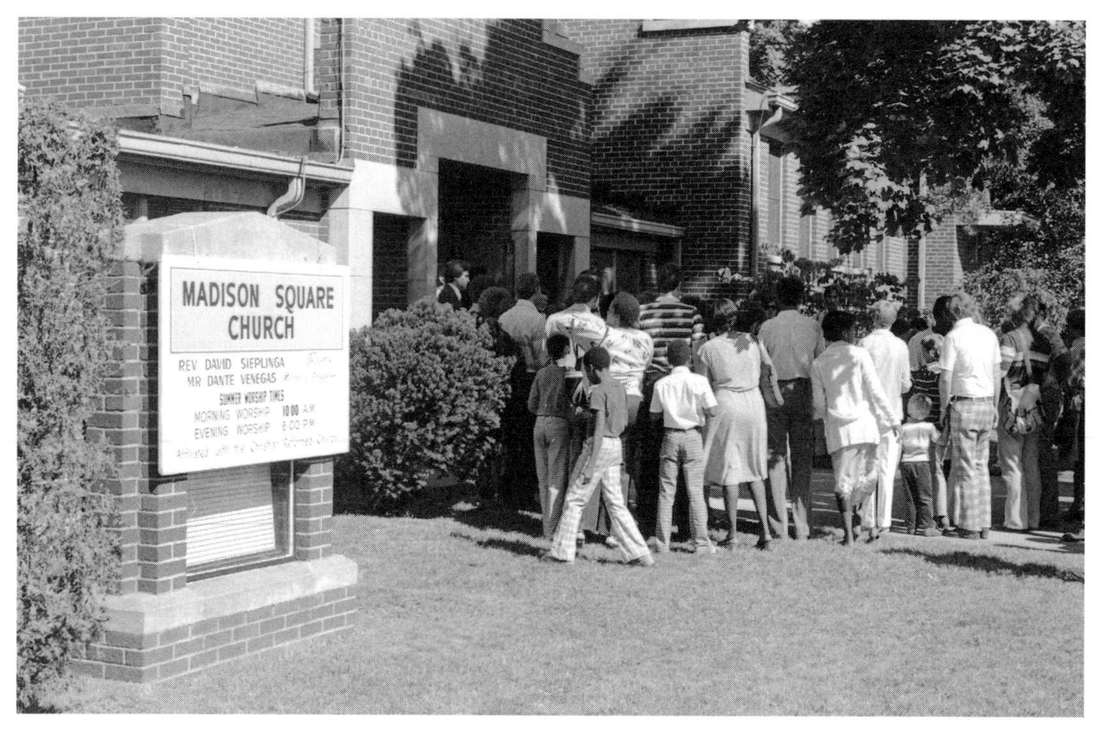

Madison congregants enter their new church home after marching from the chapel on Lafayette.

person on Madison's staff. A very able Black female graduate from a Presbyterian seminary in Atlanta, Georgia, was interviewed by Madison's council and recommended to the congregation for approval. Influenced by several strongly stated negative speeches at the congregational meeting, Madison failed to approve her for this position. No written grounds for the negative decision were ever put on paper. Disappointed with that decision, the presbytery decided to take the money held in escrow and work with the Reformed Church of America.

A Powerful Partnership

Madison's staying-in-the-city story is not an experience in isolation from other CRC churches. Change was underway throughout southeast Grand Rapids in the 1960s and 1970s, as well as in other areas of Grand Rapids and all major cities of the USA. White Flight from the cities was encouraged by a federal loan program for new homes in the suburbs, a program not available to Blacks and other People of Color.[12] Commodious suburban church construction with everything on one floor enticed many people to leave behind their old church buildings in the city. However, in southeast Grand Rapids, nine Christian Reformed Churches banded together in what was known as the Inner City Planning Committee (ICPC).

12. Robinson, *A City within a City*, 70–71.

These churches wrestled with many common concerns of White Flight, neighborhood transition, and the influx of a sizable ethnic minority population.

Together, the ICPC fought to keep Oakdale Christian School in the inner city and to make Christian education available by way of tuition scholarships for Children of Color. Many church members were encouraged to resist the White Flight and work for neighborhood stability by developing neighborhood organizations. One such organization was the Baxter Community Center, which provided day care services, family counseling, job counseling (Jubilee Jobs), free medical services, and neighborhood recreational opportunities. An old, neglected Baxter Christian School building was refurbished and remodeled to become Baxter Community Center—a centerpiece of Blacks and Whites working together. Concern for deteriorating inner city housing resulted in beginning the Inner City Christian Federation (ICCF) to remodel old houses and to build new homes. Madison members also participated in Habitat for Humanity and Home Repair Services, buying out absentee landlords to help stabilize the communities. Summer youth camps were organized for city kids. Also, Project Rehab was a powerful influence to stem the tide of drug addiction.

As a result of working together, all nine of these CRC inner city churches in southeast Grand Rapids have stayed in the city and are faithfully ministering to their communities to this day while many other congregations sold their buildings and fled the city.

In recounting Madison's history, now over one hundred years long, there is one overarching theme: *the faithfulness of God!* His hand has carried His church through failures and victories, ups and downs, ins and outs, and joys and sorrows. And Madison members and friends can only respond with praise: *To God be the glory; great things He has done!*

About the Writer

Griffioen was there! This chapter was written by **Rev. Dr. Donald Griffioen**, who has had a long and unique connection with Madison. In the mid-1940s, his father, Rev. John Griffioen, was the pastor of Oakdale Park CRC. Back then, when an organized CRC congregation began a mission outreach, the sponsoring congregation would assign families, singles, musicians, and others to support and encourage the mission in Sunday services and midweek activities. Oakdale Park

(continued on page 86)

Mary Cancler

Deloris Traylor

The Bingham Sisters

By Lorilee Craker

Deloris (Bingham) Traylor and Mary (Bingham) Cancler have been with and for each other since Deloris was born, many years ago in a little Kentucky town called Cadiz, population five hundred "counting the chickens and the hens."

The sisters giggle and snicker and hoot and holler, finishing each other's sentences. They have a long and winding shared history that eventually brought them to the same Northern state and the same mostly White church. They joined Madison Square in 1973.

But long before the sisters hitched their wagon to an eyebrow-raising choice of a church, there was growing up to do in Cadiz, also the hometown of "Yakety Sax" man Boots Randolph. Mary was eight when her baby sister was born, one of eleven children born to the Binghams, a family with roots in Europe, Africa, and Indigenous tribes of North America.

One grandfather, a Native American, was sold as a slave in Texas and came to Cadiz with whip scars on his back. Their other grandfather was a White landowner who never knew his son, their father, who could "pass for White." The girls and their siblings attended a segregated school, to which they were transported daily in the back of a pick-up truck, rain or shine, twenty miles each way.

Deloris left Cadiz when she was 17. "There wasn't nothing to do," she said.

It was 1954, and Deloris got caught up in the updraft of the Great Migration, the relocation of more than six million African Americans from the rural South to the cities of the North, Midwest, and West from 1916 to 1970. "Driven from their homes by unsatisfactory economic opportunities and harsh segregationist laws, many Blacks headed north, where they took advantage of the need for industrial workers," according to The History Channel.

According to Deloris, she had plenty to do in Grand Rapids, where she quickly found work painting car parts at Paulstra CRC, a plant that manufactured body mounts for GM, Ford, and Mercedes. According to Mary, left behind in Cadiz, Deloris had "money in her pocket and nice clothes and a nice suitcase" when she came back for a visit.

Mary, lured by Deloris's success, moved to Grand Rapids herself a few years later. She found work at Blodgett Hospital, where she met and married Lee Cancler, an electrician at General Motors. By the sixties, the couple had five children, and moved to Prospect Street in the Madison Square neighborhood.

Madison Square Christian Reformed Church came across the sisters' radar when a pastor's wife named Martheen Griffioen began tutoring one of Deloris's sons at Iroquois School on the southeast side of Grand Rapids. Griffioen's husband, Don, was acting as interim pastor at Madison, and she invited Deloris and her family to come be a part of it.

Deloris by this time had seven boys and one girl. A woman named Hilda Aukeman picked up her children every Sunday morning and drove them to church and Sunday School. Mary's children also began attending children's programs there.

On Mother's Day of 1973, the sisters attended a special program for mothers. "The Bible says 'a little child shall lead them,'" Mary said. "A little child!" She and Deloris began attending the almost all-White church and have stayed ever since. (Lee Cancler, Mary's husband, was a Methodist and preferred the Methodist church.)

It wasn't just that their children enjoyed the kids' programs. A few factors bonded two Black sisters from the South to a White Calvinist church in a denomination started by Gijsbert Haan and other Dutch immigrants in 1857.

One draw was the weekly reciting of the church's beliefs: the Apostles' Creed. "I believe in God, the Father Almighty, creator of heaven and earth . . ." That's the beginning of the code and canon Mary heard that first Sunday morning at Madison. It filled her, then and now, with substance and belonging. Simple, potent, and true, the creed gave her an identity whose roots sank much deeper than even race, gender, geography, or economics. "You know who you are" after listening to the creed, she said.

She knew who she was in Christ, and also in the body. "Back in those days we knew everyone in church," Mary said. "Pastor Vern Geurkink used to visit me all the time. He was a real sweet man."

Madison Square was different than the Black church. For one, said Mary, White people dressed much more casually on Sunday mornings than they did at her former church. "And I liked that," she said with conviction. "I *liked* that you didn't have to get all dressed up."

The Bingham sisters, Mary and Deloris, have belonged to Madison for over forty of its one hundred years, and they hope their offspring will continue to grow at church, and make it their core and foundation, until they are all together, enjoying "the life everlasting."

"One day I prayed that my children would be going here until they are in the grave," Mary laughs. "But then I realized that wasn't right. They just needed to go to a Bible-believing church."

"But you know what?" She can't help but smirk a little. "They are still all here!"

Postscript: I have written thirteen books and countless articles and blogs, but it was an especial honor to interview my dear friend, Miss Mary Cancler. I met Miss Mary about 18 years ago, at an all-ages women's Bible study at church. She told us bits and pieces of her fascinating story, of her mixed race roots and her family's beginnings in slavery and oppression. But her joy and kindness have always been the most alluring thing about Miss Mary, who signs her cards to me "Mother Mary." She is a mother to me, and to many others at Madison Square Church. I hope this story honors the brave life and grand heart of a woman I am proud to call "friend" and "mother."

Lorilee Craker

Lorilee is the author of "Anne of Green Gables, My Daughter and Me: What My Favorite Book Taught Me About Grace, Belonging and the Orphan in Us All"; "Money Secrets of the Amish,""Through the Storm" with Lynne Spears and "My Journey to Heaven" with Marv Besteman.

(continued from page 83)

followed that pattern. As a teenager, Griffioen was part of a musical group that periodically rendered special music when the Madison Square Mission was still worshiping in one of the storefront buildings.

In 1971, thirteen years after his ordination as a minister, Griffioen became director of the Grand Rapids Board of Evangelism, later known as Grand Rapids Area Ministries (GRAM). In this role he was able to focus on urban ministry concerns; at least in part due to his efforts, and with thanks to God, all nine urban Christian Reformed Churches in Southeast Grand Rapids remained in the inner city communities where they were planted. White flight fears were counterbalanced with faith and determination to minister to their changing communities.

Don and Martheen, his wife, were members of Madison for nineteen years, and each of their three children confirmed their baptism with public profession of faith at Madison. Don provided key leadership to Madison at a challenging time in its history. After Martheen graduated from Calvin Seminary, she spent two years as director of outreach ministry at Madison and worked closely with Pastor Dante. The entire family was involved in all aspects of the life and ministry of the church until they were called to other areas of ministry.

6

The Co-Pastor Years: Tension and Growth

BY REGINALD SMITH

For we are co-workers in God's service. . . .
By the grace God has given me,
I laid a foundation as a wise builder,
and someone else is building on it.
But each one should build with care.
For no one can lay any foundation
other than the one already laid,
which is Jesus Christ.

1 Corinthians 3:9–11

From 1978 forward, Madison Square Church focused on three critical themes that set the course for its long-term vitality as a church. First, the Madison leadership remained committed to multiracial pastoral leadership despite its recent setbacks. Second, Madison learned from the charismatic movement without sacrificing its Reformed identity, particularly as reflected in worship and preaching. Third, its leaders and members stayed the course in reaching out to the surrounding community. They did not retreat from evangelism; instead, they increased their efforts.

These themes are prevalent in the three successive co-pastorates, demonstrating how intentional cultivation and leadership can lead to seismic changes. Pursuing these themes was a journey of highs and lows, joy and pain. However, the persistence of the pastors and other leaders, those who saw these three themes as God-commanded and God-honoring, contributed to the uniqueness of Madison's story, not only in the Grand Rapids area but in the Christian Reformed Church at large.

Sieplinga and Venegas

The 1977 resignation of Virgil Patterson, Madison's first African American pastor, carried with it

Reginald Smith

deep racial hurt. Yet the small congregation prayerfully dared to call David Sieplinga, a young White pastor from Omaha, Nebraska. And in 1978, when African American youth leader Tom Raysor also resigned, the council authorized Sieplinga to pursue Dante Venegas from NYC.

As a Calvin Seminary intern with the Manhattan CRC in NYC (1971–72), Sieplinga served under the mentorship of Manhattan's pastor, Rev. James B. White—yes, the same James White who first taught at Trinity College and then Calvin College. Some years later he also became a Grand Rapids City Commissioner. During Sieplinga's internship he also struck up a friendship with an ex-heroin addict who had experienced a dramatic conversion in 1964 while incarcerated for a crime he had not committed.

> I met Dante Venegas very early in that time in NYC, and he graciously took me under his wing. I was a very young (twenty-two years old!), very naïve, thoroughly Midwestern, White boy . . . and Dante was a thirty-seven-year-old, streetwise, passionate, Black Puerto Rican, Pentecostal Christian born and raised in Spanish Harlem (moving to the South Bronx at age eleven). That experience in central Harlem and the tutelage of Rev. White and Dante Venegas certainly shaped my orientation to ministry and fueled a passion for being part of a church that better reflected God's goal of reconciling all people, nations, races . . . indeed, all things in Christ. And just as importantly, it exposed me to an expression of the Christian faith that was more thoroughly Trinitarian . . . that not only honored the sovereignty of God and redemption through the cross and resurrection of Christ but also sought the fullness of the power of the Holy Spirit.[1]

And so it came to pass that in August 1978 Venegas received a phone call from a still-young White preacher friend inviting him to a place he eventually and playfully called "Bland Rapids." What could a Dutch Reformed–saturated Midwestern midsized city offer a New York City–bred Puerto Rican with

1. David Sieplinga, email interview with Bob Schuyler, August 2014.

The Venegas and Sieplinga Families circa 1979
From left to right: Andrea, Jackie, Pastor Dante, Michele, Drew, Pastor Dave, Rae, and Bree

an appetite for big city life? But Venegas knew who he was: a natural evangelist.

> Dante gradually grew to realize that he had been called to something different. There was no doubt that the Lord had called and gifted him to be an evangelist. His first concern was always for people's salvation and then growing in discipleship. [He] had an incredible gift and passion for talking with people about the Lord—anyone, anywhere, at any time.[2]

Venegas was a Pentecostal Christian with a charismatic personality, amazing people instincts, and a passion for Reformed theology.

Another important gift Venegas brought with him was his ease with interracial relationships. His marriage also was interracial. In 1966, his future wife, Jackie Mulder, accepted a staff ministry position with the Manhattan CRC in Harlem. The daughter of a White CRC minister, Jackie met Dante through a ministry of the church, the Addicts Rehabilitation Center, where he was on staff. "Dante came to believe that he and Jackie were linked by God, and that they had a chance to make it as a biracial couple. He knew it would be hard work and challenging, but he had begun to cherish

2. Chris Meehan and Jackie Venegas, *Dante's Dance* (Chapbook Press: Schuler Books, 2011), 90.

Jackie Venegas was responsible for the music ministry and working with youth at Manhattan CRC. A classically trained pianist, Jackie was mentored there by a couple of African American musicians, helping to greatly expand her musical knowledge, style, and techniques of a different culture. Jackie and soloist Elease Feimster formed a White/Black duo and performed in many venues in NYC, something unusual in the 1960s and 1970s. When she arrived at Madison with her husband and family in 1978, she transported her expanded musical abilities with her, introducing a new dimension to Madison's ministry of music.

Jackie and wanted to be with her for the rest of his life."[3]

In September 1978, Dante Venegas agreed to become Madison's Minister of Evangelism and hit the ground running. He began teaching Bible studies at the Bullock House, a rehabilitation facility for recovering addicts. Sieplinga remarked:

> Dante used to say that Madison seemed to attract "the bird with the broken wing." I think that was part of the Square's DNA . . . to be a place where the broken-winged birds could find refuge and perhaps healing, where misfits could not just fit in, but even be honored. And in that, at its best, the church represented the heart of Jesus for the least, the lost, the left out.[4]

Venegas's personal testimony—deliverance from nearly twenty years of heroin addiction, crime, and prisons—plus his "presence" in the pulpit cultivated a welcoming climate for drug addicts, alcoholics, and others rejected by society. He could relate to them and speak the language of the streets, prisons, and rehab centers. He was known for his great compassion for the lost and broken.

In God's incredible wisdom, the conditions for this uncommon compassion to take root were already in place. Sieplinga deeply desired to develop Madison as a church that saw itself as the heart and hands of Jesus by welcoming people who did not fit and embracing the outcasts

The Bird with the Broken Wing

3. Ibid., 82.
4. David Sieplinga, email interview with Bob Schuyler, April 23, 2015.

of society. This vision was grounded in Sieplinga's emphasis on Luke 4:18–19 as a theme Scripture. The compassion of Jesus is the only true foundation for a recovery ministry. From the time of his arrival, Venegas, the man from Spanish Harlem, became the catalyst for Madison's evangelism vision. Barbara Jefferson—a daughter of Mama Lu Robinson, the matriarch of a large African American family at Madison—clearly saw that Venegas was an evangelist.

> Pastor Dante is approachable. You could say anything to him. He helped make an about face with that church (Madison Square). Out in the streets, he was considered a man who lifted people above their circumstances, if even for a moment. . . . He was "out of the box." In other words, he took what he preached and brought it out into the streets on a level everyone could understand.[5]

His role as an evangelist was not a secondhand position in Venegas's mind, nor did Madison see it that way. He was appointed as the person who gave leadership to recapture Madison's first love—sharing the Good News of Jesus Christ with people in the community. His role played a key part in keeping evangelism at the center of church life, not on the periphery. Evangelism is the life blood of the church.

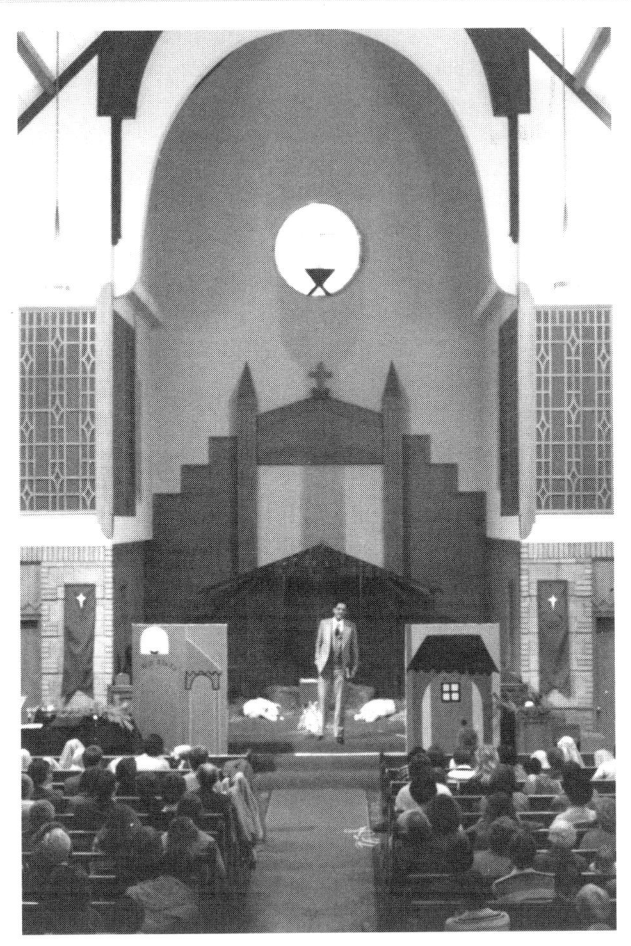

Pastor Dante preaching in the Madison sanctuary, Christmas 1980

The former-drug-addict-turned-preacher had a great love for people and a pastor's ear for listening to people's stories. He also worked through his relationship with Sieplinga; it was like any marriage, hard work and challenging. They hammered out preaching series together, called on neighbors together, and conducted

5. Meehan and Venegas, *Dante's Dance*, 94.

Co-pastoring is a unique church leadership model in which two pastors share ministry responsibilities as equals and both report directly to the supervising body, the council. While their specific assignments may vary, they work as collaboratively as is fruitful and feasible. This *multiracial* co-pastor model was initially designed by Sieplinga for Madison. It was then implemented by Sieplinga and Venegas, and it was embraced by Madison for three successive teams over a remarkable twenty-six-year period.

seminars in churches on racial attitudes.[6] They taught Bible studies on Wednesday nights, including teaching on the baptism and filling of the Holy Spirit.[7] Venegas and Sieplinga worked to model the kind of relationship that was not replicated in any other Christian Reformed church at the time. Their team ministry spoke powerfully that Madison Square Church did not shrink away from its commitment to put their money where their mouth was. Venegas even admitted that he "enjoyed team ministry."[8]

Venegas worked hard to become a full-fledged CRC Minister of the Word, including studying part-time at Calvin Seminary. His love for learning gave him the energy and fortitude to reach his goal. Sieplinga developed the plan for Venegas to be ordained under Article 7 of the Church Order, which requires the demonstration of "exceptional gifts" for ministry and "extraordinary need." [9] This article was also used in the 1960s and 1970s for the ordination of CRC Navajo leaders in Arizona and New Mexico. Under these same provisions, "Dante had to demonstrate his exceptional gifts and Madison had the burden of establishing an extraordinary need for those gifts. This represented one of the first times this article was used for an urban mission endeavor."[10] On October 18, 1981, Venegas was ordained as a Minister of the Word in the Christian Reformed Church. That was a proud day for the Venegas and Madison families.

It also was a proud day for Venegas's home church, the predominantly Black Manhattan CRC in NYC. Prior to leaving for Grand Rapids, Venegas had been a preaching elder there for a significant length of time. Clinton Ingram, Manhattan's choir director, gratefully observed that "Venegas is the first member of our congregation to be ordained (as a minister). He came a long way—from drug addiction to being ordained in the CRC."[11] Ingram, the choir, and others from Manhattan also came a long way to further enrich this special celebration.

6. "Madison Council Minutes," January 13, 1981.

7. "Madison Council Minutes," December 15, 1980.

8. Dante Venegas, "Staff Report," June 14, 1981.

9. "Article 7," *CRC Church Order*.

10. David Sieplinga, email interview, 2009.

11. Clinton Ingram, *The Banner* (November 16, 1981), 23.

Venegas and Sieplinga, with Madison and Manhattan choirs in the background, 1981

A Decade of Tension and Change

In the 1980s, the dramatic rise of AIDS and the destructive force of the crack epidemic created great societal fear and tension. At Madison, both Sieplinga and Venegas felt the tension of leading a growing church. There were people who had become new Christians through the evangelism efforts and needed discipling; on the other hand there were members who had grown up in the church and felt their needs were being neglected. In March 1980, the council "expressed the need to be more flexible for new Christians. . . . It had been expressed by many [mature] Christians that the worship, preaching, and music had been increasingly geared to new Christians and non-Christians. The needs of mature Christians are not met [with] more substantial biblical preaching, direction on Christian marital relationships, and child-rearing."[12]

Sieplinga and Venegas worked hard to both satisfy their members and not lose momentum. They taught and preached on the gifts of the Spirit and the power of prayer. The church held prayer and revival services on Wednesday evenings during the summer months of 1980, even when most church members were gone. The services began attracting people who were

12. "Madison Council Minutes," May 9, 1980.

open to asking for prayer or healing in their lives. This convinced the pastors that more needed to be done in addressing these spiritual issues. The services revealed answered prayers of healing, and people kept coming for more. The Spirit of God honored these services with unexpected growth from changed lives. However, this growth brought a new set of challenges.

The council acknowledged that the church "continued to struggle with the problem of a great number of visitors in worship. We are fearful the community residents and others whom our ministry was geared towards may be crowded out by those who might come to Madison as something of an oddity. Please pray for us."[13] The council was keeping its eye on community evangelism as paramount to fulfilling its vision and mission.

At a 1981 retreat, the council reviewed and adopted a Statement of Purpose written by Sieplinga that emphasized the inclusion of the Holy Spirit's work in all areas of life.[14]

The Statement of Purpose report also elaborated on the statement's key accent on racial reconciliation:

> Segregation in the church is not simply sad, it is a sin; it is more than unfortunate, it is heretical. We have been called by the Lord to demonstrate to the larger Christian community and to this racist society that the defeat of the enemy at Calvary also meant the destruction of the dividing wall of hostility and the establishment of a new humanity in Christ which radiantly anticipates the consummated Kingdom to be made up of every tribe and tongue and people and nation. Our style of worship and the makeup of the leadership of every program should reflect the powerful and beautiful gift of reconciliation among the races. The biracial pastoral ministry team is an important dimension of our witness to the reconciling power of God.[15]

Sieplinga and Venegas devised a nine-member team to do community calling and a seven-member team to be discipleship trainers. They were called "salt and pepper" teams. Going door-to door with multiracial teams modeled the

Madison Square Church
has been *called* by the Lord
and is being *empowered*
by the Spirit
to *be* the reconciled/healed
community of the King
and to *do* the reconciling/healing
work of Jesus.

"Statement of Purpose" Summary

13. "Grant-in-Aid Report," September 4, 1981.

14. "Madison Council Retreat Minutes," March 8, 1981.

15. *A Statement of Purpose: Madison Square Church* (1981), 2.

The Church Began to Grow

By Don Griffioen

With Venegas's love for the Gospel and his overflowing enthusiasm for evangelism, and with his gifted pianist wife, Jackie, and with Sieplinga's bold and enthusiastic leadership—when they began working together, the church began to grow in numbers, excitement and expectation.

message: Madison would not just "talk the talk" but also "walk the walk." These community evangelism efforts were blessed with strong interest and commitment from many folks in the Madison community.

This community growth, however, was outpaced by transfer growth from members of other churches in the surrounding area. In a November 1981 seminary course paper, David Beelen, then a senior seminarian and already a Madison member, reported that "When Rev. Sieplinga came to Madison Square [in 1977] there were 27 families, 63 communicant members, and 86 total members. Today there are 50 families, 135 communicant members, and 225 total members."[16] During that same time period, Sunday worship attendance was averaging around 275 in the morning service, frequently with one-fourth to one-third of the seats occupied by visitors.

Beelen also interviewed a number of Madisonites for their insights into this phenomenal growth. Here are some samples:

> Rae Sieplinga: "Five years ago a core group of women committed themselves to praying for Madison Square regularly. They are still praying today."
>
> Gail Hoekstra: "The reason the church is growing is because the Spirit is really moving in the people's hearts. I keep thinking of the time we moved [from Lafayette to Madison] and we carried a banner that said, 'The Spirit on the Move at Madison Square.'"
>
> Elder Ardie Burger: "We have a warm feeling of fellowship here. People really love each other. Also, the prayers of the people prove that they care for one another."
>
> Elder Don Huizinga: "There are two reasons: Our exciting worship experiences and Dante's gifts in evangelism and preaching."

Beelen's report continued:

> Rev. Sieplinga also recalled that during the summer of 1979, just before moving to the new building, 12 people committed themselves to receive training in evangelism and to go out into the

16. David Beelen, "Madison Square Christian Reformed Church: A Case Study in Inner City Missions," course paper, November 2, 1981, (Calvin Theological Seminary), 8.

community once a week. Each week the group would meet and receive instruction for 30 minutes and go calling for 45 minutes. Many of the current community members of the church were first contacted during that summer.[17]

Clearly, God also used Sieplinga and Venegas to lead the church into a new level of faith and freedom through expressive worship, African American Gospel music, and greater openness to the work of the Holy Spirit. Deflecting from his own impact on Madison's newfound vitality and growth, years later Sieplinga was quick to acknowledge the special contribution of Venegas and his wife, Jackie. "What Dante brought to the church was a passion for sharing the Reformed theology and infusing that great theological framework with a Pentecostal enthusiasm. Dante came to Madison Square and, along with Jackie and the music she played, brought a different style of worship that put us near the forefront of our denomination."[18] Madison Square Church never looked back at the once struggling church that almost closed its doors.

Vince Bivins, 2006

Long-Term Volunteers

As new doors opened for ministry, Madison attracted young men and women with a heart for the city dwellers. Under a program called Long-Term Volunteers, aspiring young leaders could sign up as unpaid workers, live on a small stipend through CRC Home Missions, reside with families from a church, assist in a variety of ministries, and even start new ones.

In February 1978, a quiet young man from Paterson, New Jersey came to Madison as a Long-Term Volunteer. Vince Bivins was paid $3.00 an hour for eighteen weeks of service. His job was to do community calling among the young people in the neighborhood. The year before, when Reggie Smith (from Chicago and now an ordained CRC minister) served on Madison's Summer Workshop in Missions

17. Ibid, 9–10.

18. Meehan and Venegas, *Dante's Dance,* 107.

Ruth Apol Zoodsma

(SWIM) team, Bivins was one of the team leaders.

Community response pressured Madison to find more workers for its garden. In 1981, Madison brought on additional Long-Term Volunteers Phil Apol, a White CRC preacher's kid, and Tom Fiet, also White, who loved youth ministry and diaconal work. Marjorie Boot also served during this time.

In 1982, Ruth Apol Zoodsma, a young Anglo woman with strong administrative skills, came aboard as a volunteer. Later she was brought on as paid staff and helped put feet under many existing and new ministries. Ruth served on staff until 1991 as Madison's secretary and administrator during its explosive growth.

These amazing young people gave Madison affordable, yet crucial, supplementary leadership in a time of rapid growth and great challenge.

Venegas and Beelen

In June 1982, Sieplinga felt the call of God to go to West Chicago; an inner city ministry, Garfield Christian Reformed Church, drew him away from Grand Rapids. What now? Would Madison turn away from a multiracial pastoral team? The council quickly began a search for a new co-pastor, and the administrative team developed a job description for "team ministry."[19] Both Venegas and Sieplinga served on the search team prior to Sieplinga's departure for Chicago. The names of twenty applicants were narrowed to two persons recommended by council. Madison then selected twenty-seven-year old David Beelen, a recently approved CRC candidate for minister of the Word.

Beelen and his wife, Melanie, had officially joined Madison Square in August 1981. They had already been serving as volunteers, helping with the young people's group and calling on people in the community. No doubt these involvements favored his selection. Beelen also received a call from another CRC

19. "Madison Council Minutes," June 8, 1982.

Melanie and Pastor David Beelen

church in the Grand Rapids area but was led to accept Madison's call with seriousness and humility. In Beelen's letter of acceptance he wrote, "When we were with Madison folk, we felt a strong pull to minister [here]. . . . So it is with . . . joy that we can tell you we accepted the call to serve our Lord and His church at Madison Square."[20]

Venegas was twenty-two years older than his new partner and had been educated in the school of hard knocks and hard time. Beelen grew up as a CRC preacher's kid, attended Christian schools, and knew the ins and outs of the Dutch Calvinist pastoral life. How would this partnership work?

Venegas and Beelen would make mistakes, spend time talking through the problems, and then would walk together again. They were not just "salt and pepper;" they were polar opposites. Their relationship was complicated at a time when the numerical growth of the church was shooting through the roof. What were some of the high points and growing edges that served the church and their pastoral relationship well?

The year 1984 was crucial for Venegas and Beelen. This was the year that Madison broke the four hundred attendance barrier for the first time. In Grand Rapids, all eyes were on this multiracial church that was growing by leaps and bounds. Venegas and Beelen contributed to Madison's multiracial growth as they gave leadership to the council and congregation, but they also had to grow in their multiracial relationship themselves. They had to learn how to be a team.

In their early years it was difficult to find time to get to know each other. Along with regular pastoral duties, Venegas was running Bible studies at the Ionia Correctional Facility, conducting Square Entry classes at the church, and writing guidelines for training members for evangelism. Beelen was finding his voice with preaching and getting to know people in the church. But they did meet to pray together before each Sunday

20. David Beelen, "Letter of Acceptance," July 1982.

service. This was a small thing that made small deposits of trust between them.

In addition, they planned and preached sermon series together. Beelen recalled "I believe that one of the reasons our co-pastorate works so well is that Dante and I continue to plan and preach series of sermons together. We are then forced to communicate—especially about the direction of the church and how we hear from God."[21] Venegas expressed that the partnership took time. He said, "Brother Dave and I still have a long way to go in becoming everything God wants in a team ministry, but I believe that we are far ahead of the usual. We are exploring, we love each other, and we enjoy being together."[22]

Both readily admitted that maintaining a friendship was hard work, but they never allowed their struggles to spill over into the public arena. In fact, in early September 1986, Venegas again expressed renewed confidence to the council about working with his ministry partner: "I am excited about a new year at Madison. I look forward to preaching with Dave and I feel good and confident with all that the Lord has led me through and given me to teach."[23]

Pastors Beelen and Venegas

However, within days of this report there was an "incident" that rocked their relationship. Beelen and Venegas were conducting the wedding rehearsal of a couple who were not familiar with the church. Both pastors participated in everything together from pre-marriage counseling to the ceremony. However, at the beginning of the wedding rehearsal, Beelen inexplicably referred to himself as "the pastor of this church." Venegas was standing beside him when he made the comment.

This was deeply hurtful. Somehow Rev. Al Mulder was invited into the matter. Mulder was a member

21. David Beelen, "Staff Report," January 1984.

22. Dante Venegas, "Staff Report," March 13, 1984.

23. Dante Venegas, "Report to Council," Sept. 9, 1986.

at Madison, a friend of both pastors, and a denominational leader with a heart for racial reconciliation. Whatever else went on behind the scenes, Mulder reported to council that the incident "served to bring some issues of black-white co-pastorship out into the open. It was significant and had repercussions on the team ministry of the two partners."[24]

As their partnership continued for another ten years, Venegas and Beelen continued finding ways to listen again, forgive again, and still lead a complicated church during its phenomenal growth. The truth is that this kind of co-pastorate was not attempted by many churches, whether in Grand Rapids or elsewhere. Their leadership timing was impeccably providential because their pastoral team was a large contribution to the growth of the first ever *large* multiracial church that happened to be Christian Reformed.

Managing Growth

In November 1986, the council convened a task force on church growth to recommend solutions to the overcrowding in Madison's Sunday morning worship services. The team came back with three options: (1) plant a new satellite church, (2) start another morning service, or (3) buy a new building.[25] Madison believed the Lord was expanding her tent to reach more people for Jesus Christ. The leadership recommended moving to two morning services in December, in the confidence that the Lord had not brought them this far to leave them.

With the continuing rapid growth of the congregation, the issue of overcrowding came up again in 1987. Growth was happening across the board—from community visitors, college students, and others driving in. The two morning services were breaking the five hundred attendance barrier consistently. This time the Church Growth Task Force, along with strongly recommending that Madison add a third Sunday morning service, also proposed to "study the multisite church model . . . (as) the solution to address our space problem."[26]

Curiously, talk about a multisite church model did not surface again for another 18 years. But Madison did soon begin exploring the idea of constructing a new sanctuary. And simultaneously, there was increasing momentum for starting

24. Al Mulder, "Letter to Council," Sept. 17, 1986.

25. "Task Force on Church Growth Minutes," Nov. 4, 1986.

26. "Madison Council Minutes," November 1987.

George Davis leading choir rehearsal

George Davis came on staff with Madison in September 1988 with a two-fold assignment: To develop, direct, and maintain a Gospel Choir and to lead the congregation during one of the worship services each Sunday. During his seven years on staff, membership swelled from 339 to 1052. The transfer growth due to people from other CRC congregations was matched with growth from other churched and unchurched folks from miles around. One of the contributing factors for this growth was Davis's skilled leadership as the anchor of the music ministry. Things were humming along for Madison, which was considered the "go to" church for good worship and good preaching. In 1995, God ushered Davis into another rich chapter in cross-cultural ministry, this time with Oakdale Park CRC.

a daughter church. In December 1989, the council reported that it was seriously exploring "the possibility of planting a new church."[27] Meanwhile, membership rolls continued to climb and worship and ministry space issues became increasingly challenging. In 1990, the congregation made the decision to construct a new sanctuary. In January 1992, Madison moved into its new and expanded worship center and returned to two morning worship services.

In the midst of all the attention being given to growth, Venegas never relinquished his prophetic call that the church must keep its focus on the people within its geographic boundaries. Already back in July 1989, Venegas had challenged the council with these questions: "Are we as a church committed to evangelism ministry? How do we train and involve the church in such ministries as Project Rehab and neighborhood calling?"[28] Venegas felt it was his mandate to remind his fledgling church not to forget her calling to evangelize her neighbors. Venegas, along with Beelen, worked together to keep the church close to its mission to reach the people in walking distance.

Madison's numerical growth created not only organizational struggles but also struggles in remaining true to its mission—true to its calling of creating place and space for members of the community. Mary Stamps, an African

27. "Madison Council Retreat Minutes," December 2, 1989.

28. "Madison Council Minutes," July 11, 1989.

New sanctuary being constructed in 1991

American woman, served as director of community ministries for a period of time. Upon her leaving, Madison found new ways to move forward as a difference-making presence in the neighborhood. In 1994, the church approved two new ministry positions filled by persons whom Venegas playfully referred to as his "Dream Team." Earl James, an African American with management skills learned from two decades of working with the Michigan Department of Corrections, was hired as director of ministry and communication. Bonny Wynia (now Mulder-Behnia), a White CRC preacher's kid who grew up in cross-cultural mission churches in the Southwest and was a part-time seminary student, became the new director of children's ministries. Both were appointed to "demonstrate commitment to our multiethnic, inner city environment."[29] Through seeking wisdom from the community and the leading of the Holy Spirit, Madison was indeed rooted in the community and willing to commit resources to back up its claims.

A Very Painful Period

In 1993, Greg Cumberland was hired as Madison's new youth pastor. Unfortunately, he began his ministry under a heavy cloud of controversy, not of his own making, and without the full support of the council or the congregation. After struggling to carry out his responsibilities, he was granted a leave of absence in 1995 and resigned his position in 1996. (For a more detailed account of this painful period, see chapter 10.)

29. "Madison Council Minutes," April 12, 1994.

An Alternative Direction for Pastor Dante

The truth be told, the fallout from the 1993 youth pastor conflict deeply wounded Venegas. Only a few ever knew of his struggle; he never spoke of it publicly. He continued his ministry as before, but it was difficult for him. His strength of character and total dependence on God enabled him to persevere. However, in early 1996, having fulfilled his promise of staying on for three years following a sabbatical, Venegas requested a meeting with the elders to ask their permission to seek another ministry. With great sadness, they granted their permission and gave him their blessing. In his farewell sermon later that summer he said, "I knew in 1993 that I had to leave Madison. Now the Lord is bringing me back full circle to where I came from."

In the course of this painful process, God opened a door to Venegas for a new direction. Or make that Alternative Directions. The church celebrated his ministry among their midst and sent him off with their blessing. At Alternative Directions, Venegas became their new director of chaplaincy, providing spiritual counseling and his well-worn wisdom to those trying to overcome a life of drug and alcohol addiction. He returned to his first love of sharing the Good News with those far from God.

My Dream, My Desire

A reflection in Pastor Dante's 1996 farewell sermon offers a special window into the origin of the recovery ministry at Madison: "I have had this burning desire to see a church where the broken, the disenfranchised, the addicted, the prostitutes, the non-descripts, the ne'er-do-wells can come and *feel* that they've been in the presence of God, and *feel* that they've been accepted, and *feel* that they have heard a word from the Lord. That has been my dream. That has been my desire."*

*Dante Venegas, Farewell Sermon, August 4, 1996

Madison's celebration of Venegas and his ministry was held on October 19, 1996. One of the speakers on this occasion was Elder Donald Huizinga, one of the White leaders who had voted to invite Venegas in 1978. Huizinga described the overall impact of this Black Puerto Rican pastor from New York City on the emergence of Madison's current ethos:

> 1978 was not only the turning point for you and Jackie but also for Madison Square. . . . You preached Jesus Christ with the demonstration of the Spirit's power. . . . Your leadership at Madison has been crucial for the CRC denomination. . . . You were willing to place yourself in that crucible and be a powerful witness. . . . You stuck it out where many would have quit.[30]

Huizinga also acknowledged Venegas's influence on Madison worship: "You taught us to worship with our whole selves. The effect that

30. Donald Huizinga, "Remarks at Venegas Farewell," October 1996.

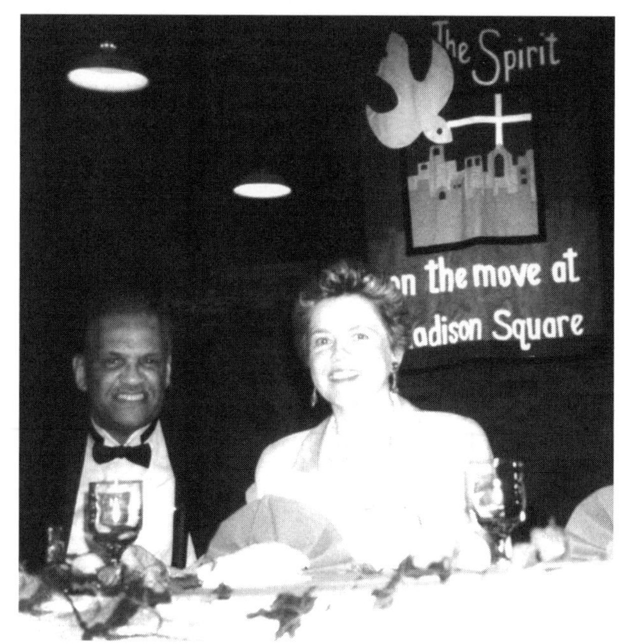

Venegas Farewell Dinner, 1996

had on allowing the Holy Spirit to bless us is evident from the number of people who have been attracted by the Spirit's presence in our worship services."[31]

Another former Madison elder and close friend, Joel Huyser, wrote of Venegas:

> It is not hyperbole . . . to say that people like Dante helped break cultural barriers and pave the way for racial change in the church as well as in society. . . . He was in many ways an unsung hero. . . . He became a living example of what it truly means to cross racial and cultural barriers. Dante had something special and unique. He was able to communicate a freshness and an aliveness to the Gospel that a lot of people had never experienced.[32]

Venegas's eighteen years at Madison was one of the most significant movements of the Holy Spirit that set the once small chapel to become a model of a multicultural, multiracial Reformed witness on the Grand Rapids religious scene.

Beelen and Reeves

Madison was at a leadership crossroads once again. How would another new pastor fit into the leadership at the Square? What was the Holy Spirit up to? With the departures of Venegas, Cumberland, and Davis—all within one year—there was no paid Black leadership in worship and preaching roles at Madison for the first time in decades. What did the Spirit have in mind?

In November 1996, the search team for a new pastor debated the wisdom of continuing with the co-pastorate model of leadership. This biracial, co-pastorate model was a powerful witness to a racially diverse community and congregation. At the same time, it was beset with racial misunderstandings and seemed to bring wounds to leaders and members alike. Ultimately, however,

31. Ibid.

32. Meehan and Venegas, *Dante's Dance*, 147–48.

advocates for continuing this unique leadership model won the day.[33] A nationwide search was initiated; candidates were interviewed by the council and appeared before the congregation. In 1998, Madison extended a call to Samuel Reeves to serve as co-pastor with Beelen.

Reeves hailed from Monrovia, Liberia, West Africa. He had prior Christian ministry experience in the oldest church in Liberia, Providence Baptist Church, but had left the country for his personal safety due to the throes of political unrest there. In the United States, Reeves pursued and obtained a Master of Divinity degree at Princeton Seminary. During his years at Madison, he also completed a Doctor of Ministry degree that was awarded him in 2002. Reeves brought a global leadership perspective to Madison. His style of preaching that was almost musical in its cadence, his encouragement of a global awareness, and his emphasis on holy living all deeply influenced Madison.

Through the leadership of Beelen and Reeves, Madison ventured into both familiar and unfamiliar waters by: (1) recommitting to increasing ethnic minority leadership on the council by 50 percent; (2) approving a church planting strategy to expand its vision to "discover fresh and contemporary ways for relating worship to all aspects of life;" (3) seeking to center all ministry on the Four Rs—Reach Up, Reach In, Reach Across, and Reach Out; and (4) forming an intentional partnership with Providence Baptist Church to promote "international reconciliation."[34] These initiatives fueled and focused the church's efforts to retool her impact beyond the front doors of the church.

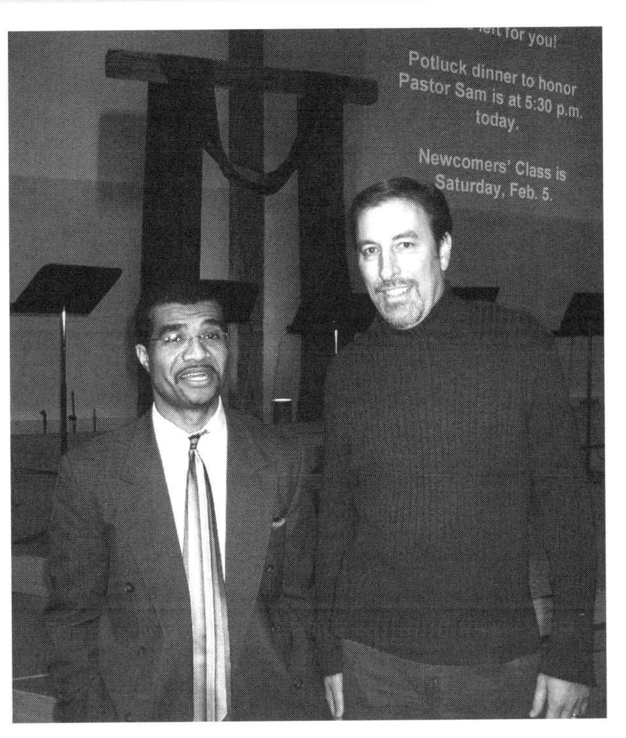

Pastors Reeves and Beelen, 2005

The sister-church relationship with Providence Baptist Church in Monrovia, Liberia took off quickly with a devoted team that championed prayer, letter writing, and

33. David Beelen, telephone interview, June 2016.

34. "Madison Council Minutes," December 7, 1997; March 10, 1998; May 12, 1998; August 2, 1998; August 11, 1998.

Pastor Sam and "Delicious"

"Pastor Sam-isms"

"I stopped by on my way to glory this morning to preach to you."
"I would like to introduce you to my delicious wife, Alice."
"I'm glad you asked."
"Put on your sanctified imagination and come along."*

*With thanks to Audrey Laninga

annual visits back and forth between the cross-continental congregations. Every other year or so, a delegation of Madison staff and volunteers would visit Providence to learn their ways of doing church and sharing God's love through reconciled relationships. On the off years, a Liberian delegation would visit Madison to participate in Madison's culture and to share their own culture. They stayed in each other's homes and shared each other's food. They fellowshipped in new ways. And, more importantly, they all loved the same Father, Son, and Holy Spirit. Folks from the two churches found that they had more important, foundational common ground in comparison to their minor surface differences.

Reeves's dream of assisting Madison Square Church to further her reach took on a new look and feel. Reeves reflected that Madison was

> deeply rooted in God's intention for His church; a dream that was seen clearly, felt deeply and taken seriously. A dream that this church will be transformed into a new community: not a black community, not a white community, not a Dutch community, not an African community, but a new community, a multiethnic, multicultural, antiracist community where the Gospel will be preached, lost people will be found, believers will be equipped, poor people will be served, lonely and broken people will be enfolded, and where God will get the glory for all of it.[35]

As community and global evangelism evolved for Madison in the new millennium, the Venegas legacy of knocking on doors, talking with neighbors, and sharing the Good News of salvation had never gone silent. Through the leadership of Beelen and Reeves, God also ushered in a new dimension of ministry in Madison's journey—beyond its prior racial and socioeconomic limits. Madison now began to imagine building relationships that extended its vision and mission to reach and

35. Samuel Reeves, *Congregation-to-Congregation Relationship: A Case Study of the Partnership Between a Liberian Church and a North American Church* (University Press of America, Inc., 2004), 26.

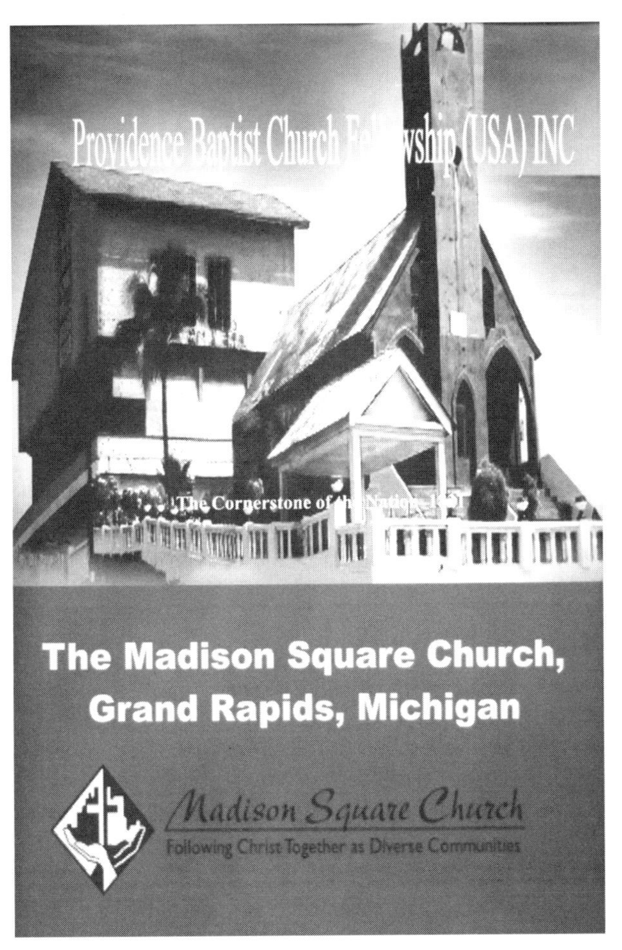

Madison/Providence Partnership

reconcile with people *outside* as well as *inside* her city walls.

In 2004, to the surprise and admiration of Madison Square Church, Reeves answered God's call to once again serve the Providence Baptist Church in Monrovia, this time as Senior Pastor. He made the move in 2004, encouraged by the prayers of the people and the promise of a continuing partnership.

The Madison/Providence Partnership

Reflections by Pastor Sam

The church and its witness to the Gospel is multifaceted and multidimensional, and as believers we sharpen our understanding when we encounter other Christians across cultural, geographical, denominational, and theological lines. The importance of social relations is not bound by culture. We are social beings, and how we interact with those around us is a universal concern. However, there are substantial cross-cultural differences in our interaction, and these differences ought not to be reasons for more alienation but occasions for a greater cooperation on our part. In June 2000, Madison Square Christian Reformed Church (Grand Rapids, West Michigan) and Providence Baptist Church (Liberia, West Africa) entered into a congregation-to-congregation relationship, believing that this relationship is an opportunity from God to live out our Christian faith globally by entering into this partnership. As part of our common heritage, we share the fellowship of the Holy Spirit, for "There is one body and one Spirit, just as we were called to the one hope that belongs to our call, one Lord, one faith, one baptism, one God and Father of us all, who is above all and through all and in all" (Eph. 4:3–6).

Congregation-to-Congregation Relationship

Reeves's book by this title is a profound, refreshing, and penetrating look at how faith, mingled with a daring outreach agenda and mixed with a caring disposition, can nurture cross-cultural contacts, interactions, and relationships in its search for the Good News. Here a hope-filled vision of how two very different communities of faith, a Baptist congregation in Africa and a Christian Reformed church in Michigan, came together to form a relationship of mutual giving and receiving. We see in this moving account a story of building bridges across oceans and cultures and traditions—bridges of mutual respect, of two-way sharing of resources, and of visits on one another's turf.

Even though both congregations have relationships with congregations in their respective denominations (the Christian Reformed Church of North America and the Liberia Baptist Missionary and Educational Convention, Inc., of Liberia, West Africa), we believe that this cross-cultural relationship between these churches and peoples will expand their understanding of the local and global kingdom of God. This multicultural experience will deepen our love for all disciples of Christ and enhance the ministries of both congregations.

In order to facilitate the growth and maintenance of this relationship and fellowship, the pastors, elders, deacons, and members of both congregations covenanted to do six things:

Remember and pray for each other corporately.

Encourage the exchange of prayer concerns.

Exchange greetings semi-annually in the form of letters and publications.

Promote and develop person-to-person relationships.

Implement joint ministries.

Renew this relationship annually.

Both congregations believe that, in Christ, they can be of mutual blessing to one another and hold each other accountable to continue growing in the grace and knowledge of our Lord and Savior Jesus Christ.[36]

About the Writer

Rev. Dr. Reginald (Reggie) Smith served on a youth mission at Madison in 1977. When he became a student at Calvin Seminary, he attended Madison from 1988–1992, married Sharon at Madison in 1990, and served as Madison's pastoral intern in 1991–1992. He was co-pastor at Northside Community CRC, Paterson, New Jersey from 1993–1994 and senior pastor at Roosevelt Park CRC, Grand Rapids, from 1994–2015. He received an M. Div. degree from Calvin Theological Seminary in 1992 and a D. Min. degree from Western Theological Seminary in 2004. Reggie and Sharon have three daughters, Janelle, Katrina, and Mariah.

36. Reeves, *Congregation-to-Congregation Relationship*, 2, 3, 65.

7

Lord, We Lift Your Name on High

Part One: Worship

BY AUDREY LANINGA

Come, let us sing for joy to the Lord;
  let us shout aloud to the Rock of our salvation.
Let us come before him with thanksgiving
  and extol him with music and song. . . .
Come, let us bow down in worship,
  let us kneel before the Lord our Maker;
for he is our God and we are the people
  of his pasture, the flock under his care.

Psalm 95:1–2, 6–7

The overall goal of worship at Madison Square Church is to create God-honoring, Christ-centered worship. Although this goal was not articulated in this way until more recently, it certainly has been foundational to worship at Madison throughout its history. Likewise, Madison's worship has always been multicultural, multisensory, and multi-participatory in nature—a part of its DNA—when understood within its context. Since 2005, these specific strands have been identified increasingly as important supportive goals for worship.

Increasingly Multicultural

In 1977, Madison's first African American pastor, Virgil Patterson, resigned. Youth leader Tom Raysor, also African American, left in 1978. The community was increasingly African American, and Raysor introduced music new to the congregation, both Gospel and contemporary styles, often using tapes with large speakers for accompaniment. During this period, the morning worship songs were primarily from the *Psalter Hymnal* with Gertrude Door at the organ. In the 1960s and 1970s, Linda Vander Lugt Brooks

Audrey Laninga

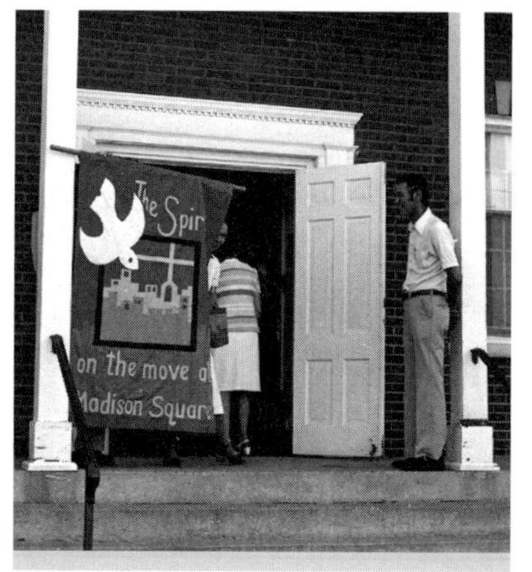

Preparing to march from the chapel to the church, August 1979

played the piano for evening services. Songs were selected from various songbooks, including a spiral-bound book, *The Dove*, which was purchased by Rod Mulder.[1] Published in 1975, *The Dove* added a tinge of contemporary flavor.

Patterson was succeeded by David Sieplinga, a Dutch-American from western Michigan, and Tom Raysor was followed by Dante Venegas, a Puerto Rican from New York City. Years later, Sieplinga recalled that almost immediately Venegas sparked greater spontaneity. "Pastor Dante was a worshiper before he was a preacher. His creativity, infectiousness, and passion for praise brought fresh worship expression to the congregation, such as coaxing 'Amens' from people, urging us to raise our hands in praise, incorporating a 'call and response' pattern, Black Gospel music, altar calls, and spontaneous prayer."[2]

Sometime after Venegas arrived, as he was leading a worship service in the chapel, he unexpectedly called his wife Jackie to the piano. He began singing "I'm So Glad Jesus Lifted Me," a chorus they had sung often in African American churches in NYC. Jackie joined in with him, and the congregation soon joined them in singing this chorus that was previously unknown to many. There was a stir in the congregation, and the passing of the music baton had begun.

The Passing of the Baton

Gertrude continued playing the organ for parts of the morning service; at one point, she asked Jackie to begin playing for some of the singing. Linda and Jackie were the pianists at the evening service.

1. *Psalter Hymnal* (CRC Publications, 1959) and *The Dove Songbook* (Home Publishing Co., 1975).

2. David Sieplinga, email interview, November 2015.

Pastor Dante taught the congregation to worship with their whole selves—body, soul, and spirit.

Evening worship started with a song service and people were given the opportunity to choose any song they wanted. As Jackie began to play more regularly, Pastor Dante would spontaneously start singing easy-to-learn choruses like "I Will Trust in the Lord," memorable Gospel songs such as "We've Come This Far by Faith," and well-known hymns like "Leaning on the Everlasting Arms" and "Hallelujah, Praise Jehovah."

Very soon "We've Come This Far by Faith" became a rallying cry for the growing congregation. In August 1979, the congregation left the chapel at 1164 Lafayette SE and marched to their new location at 1441 Madison Ave. SE. They sang this song over and over again as Pastors Sieplinga and Venegas led the procession carrying a banner with these words: "The Spirit on the Move at Madison Square."

The congregation's marching song was "We've Come This Far by Faith." As the people filed out of the chapel, Jackie played that song repeatedly until the last person had left. She then ran ahead to the new site and began playing the same song in the new sanctuary as the marchers entered, providing a musical faith-bridge between the leaving and the arriving.

Twelve-plus years later, in January 1992, on the occasion of dedicating the newly constructed sanctuary at 1441 Madison, Venegas recalled the 1979 move:

> We came here by faith! Marching across Hall onto Madison, 120 people strong (members and guests). Moving into what appeared to be a "very large sanctuary." Before we left 1164 Lafayette, we were given rocks on which to write our names and any message we wanted. We carried those rocks ("Ebenezer. . . . Thus far the Lord has helped us." 1 Sam. 7:12) and we deposited them on a pile in the front of the sanctuary. We still have those stones. . . . "He brought you water out of hard rock." (Deut. 8:15)[3]

3. Dante Venegas, sermon preached at the dedication of Madison's newly constructed and expanded sanctuary at 1441 Madison, January 11, 1992.

Marching "This far by faith"

The 1979 transition from the small chapel to the larger sanctuary at 1441 Madison was overwhelming. In the 1992 service of dedication for the now even larger sanctuary, Venegas continued his reflection on the 1979 move. For the evening service, he said:

> We started to worship in the basement where the janitor's office and some of the washrooms are located. But God said, "No, take the tartar sauce with you. Go back into the sanctuary." Mind you now, this is a group of folks whose budget several years before was a mere twenty thousand dollars. We are talking about having to ask the parishioners for extra money because we couldn't pay the pastor at that time.[4]

The congregation continued to grow rapidly in the new building. A worship committee was formed and began helping plan the worship services: themes, music, leaders, banners, and the sharing of joys and concerns. As worship became more complicated, it also became more difficult for Gertrude Door. In a meeting of the committee in 1982, someone suggested that Jackie speak with Gertrude about stepping down. Jackie, however, was uneasy with showing Door the door and advised, "Instead, let's pray that the Lord speak to her about when to step down." In a couple of months, Door told the church that she was ready to pass the baton to Venegas; a bit later she was honored for her

Gertrude Door loved Madison Square Gospel Chapel. When she began playing in the late 1930s, she offered her gifts to the church because of her deep love for Jesus, a love for reaching people with the Gospel, and a love for music. Affectionately given the middle name "Faithful," Gertrude played the organ for some forty years. She knew the hymns of the church that anchored her childhood as a member in the Christian Reformed Church. The Psalter Hymnal matched her playing style and ability, and essentially it was the soundtrack of a church that was about to undergo significant cultural change.*

*This profile was compiled by Reginald Smith.

4. Ibid.

"Thus far the Lord has helped us."

nearly forty years of faithfulness. With the Door/Venegas transition, Madison made the musical shift from the early twentieth century poor White context to the new urban African American scene that had a different history and moved to a different musical beat.

In the new sanctuary, the book racks held the *Psalter Hymnal* and *The Dove*. So many other songs were introduced that eventually Madison produced them—words and chords—in printed form with a hard red cover, affectionately called *The Red Book*. The first version had fifty-six songs, the second version one hundred and one songs. They contained hymns, choruses, Scripture songs, Black Gospel songs, Spirituals, and contemporary songs. Eventually (and for many years, even in the current sanctuary), these books were replaced with lyrics printed on transparencies that were shown on the front wall via an overhead projector.

Worship was also supported with banners. During the chapel days, a worship committee existed and the people were very involved; part of that included a small group of women who designed and put together a wide variety of banners. In 1977, professional artist Rae Sieplinga, with the help of many others, began creating banners for the chapel walls. In 1979, then in the new sanctuary, many more banners were created to transform the brown and grey walls and to cover the windows that had been stripped of their stained glass. Some banners were designed to fit with sermon series as well as the various seasons; these were hung from poles anchored in the wooden arches in the sanctuary (now the lobby). Single banners hung on the walls on each side of the pulpit.

A particular challenge was the large circle window—stripped of its stained glass—far above the pulpit. Initially, Rae designed a translucent fabric banner to cover the window's plain glass. Later on, she designed the stained glass image of the Holy Spirit hovering over the city as a dove. Madison member Mike Westra then assembled it, constructed its wooden frame, and placed it in that window above the pulpit.

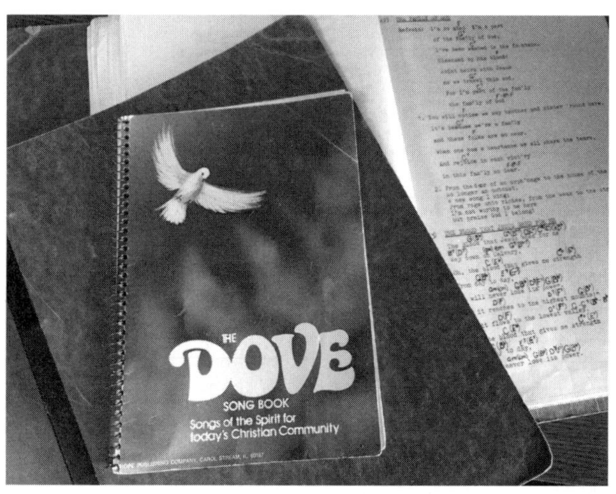

The Dove and *The Red Book*

Embracing Inequality

During the early years in the new sanctuary, the music ministry grew slowly and steadily. More pianists, more soloists, and more instrumentalists began using their gifts. Jackie developed an anthem choir, with Joel Niewenhuis eventually assisting as director; she also started a children's choir with assistance from Jeaninne Butler-Sytsema as director. And to expand the congregation's musical range, Jackie started an informal Gospel choir.

One Sunday in 1984, just as a Gospel choir rehearsal was ending, some folks walked into the room with Alice Finley, an African American musician, introduced her to the choir, and announced that Finley would now be their director—effective immediately.

Subsequently, the question arose about whether Finley should be paid. This became a point of tension. In March 1988, a study committee recommended that, since the anthem and children's choir directors were not paid, the Gospel choir director should not be paid either. The council agreed. However, upon reporting this to the congregation in July 1988, council received pushback and was urged to make a stronger commitment to reaching the community in more relevant contextual ways.

The council listened. In its report to the congregation in September 1988, it declared:

> Madison Square is a multiracial congregation and must maintain a good balance in the styles that nurture the congregation. In order to address the lack of balance in our present worship style, we must spend the money and give support to a gifted Black musician who has excellent leadership abilities. Even though it creates inequality with only one paid director, [and in keeping with] the goals of our church and mission to provide a worship service which reaches a multiracial community, we believe that this inequality is wise.

However, Finley had resigned in August, just prior to this report.

Simultaneous with the September decision to embrace the inequality of paying only one choir director, Madison hired George Davis as its first director of Gospel music. Davis was given the responsibilities of developing and directing a Gospel choir and leading the congregation in worship. Overall, the congregation responded positively to Davis's music and worship leading. Under his leadership the Gospel choir was invited to other venues as well, such as the CRC's Multiethnic Conference, the Grand Rapids Festival of the Arts, and even the Muskegon and Ionia Correctional Facilities.[5]

Creating Sacred Space

In 1992, after the congregation moved into the new and larger sanctuary, God used a team of artists from Madison to beautify it by visually creating a sacred space for worship. Frank Speyers, a professor of art and art history, agreed to design a motif for the windows in the sanctuary side walls and a cross for the front. He described the creative process in this way:

> The idea of the cross came during an initial meeting with a group of artists convened by Jackie Venegas. The large blank wall space behind the platform obviously needed a focal point for the congregation. I offered to create a large cross but had no equipment to create it. I turned to Mike Westra who enthusiastically supplied a router and the Styrofoam; he also knew of a downtown Grand Rapids

5. The narrative under "Increasingly Multicultural," "Passing the Baton," and "Embracing Inequality" were informed by an early draft of chapter 6 which was written by Reginald Smith.

warehouse wherein I could do the work. There I routed out the Styrofoam to simulate the wood of a large rugged cross. The upright became a 14 feet tall, 12-inch square beam and the crossbar an 8 feet wide, 8-inch square beam. The white Styrofoam, however, was not much to look at; so I brought along my leftover grey house paint and painted the cross to simulate time-worn barn wood. It worked! When I doubted whether the large cross could sustain its vertical position without support, Mike suggested inserting a four-by-four beam into the back of the cross to stabilize it. The cross became stable yet remained light enough to be moved if needed.

The windows came next. I drew out a cross section of a galaxy of stars. The windows were to be a deep shade of cobalt blue with the stars inserted as white lights in the night sky (Mary Katerberg cut the glass and Mike Westra implemented the design). God used General Revelation, the stars, to lead those outside the covenant of Israel to Special Revelation: Jesus Christ. And so the stars in Madison's sanctuary are meant to lead men, women, and children from the margins forward—not to a cradle but to a cross. The cross, that instrument of great shame, became the great symbol of triumph for Christians throughout history.[6]

Mary Katerberg

Frank Speyers

Several other artists created works that still bless Madison. Mindi Zylstra and Liz Kramer continued the new banner committee. Brett Likkel created the stained-glass candleholders for Advent, Dan Beelen the copper crosses, Ron Irvine the wooden crosses above

6. Frank Speyers, email interviews, October 8, 2015; June 24, 2016.

Advent Candleholders

all the sanctuary doors, and Ron Nykamp the baptismal font and communion table. The communion table in particular was designed to reflect a multicultural body, with different woods from the seven continents of the world, underscored by the words etched in the table's front: "Every Nation . . . Every People."

Moving into the new sanctuary also prompted improvement in the quality of the music, drama, and dance ministries. Madison purchased a baby grand piano, a Hammond organ, and a new sound board, while continuing to use overheads rather than hymnals. Later on, the church switched to a ceiling-hung digital projector and a computerized song database system. The expanded worship space, and the consequent loss of intimacy and community, increased the urgency for worship leaders to engage worshipers from the first to the last row

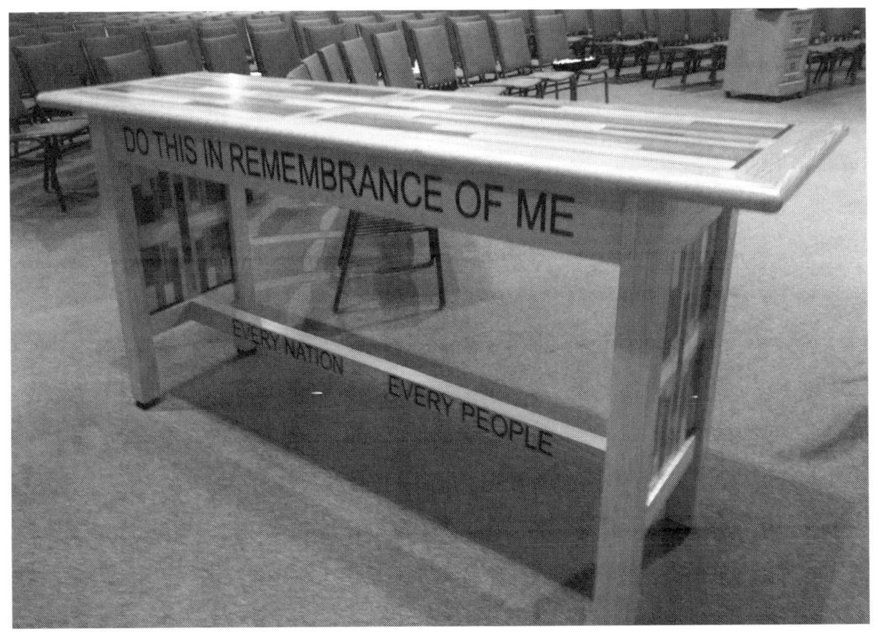

The Communion Table

of a six-hundred-seat sanctuary! Likewise, dance, drama, and worship teams needed to be better seen and heard, which led to a higher platform plus improved lighting and sound. What remained constant in the new sanctuary was Madison's inclusion of the marginalized, vibrant and enthusiastic singing, solid and authentic preaching of the Word, and spontaneous worship.

Twenty Years of Dance, Drama, and Design

Dance and drama ministries, which already existed in the 1980s, became more intergenerational in the 1990s under the leadership of Altia Legters, Lori Silvey, Amy Stoner, and Audrey Laninga. Children, youth, and adult dance teams were formed to participate in leading worship. Dance ministry also teamed up with drama ministry as a means for telling the Good News of Jesus through musicals and plays.

- 1994 and 1999: *The Lion, the Witch and the Wardrobe*—performed on Easter Sunday morning before large crowds and with a powerful community impact.
- 1995: *The Best Christmas Pageant Ever*—a delightful retelling of the Christmas story through the eyes of children.
- 1996 and 2002: *Godspell*—performed on Easter weekends, with thousands in attendance and a number of people coming to a newfound faith in Christ.

Henry Salley as Aslan (*The Lion, the Witch and the Wardrobe*)

God Is Not Blond

By Henry Salley*

Aslan is not a tame lion. He is a creature we cannot control. Myself as a Black person playing the part of Christ or Aslan says God is not blond with blue eyes. It helps the community to have hope and see Christ in them.

*Henry Salley, *Grand Rapids Press*, April 4, 1999

- 1997: *Heaven's Gates and Hell's Flames*—a dramatized call to repent and believe in Jesus Christ.
- 2000: *A Woman Called Truth*—the story of abolitionist Sojourner Truth.
- 2004 and 2006: *God's Trombones* by James Weldon Johnson—a story of God's great rescue plan with a Gospel flavor.
- 1998 and 2014: *Stand and Deliver*—the inspiring story of Jaime Escalante, a teacher from Bolivia who excelled in teaching math to core-city students in California. It also was presented in collaboration with local Master Arts Theatre as a matinee for six hundred public school and Christian school children.

In addition to the impact of the events themselves, their intergenerational and multicultural casts also built community within the body of Christ. What Beelen wrote of *Godspell* in 2002 could well have been written about the other presentations: "I witnessed how so many gifts of the people of God were utilized as more than a hundred people were involved in the projection and implementation of this ministry. God is glorified as we work together to

Greg Niemeier, Sound Designer

Ricardo Tavarez as Jaime Escalante and Xavier Edwards as Angel Guzman (*Stand and Deliver*)

The cast of *Godspell*, 1996

bring the Gospel of Jesus Christ to the people who are in such need of the saving grace of God."[7]

Expanding the Visual Arts

Liz Kramer, a Madison artist and visual arts committee member, explained that the visual arts continued to develop at Madison due to three primary influences:

Eric Nykamp formed a Sunday School class that explored Christian worship and the arts.

Audrey Laninga was hired as the director of arts and worship.

A committee was formed of people who led worship in all areas of the arts.

Blessed by these three influences, Madison has visuals that complement the sermon series, pastors who are more appreciative of the visuals and refer to them at appropriate times, and PowerPoint presentations that incorporate visuals into their design.

Mindi Zylstra, also a visual arts committee member, reflected specifically on their work with banners: "Sometimes we felt overwhelmed with the amount of work that needed to be done in a short amount of time, but one of the things we have learned and have come to depend on is the completing work of the Holy Spirit."[8]

7. David Beelen, personal letter, March 20, 2002.

8. Liz Kramer and Mindi Zylstra, email interviews, November 2015.

The Golden Lampstand

Worship and the Tabernacle

In the 1980s and 1990s, Venegas and Beelen continued to encourage freedom of expression in worship. Always from a Reformed perspective, their emphasis included sermons on the presence and gifting of the Holy Spirit, and multiple presentations of "Seven Ways to Praise."

In the late 1980s, Beelen began taking on greater responsibility related to worship. He formed and supervised the first volunteer team of musicians and singers: Steve Assink, Dan Beelen, Elaine Drenth, Bob Hartig, and Sue Vigh. In 1990, on Beelen's first sabbatical, he focused on a particular model for worship. Earlier he had studied two books by Barry Liesch: *People in the Presence of God* and *The New Worship*.[9] God strongly attracted Beelen to this Tabernacle Progression model for worship. This model, which still guides Madison's worship planning and practice today, is designed to show the progression from the Outer Courts (thanksgiving) to the Inner Courts (praise) to the Holy of Holies (intimate worship). Worship leaders were to imagine leading Madison's worshipers on a shared journey through the Tabernacle to the Holy of Holies, with the destination of becoming aware of the manifest presence of the Triune God.

In 2011, Madison undertook a major creative worship project with the help of a $12,000 grant from the Calvin Institute of

9. Barry Liesch, *People in the Presence of God* (Grand Rapids: Zondervan, 1988) and *The New Worship: Straight Talk on Music and the Church* (Grand Rapids: Baker Books, 2001).

The Bronze Basin

Wes Walker plays the role of the high priest.

A Unique Worship Experience

A congregational highlight was a winter retreat, which was held despite a fierce snowstorm and no heat or electricity. Folks came and—after cleansing their hands in the bronze basin, seeing with the light of the seven-branched lampstand, smelling the sweet aroma of the altar of incense, and looking in at the Ark of the Covenant inside the Holy of Holies—worshiped the Most Holy God in unamplified song led by Ken Reynolds. The sermon by guest pastor Marvin Williams, held in the Holy of Holies,* reminded everyone that Christ was the sacrificial lamb who was killed, and whose blood has purchased people for God from every tribe and language and people and nation (Rev. 5:9).

*This Holy of Holies replica was built by Bob and Heidi Bengelink and team.

Christian Worship. The stated objective was to "seek to renew worship from a spectator-performance to experience the complete, active participation of each worshiper of every ethnicity and age."[10] The goal was to expand the understanding of the Old Testament Tabernacle Progression approach set forth by Beelen in his 1990 sabbatical, and the method was to experience ancient worship as practiced by the Israelites in the Old Testament through the New Testament lens

10. Audrey Laninga and V. Cummings, "Proposal to Calvin Institute of Christian Worship," December 2011.

Children and Intergenerational Worship

By Kristen (Buurma) Lewis*

In all our children's ministry programs, we encourage kids to pray in front of the group, to lead in motions, to read Scripture, to teach and do registrations, so that the children are learning their gifts and are prepared to use these gifts to bless their church family. We then give them opportunities to do these things, not just in our children's ministries but also in front of the entire congregation.

*Kristen Lewis, email interview, November 5, 2015. Lewis is Madison's children's ministry pastor.

of multicultural and multisensory worship. Volunteers created a realistic full-scale tabernacle—complete with furnishings—in full view during congregational workshops, retreats, and even worship services.

In the course of the grant year, Madison learned that both the ancient and contemporary forms of worship share the overarching purpose of restoration and renewal in Jesus Christ. It also was observed that ancient worship seemed to be more participatory and Madison worship more multicultural. Ancient worship has much to tell about more fully using our bodies in the worship of God! Looking back on that year, Madison realized anew that the entire Bible—from Genesis to Revelation—tells one great story of God's love for His children and His amazing rescue plan.

Ken Reynolds Sr. and Ken Reynolds Jr.

Twenty Years of Worship Leadership

George Davis resigned in 1995, having accepted a worship leadership position with Oakdale Park CRC. Given his seven years as an up-front music and worship leader for Madison, some wondered if his years of abundance would be followed by seven years of famine.[11] Once again God provided a capable African American musician, a young man by the name of Ken Reynolds. He

11. A reference to Genesis 41:29, with seven years of abundance followed by seven years of famine.

Charsie Sawyer

Nick Hopkins

Leslie Montgomery

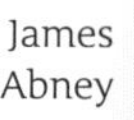
James Abney

had training and experience in a variety of musical styles and brought musical family members with him to Madison. He gathered and directed a powerful Gospel choir and, in 1998, convinced them to record their first-ever Gospel CD. During his years at Madison, Reynolds grew in his ability to draw people into worship in ways that were biblically informed, culturally relevant, and God-honoring.

Reynolds' ministry even took on a global emphasis. In 1999, Ken traveled to Liberia to lead worship workshops and teach favorite Madison songs to brothers and sisters at Madison's partner church,

Eric Nykamp at the Piano, 2005

Providence Baptist in the capital city of Monrovia. And it is noteworthy that a song he wrote at Madison – "Does Anybody Here Want to Praise the Lord with Me?" – was translated into Korean, Portuguese, and Spanish, and sung all over the world. In 2001, Reynolds accepted a full-time ministry position with Resurrection Life, a megachurch in Grandville, Michigan.

In the years since then, Madison again was blessed with a wonderful procession of Gospel choir directors, each of them contributing to the music and worship ministry in a variety of ways.

- Charsie Sawyer, 2001–2006, who was a member of the Calvin College music faculty.
- Nick Hopkins, 2006–2010, then a seminary student, now pastor of the Shawnee Park CRC.
- Leslie Montgomery, 2010–2012, who also participated in the yearlong Tabernacle experience.
- James Abney, 2013–present, a well-known and charismatic director and composer.

During this same time frame, the worship services were led consistently by a wide array of worship teams. The teams worked hard at reflecting cultural diversity—vocalists and instrumentalists alike. Laura Carpenter Pritchard, one of Madison's longtime ministry directors, modeled these values in the leadership of her worship team called "The Love Team." A gifted worship leader and Gospel vocalist in her own right, Laura had an especially influential role in encouraging and shaping all the worship leaders to incorporate African American music with a Gospel flavor into congregational worship.

To add to the diversity in music, Linda Naranjo-Huebl, along with husband, Scott, and their team, introduced worship music with a taste of Latino salsa and a touch of Southwest flavoring, including some songs in Spanish. More recently, worship leaders Attah Obande and Paul Sokomba, both from Nigeria, have taught songs from their native church experience to other worship leaders and the congregation.

Impacted by these and other global emphases, Eric Nykamp, a gifted pianist and artist, created the

“The Parting of the Red Sea” by Michael Harris

Ubantu Drum Circle ministry. He collected drums and other percussion instruments from all over the world and even constructed very good imitations. Periodically, children and adults alike were offered instruments as they entered the sanctuary and participated enthusiastically as Nykamp led the congregation in worship and praise with an energetic beat and dramatic flair. While many appreciated the opportunity to worship in a new way, there were some who couldn’t participate because the volume was too loud for their sensitive ears. So even while Madison was attempting to be diverse, their eyes and ears were being opened to consider a broader picture of how people are different.

For the last decade and more, Beelen has invested increasingly in training members for effective worship leading. This included a weekend retreat in 2011 in which the biblical roots of multicultural worship were traced. He also developed additional training modules with two primary purposes in mind: Ensuring that each worship team reflects diversity in gender, culture, and age, and that the congregational singing times are multicultural, multisensory, intergenerational, and participatory.

Finding Jesus in Every Book

During ministry year 2013–2014, the pastors preached a yearlong series of sermons on the theme “Follow the Scarlet Thread: Finding Jesus in Every Book of the Bible.”[12] Each message was illustrated with an original painting by African American artist Michael Harris, who created one new image for each of the forty-two messages. These remarkable paintings served as a visual during the message, became pages in a coloring book for children, and were part of a weekly

12. Sally Lloyd-Jones, *The Jesus Storybook Bible* (Grand Rapids: Zonderkidz, 2007). This book was a key resource for this series.

devotional. Harris's extraordinary work also won entrance into a Christian national juried art show in 2015 and has been exhibited throughout the greater Grand Rapids area.

When asked what was one of the most impactful sermon series since 2000, Pastor Beelen chose this series because "it taught the congregation how to read the Bible through the Jesus lens, with the artwork and the intergenerational focus tying everything together."[13]

Madison Worship and the Future

In October 2015, Beelen also was asked what he imagined for Madison's worship in the future. He responded with a series of questions of his own.

> How do we become more proficient at being truly multicultural and more welcoming to the Spirit and also to the spirit of other cultures? How do we stay authentic in a world that tries to produce authenticity? How do we do multi-generational worship well? How do we train a new group of worship leaders in our sites and make this focus travel to other sites as well?[14]

13. David Beelen, email interview, October 27, 2015.
14. Ibid.

When Less is More

In 2005, Madison decided to switch to a three-service schedule in response to consistent strong attendance. While this arrangement helped Madison touch more lives, questions arose about the overall impact. The schedule was long and complicated for worship volunteers, and the worship services were becoming less multiracial and multicultural. After prayerful consideration, in 2012 Madison returned to its prior pattern of two morning services.

God-honoring, Christ-centered worship is essential to the vitality of a congregation. In keeping with its history of Holy Spirit–empowered worship and its longstanding commitment to racial reconciliation with justice, Madison continues to pray that God will so guard and guide its worship times that "to him be glory in the church and in Christ Jesus throughout all generations, for ever and ever! Amen." (Eph. 3:21).

About the Writer on Worship

Audrey Laninga married Jay Laninga in 1968 after she graduated from Calvin College. She also obtained a masters in communications at Western Michigan University and taught at Unity Christian High School and Calvin College. In 1992 they joined Madison with their children Aaron and Lisa, who also became active professing members at Madison. As a volunteer Audrey directed worship planning and several dramas. From 2005 to her retirement in 2015, she served successively as executive director of ministries, director of education, and director of worship arts. Aaron and his wife Cindi have given them three precious grandchildren.

Mike Westra, Sue Carruthers, and Liz Kramer by the stained glass window in the Gathering Room

A Beautiful Window Finds a New Home

With the construction of the new sanctuary, the remarkable stained-glass window high above the pulpit in the original sanctuary was removed and placed in storage. More than a decade later, in 2012, Mike Westra, who had also created the original framing, made it possible to relocate this special window in the Gathering Room adjacent to the lobby. This same beautiful window graces the cover of *This Far by Faith*.

Part Two: Prayer

BY LOIS MEYNE

> And pray in the Spirit on all occasions
> with all kinds of prayers and requests.
> With this in mind, be alert and always keep on praying
> for all the Lord's people.
>
> Eph. 6:18

Everything of God begins in prayer and worship. Everything born of God goes through a process: worship, prayer, conception, gestation, travail, and birth. As a church, we must always begin in prayer. At the place of thanksgiving and praise, God conceives within us His heart and mind for the church." This is how Madison's total dependence on God was expressed around 1985 by Pastors Venegas and Beelen in a several page handout for the congregation entitled "Developing Our Vision."

The handout continues: "The pastors' vision: We see all ministries bathed in prayer. We see a congregation deeply dependent upon God and our prayer life characterized by humility and joy. We see a church which is full of prayer warriors and intercessors." Without God, this so-called "sociological nightmare" of a church (see chapter 10) would surely have died. But God miraculously kept it alive and has used it powerfully to nurture believers for serving here in Grand Rapids and in all parts of the world.

"All Kinds of Prayer"

Prayer ministry was given special prominence under the leadership of Madison's first co-pastor team, Sieplinga and Venegas. What a "salt and pepper" team God put together! In the diversity of their leadership, they modeled not only racial reconciliation but also the power of the Gospel and of prayer.

To fan these flames, Venegas invited a small group to his home on Saturdays to spend the entire morning in prayer—a practice that

Lois Meyne

continued for about two years. Around the same time, Rosie Hair, an experienced prayer warrior and lay leader, authored Madison's first prayer manual. With God's blessing, the strength of Madison's prayer ministry, even today, can be attributed to Venegas and Hair. God used both of them to teach the prayer leaders many things: Learning about prayer as spiritual warfare, learning about the Holy Spirit and His gifts, and learning how to serve as intercessors. They also taught them how to trust God more and to be bold in the power of the Spirit, how to listen more in prayer, how to serve people in crisis and with chronic needs, how to pray for both physical and spiritual healing, and how to respond to requests for house blessings and house cleansings. Some came early on Sunday mornings to cover the entire church with prayer. Others spent entire worship services praying that God's Word would touch people at their deepest needs. These intercessors also met regularly for prayer and instruction.

While lead responsibility for the prayer ministry remained with Venegas after Beelen arrived in 1982, Beelen also was a prayer leader and consistently modeled prayer as a priority—with concentrated time in prayer weekly, a week-long prayer retreat annually, and a habit of encouraging leaders around him to do the same.

Prayer and Healing

As Madison was growing in size and in ministries, and as the leaders sought to address people's needs in a holistic manner, they initiated the practice of praying with people at the conclusion of the worship services. These were key opportunities to come alongside people who needed the healing touch of the Lord and to bring new converts into the fold. As was soon discovered, invitations for healing prayer became the catalysts for people from all walks of life who were looking for a place to bring their pain and suffering and to find Jesus as Savior.

In 1984, Venegas and Beelen stressed to the elders that they had to "make the first move," which would encourage other people to come up for prayer after the preaching of the Word.[15] For a while, only elder-deacon teams

15. "Madison Council Minutes," April 10, 1984.

were stationed in the front of the sanctuary after the services for people to come forward to and be "prayed over." Both pastors trained these spiritual leaders to open themselves to praying and providing spiritual care that spoke to the needs of members and seekers. Soon additional members were invited and trained to become prayer servants as well.

In 1986, the elders and pastors developed a process of prayer and healing that became a permanent piece of Madison's worship life. They laid out seven steps for prayer servants to follow in their ministry of healing prayer.[16]

Step 1: Pastors and elders ask, "What do you want prayer for?"

Step 2: Tell them Jesus loves them and wants them to heal deeply.

Step 3: Dedicate the oil of anointing in Jesus's name.

Step 4: Apply the oil in the sign of the cross, pray for the person's need, and lay hands on them.

Step 5: Allow for a few seconds of silence and ask the person to thank the Lord.

Step 6: Tell them a sign of their faith was stepping forward and asking for prayer.

Step 7: Tell them Jesus loves them.

16. "Process of Prayer and Healing," 1986.

Rosie Hair

All Kinds of Prayer Leaders

Over the years, Madison's prayer ministry continued to develop under a series of lay leaders. Claudie Baldwin filled a staff role specifically for the prayer ministry from March 1995 through December 1996. She also taught a ten-month class on prayer counseling, focusing on the deep healing power of the Holy Spirit. In response to a call of a different kind, Baldwin moved to Texas shortly afterward to live with her new husband, Ken Vos.

At this point in time, Hair had already left to minister in another local church. Don and Beth Swanger, who had been trained by Hair, were next invited to lead Madison's prayer ministry. Under their

Claudie and Ken Vos

leadership, and fueled by multiple external movements, the prayer ministry explored new dimensions of spiritual warfare, spiritual mapping of strongholds, and prayer walking. For a brief period, a small group also experimented with all-night prayer watches.

Other initiatives included establishing houses of prayer in the neighborhood, modeled after a program in India. Cheri Niemeier introduced "Fresh Fire," modeled after the ministry of the Brooklyn Tabernacle in New York City. The Freedom in Christ ministry was introduced, based on *The Steps to Freedom in Christ* by Neil Anderson.[17] For a church with an identity of being strongly rooted in the Reformed tradition, these changes brought both inspiration and enrichment to Madison's preaching, teaching, and prayer ministry.

After Venegas left in 1996, God provided a new co-pastor to team with Beelen, the Rev. Samuel Reeves, a native of Liberia. Although Reeves had a very different life script from either Venegas or Beelen, providentially he also was a strong person of prayer.

Changes also occurred in the prayer ministry leadership. Eventually the Swangers left Madison, and Gordon Griffin—a longtime Madison member and one of its gifted musicians—picked up the prayer leadership. He personally took many people through the "Steps to Freedom" process and worked hard at recruiting new prayer servants. Eventually he also left Madison, exhausted.

Gordon was followed by Steve King, a psychiatrist, a gifted leader, and also a strong prayer warrior already serving in the prayer ministry. Steve gave great support and encouragement to other prayer servants; he also was gifted in teaching and in working to bring unity. But God had other plans for Steve and suddenly called him home to heaven in July 2005.

The mantle then fell on staff member Paula Seales, another strong person of prayer. Paula worked hard at having prayer

17. Neil T. Anderson, *Steps to Freedom in Christ* (Bloomington, MN: Bethany, 2015).

warriors meet together and be accountable to one another. She promoted more scheduled times for corporate prayer and gave leadership to prayer servants who would meet at church in the summer and then fan out to pray with Madison's neighbors. It was a high priority with Paula to unite prayer and outreach. However, she relinquished her mantle in 2011 to become a full-time student at Calvin Seminary.

By this time, Claudie Baldwin-Vos and husband Ken had returned to Michigan and to Madison; again she was tapped to lead the prayer ministry. In this new phase, a prayer leadership team was established to provide unity, support, encouragement and accountability. The Freedom in Christ ministry was re-energized. The prayer chain regularly sent out prayer requests to about one hundred intercessors. The pastors, worship teams, and worshipers were lifted up. Prayer teams were at the front of the sanctuary after the services. Healing services were held the third Sunday evening of each month. Special prayer training events were held three times a year. The neighborhood prayer teams and Soul Food Sundays were covered in prayer.

In 2014, Pastor Darrell Delaney became the campus pastor at the Madison Square campus—alongside Beelen, who then transitioned to the role of senior pastor of Madison as a multisite church (see chapter 11). As only God can orchestrate, Delaney and his wife Kia are both passionate prayer warriors. From the beginning of his tenure as pastor, Delaney has sought opportunities both to pray for people and to teach them about prayer, the Holy Spirit, and God's healing power. With a kindred passion, Kia initiated a prayer ministry called "Saturate," designed to create a safe place for women to seek healing from deep hurts.

Kia and Pastor Darrell Delaney

Throughout the generations God has blessed Madison Square Church tremendously with anointed prayer leaders and prayer servants—those named above and scores of others not named.

But who is the hero in this story?

As foundational as their prayer ministry was, it is not Pastor Dante Venegas or Rosie Saverson-Hair. Even though he has served Madison longer than any other pastor, it is not Pastor David Beelen. Although he has been a prayer warrior for over fifty years, it is not Ardie Burger. Despite their many hours each week in prayer ministry, it is not Claudie and Ken Vos. And notwithstanding his passion for prayer, it is not Pastor Darrell Delaney. Nor is it any other prayer warrior among us, past or present. The hero of the Madison story is none other than God Himself.

Everything begins and ends with God. We were dead and He reached out to pick us up. He breathes life into us. He cleans us up—not once, not twice, but continuously. And He Himself sustains a living relationship with us. We can't even do that! So we come back to where we started: "Everything of God begins in prayer and worship." All praise, honor and glory belong to Him! May we ever continue to grow in our relationship with God. And with our eyes fixed on Him, we step into the future with confidence.

About the Writer on Prayer

Lois Meyne first attended Madison as a Calvin student in the mid-1960s; she also taught Sunday School and helped with a Saturday afternoon play group for neighborhood kids. She and husband Marty joined Madison in 1970. Over the years, Lois has engaged in prayer ministry, children's ministry, council, care groups, pastoral care, outreach ministry, and multiple committees. Their children, John married to Kelley and Michelle married to Brett Ransom, have given them five wonderful grandchildren.

A Prayer of Gratitude

Dear Lord, we thank You as we remember the life-giving experiences of worship and prayer at Madison in recent decades.

We thank You for pastors whom You placed among us for new seasons and fresh perspectives, weaving together "what was" with "what was becoming." We thank You for worship leaders and prayer leaders whom You placed among us to deepen our understanding and expressions of worship and prayer and to call us to become personal sanctuaries of praise and prayer.

We thank you for the unity in diversity You provide us in worship and prayer through brothers and sisters with different faces and from different places in our local context and from around the world.

We thank You for hearing our prayers in the powerful name of the Father, the Son, and the Holy Spirit. Amen!

By Claudie Baldwin-Vos

8

Equipping God's People for Service

BY AL MULDER WITH CHRISTY CARLIN KNETSCH

> So Christ himself gave the apostles, the prophets,
> the evangelists, the pastors and teachers,
> to equip his people for works of service,
> so that the body of Christ may be built up.
>
> Eph. 4:11–12

Madison became an organized CRC church in 1970 under the leadership of Pastor Vernon Geurkink. When he left in 1974, the congregation—now sixty years old—did two things it had never done before: It selected its own pastor, and this pastor was African American.

The Rev. Virgil Patterson was first a Methodist pastor, then Presbyterian, and subsequently Christian Reformed, serving on staff at the Fuller Avenue CRC. At Madison, more African American families soon began attending and were baptized. Tom Raysor, also African American, was the youth pastor and part-time worship leader. Madison found its voice. Prayers went up. The Spirit came down. But change and challenge from within and without were overwhelming, and in 1977 Patterson resigned.

Within months, Madison chose a new pastor, the Rev. David Sieplinga: White, Dutch American, CRC, and young. When Tom Raysor left in 1978, Sieplinga proposed pursuing Dante Venegas—a Black Puerto Rican, a Pentecostal who loved Reformed theology, and fifteen years Sieplinga's senior. The two had met when Sieplinga had a one-year urban ministry internship with the Manhattan CRC in New York City from 1971–72. Venegas was uniquely endowed with gifts of the Spirit and had been a preaching elder at the Manhattan church.

A New Paradigm

Decades later, Sieplinga observed that forming a rationale in the late 1970s for Venegas becoming ordained in the CRC led to a paradigm shift in Madison's approach to developing leaders. "We were convinced that it was important for Dante to be ordained as a Minister of the Word, and we recognized that it wasn't reasonable for him to take the traditional CRC route to ordination—given both his age [forty-five] and the urgency of the matter."[1] These considerations led Madison to explore a seldom-used provision of CRC church governance, which stipulated that "Those who have not received the prescribed theological training, but who give evidence that they are singularly gifted as to godliness, humility, spiritual discretion, wisdom, and the native ability to preach the Word, may, by way of exception, be admitted to the ministry of the Word."[2] In summary, it was possible for an especially gifted person to be approved for ordination as a Minister of the Word without having obtained all of the required seminary training.

Madison was attracted to this gift-based approach as an authentic alternative with its own advantages. Quoting Sieplinga again, "This paradigm shift regarding an alternative route to ordination coincided with the congregation's growing awareness of the power of the Holy Spirit and our study of the gifts of the Spirit." In retrospect, God used this occasion and this pastoral team to usher Madison into a more gift-based paradigm for developing leaders.

1. David Sieplinga, email interview, 2009.
2. *CRC Church Order,* Article 7.

Sowers Went out to Sow

Matthew 13:3

Of all the people whom God has equipped for service through Madison, here are several persons who reflect on God's equipping them for service beyond their Madison experience.

Samuel Cooper

The congregation had just moved "by faith" to 1441 Madison when I began attending. Shortly before graduating from Calvin College, I heard Pastor David Sieplinga speak at a weekday chapel service. Truth be told, that's why I came to Madison. I stayed because I found in the congregation that same authenticity, spontaneity, creativity, and charisma—the Spirit on the move.

Pastor Dante and Sister Jackie, with daughters Andrea and Shelly, had just come from NYC. Through them I learned that serving and leading meant "staying on my knees

Samuel Cooper

to pray" and "trusting in the Lord 'til I die." One learned at Madison to serve genuinely and lead humbly from those who were already serving and leading in many ways.

From Ardie Burger, to pray boldly.

From Bobbie Riley, to serve practically and joyfully.

From Rod Mulder, to love justice.

From Rosie Hair, the realities of the Spiritual world.

From Al Mulder, to walk humbly.

From Jeffrey Butler, to shout Hallelujah!

From Jud Smeelink, what generosity was.

From Henry Salley, to give thanks in all circumstances.

From Jeannie Huyser, to love and serve young people.

From Jackie Venegas, the power and beauty of the Gospel in music.

From Ruth Zoodsma, to love the neighbors and the neighborhood of Madison Square.

From Ruth Bandstra, to be dependable.

From Dorwin Gray, that God has no favorites.

From Louise Price, to hear God's voice.

From Elaine Smeelink, to listen to others carefully.

From Melanie Beelen, that everyone can make a difference.

From Earl James, that gentleness is an enormous strength.

From you, my brothers and sisters, I learned to kneel, to raise my hands, to open my hands *and* my eyes to receive God's benediction; to use my body to train my soul.

From Pastor Dave Beelen, I learned the beauty and power of preaching and teaching that is faithful to the text, Spirit-directed, and meaningful—not just for my own spiritual growth but for the transformation of a community and a city.

From Pastor Dante, I learned the beauty and power of

testimony that is full of outrageous grace, genuinely relational, and absolutely dependent on the work of the Holy Spirit. Whether doodling on a restaurant napkin, cooing with a baby, teaching a small group to share their faith with neighbors, or testifying joyfully and enthusiastically, Pastor Dante taught me to be bold and unashamed of the One who saved and blessed us to be a blessing. I came to Madison Square Church aware of my own internal call to parish ministry but fearful and uncertain about surrendering to such a vocation. In God's providential care, He surrounded me with brothers and sisters—Jesus with skin on—who recognized my gifts and calling and urged me forward.

In 1993, my wife, Leanne, and I were called to our first pastoral charge in Toronto, Canada. Some twenty-five members of the Madison community joined in our ordination service. It gave us a glorious start and apparently a gracious longevity. In the words of Isaiah, "All that we have accomplished, you (God) have done for us." (Isaiah 26:12)

Cindy M. Vander Kodde

Cindy M. Vander Kodde

I was a single mom with five children, attending Calvin College. I had a strong relationship with the Lord but was struggling with how to live it out. Although I was active in another church, I was attracted to Madison by the style of worship, and because Jackie and Dante were from my home church in New York City. When I began attending full-time in 1984, Pastor Dante was very instrumental in helping me walk with the Lord faithfully. He taught me to take myself off the throne of my life and put Jesus there.

Around 1985, the Madison elders were concerned about the noise going on before worship and approached me to be a pre-worship leader to help bring people into the presence of the Lord before the service started. It seemed to help. More pre-worship leaders were added and eventually worship-leader teams were born. Pastor Dave Beelen trained us in worship leading: entering the outer courts, ushering into the inner courts, and ushering out to serve in the world.

I led a children's choir for fifteen years, and when they became teens we started a teen choir called "The Voices of God." Their performance of "Friends Forever" really brought them together and blessed many people. Another ministry created under my leadership was "Let's Come Together Ministries" in response to a sermon on race by Pastor Dave. I began meeting with a small diverse group to learn about our biases and also how to communicate and love each other better.

After Madison I worked for Calvin CRC as coordinator of evangelism and outreach. I've also served as a volunteer in various CRC denominational ministry-related roles: the board of trustees, the disabilities committee, the 150th anniversary committee, and in antiracism training. More recently, I also was involved in DeColores, Bible Study Fellowship, and Prisoners in Christ, a ministry to prisoners and returning citizens.

When I came to Grand Rapids, I was looking for spirituality. I give all honor, praise, and glory to my faithful Savior who led me to Madison and knew what I needed. Pastor Dante and Pastor Dave patiently nurtured

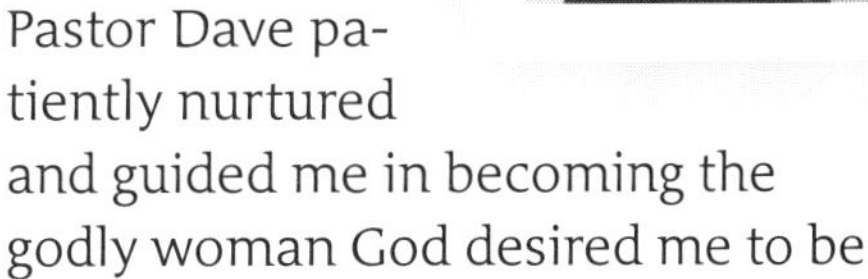

and guided me in becoming the godly woman God desired me to be.

Cheri Niemeier

Cheri Niemeier

Greg and I first walked into Madison in the fall of 1985. Ardie Burger hugged us both and welcomed us as a son and daughter. From Ardie's love and the Holy Spirit's presence, we knew we were home.

We had just started dating and were very broken. I had been divorced recently and was still dealing with the wreckage. Greg was further from his divorce, but he had not forgiven himself for the failure of his marriage. Soon we were invited to a care group with Pastor Dave and Melanie, Rod and Lu Mulder, and others. God used these initial relationships to mentor us and begin our healing process. Premarital counseling with Pastor Dave helped me admit and expose my sexual abuse as a child. Counseling with Rod Mulder helped us deal with the fallout of alcoholism and unfaithfulness and divorce in our families of origin. God gave me immense freedom as I was led to forgiveness of others and myself. My first ministry role at Madison was as a teacher in Madison Girls, and then I became a care group leader. Later I was very active in Madison's choir and became a prayer leader for ministering to one another at the conclusion of our rehearsals. My passion for prayer grew through a ministry called Households of Prayer; we would go to a home to pray after going to three other homes to gather prayer requests.

In 1997, I began the children's ministry called Pebbles and Stones, and through 2009 I watched the lives of children, teens, and adults being transformed through the power of listening prayer. I also served as a Madison elder for five years and believe that discernment and prayer was the reason God called me into that position. God used the Madison family, under the leadership of Pastor Dante, Pastor Dave, Pastor Sam, Pastor Joy, Laura Pritchard, Ardie Burger, Christy Knetsch, and many others, to transform me into the leader I am today!

At this writing, Greg and I are members at Impact Church, where I serve on the leadership accountability team as an elder and as the prayer ministry leader. Even though God called us to Impact in this season of our lives, Madison will always be our home!

Chris Schoon

I transferred into Calvin in 1993, in my third year of college. Hennie and I had just started dating, and the first time we attended worship together was at Madison. I had heard of Madison's inspiring worship, its commitment to racial reconciliation, and the preaching from Pastor Dante and Pastor Dave. I had an inkling God was calling me toward ministry, but I was not sure what that would look like.

Madison leaders invested in me in numerous ways. Audrey Laninga encouraged me to use my gifts in drama within worship. Greg Cumberland, Earl James, and Bonny Mulder-Behnia encouraged me to participate in youth ministry. In 1996, I started at Calvin Seminary, and Pastor Dave mentored me and a few other seminary students. Along the way I collaborated with Renita Reed, Andy Schrier, and Earl James in starting the Hattie Beverly tutoring center. I served as co-chair with Laura Pritchard on Madison's first antiracism team. Bob and Renita Reed inspired me by their persistent commitment to the neighborhood in which they lived. The mentoring and guidance of Pastor Dave and Pastor Dante, and to some extent Pastor Sam, profoundly shaped my understanding of pastoral identity and calling.

Chris Schoon

There have been ample opportunities to pay it forward. Serving as a pastor, initially in Grand Rapids and currently in Hamilton, Ontario, I have consistently mentored others preparing for ordained ministry. My advanced studies in mission, worship, and evangelism have opened many doors for training others through workshops, conferences, and courses in university and seminary settings.

God has shaped my understanding and vision for ministry through relationships and experiences at Madison in at least three ways:

- The role of a pastor is to help all God's people discover ways in which God equips them to participate and contribute within His church and kingdom (Eph. 4).
- Being God's people together always has a messy element to it, and loving one another in Christ requires vulnerability, patience, and lots of ongoing dialogue.
- Reconciliation with God calls for reconciliation with others. We faithfully embody the Good News of Jesus Christ only when we consistently expose and challenge the many pervasive ways in which racism and classism diminish all of us.

After serving elsewhere for fourteen years, Madison still feels like home every time we come back.

Ministry by Reliable People

2 Timothy 2:2

Many of our members became congregational servant-leaders after first meeting Christ or experiencing a deepened relationship with Christ at Madison, and then continued to invest their gifts and passion in ministry opportunities and needs under Madison's umbrella.

Don Huizinga

In the fall of 1969, during my first year in seminary and less than two months after being married, Dorothy and I were in a serious car accident in which she almost lost her life. In addition to many months requiring twenty-four-hour care, Dorothy needed to still remain near her doctors the next summer, which became the occasion for the

Don Huizinga

seminary appointing me to an internship at Madison.

Dealing with the long-lasting effects of the accident while attending seminary, up-close observation of Pastor Vern Geurkink's gifts and responsibilities, along with the experiences of preaching and co-leading a summer youth program, made clear to me that I could better serve God as a teacher than as a pastor. At the same time, however, Dorothy and I were immediately attracted to this core urban setting and this racially integrated fellowship of Christians—a relationship that has now lasted forty-six years.

In the early 1970s, when our fellowship had fewer members, the need for filling leadership positions became opportunities for me to serve as elder and as youth leader.

In the early 1980s, exciting pastors such as Dave Sieplinga, Dante Venegas, and Dave Beelen provided attractive, racially integrated leadership that contributed to vibrant worship and rapid growth, once again drawing me into serving in a variety of roles as needed.

In the early 1990s, in the context of heightened racial conflict, the council asked Earl James, an African American, and myself, a White person, to co-lead a team that would help Madison turn this conflict into a time of beneficial reflection and spiritual growth for the congregation. Earl exhibited inspirational leadership. Competent, organized, sensitive, and articulate, he steered the church (and me) toward healing and growth at a crucial time. His service was a model and motivation for me.

Around the year 2000, Andy Schrier founded a much-needed tutoring ministry named after Hattie Beverly, the first African American schoolteacher in Grand Rapids. Andy's dedication and sacrifice for that ministry, plus the fact that he became my son-in-law soon after, planted in me the desire to participate in that ministry—something I have done since my retirement from professional teaching.

Now that God has blessed Madison with many talented servants, I get to serve in ways that better fit my gifts and desires: teaching, tutoring, participating in short-term committees, or even painting walls and doors.

Dawn Niewenhuis

The first time I attended Madison was in the early 1980s. It still amazes me that a young Catholic girl from a broken, violent, abusive home on the northwest side of Grand Rapids would end up at Madison Square Christian Reformed Church. I knew the preaching was pretty good, but I never imagined what more God had in store for me. What I found was not just a group of people who gathered to worship Jesus but also "a church of the broken wing." I found a diverse family of God who cared and prayed for each other and who shared their lives with one another. As broken-winged people, our loving Father shapes and molds us until we are ready to receive our Savior's healing that we so deeply need.

In 1984, I joined a household (care group) by the odd name of Living Stones. Led by John Dodge, our household was made up of several college-age students, some single young adults, and an older couple in their sixties—Doré and Dolores Westra, who were the mom and pop of our group. This household family walked with me when I needed healing from my past. This family challenged me to read Scripture daily and to deepen my walk with the Lord. This family introduced me to Joel, whom I grew to know and love and who is now my husband.

Dawn Niewenhuis

Madison Square has consistently encouraged leadership development, but I never saw myself as a church leader, only a teacher and a musician. Yet God used Pastor Dante's testimony to help me see how He uses broken people. Sometimes God puts us in positions where He can stretch, mold, and carve us into the person He wants us to be. God has seen fit to use me in co-leading a care group, in co-leading the Madison Square Home Schooling ministry, and in singing, song writing, and worship leading.

God has also sustained me through Pastor Dave's teaching of Scripture and church doctrine. The many practices he has urged us to incorporate into our lives—memorizing and meditating on Scripture, refueling through retreats, fasting, listening prayer, practicing forgiveness, confession, prayer journaling, embracing racial reconciliation, nurturing my family, asking for the Holy Spirit's guidance, and being *still* before a mighty God—have fortified my relationship with God and enhanced my leadership journey.

Ben McKnight

Ben McKnight

My wife, Kimmie, and I started attending Madison Square Church late in 1983. We had been told that Madison had a great preacher, Pastor Dante Venegas.

We had been married three years at this point and were going through some difficult times relating to our jobs, which also affected our marriage. In addition, we were going to go through an adoption process and needed to become members of a church.

I was not saved at the time.

From the beginning of our attending Madison, Pastor Dante welcomed us—just as we were. He also connected us with Joel and Jeannie Huyser. Through them and many other folks leading me and praying for me, I accepted Jesus on March 11, 1984.

The Lord, through the powerful working of the Holy Spirit, has blossomed us into faithful followers of Jesus. With the gifts that God has given me in organization and administration, I have been able to use them in the various roles I was blessed to have received: deacon, elder, council chair, Sunday School class leader, and more.

As of 2015, I have continued to use the gifts God has given me to help Madison and its ministries in any way possible. God's gifts and grace also provide a foundation for dealing with other situations that I am involved in on a daily basis.

Having been at Madison for over thirty years, I feel so blessed to be a part of this church. With the Holy Spirit always pushing us out of our comfort zones, I will continue to allow the Holy Spirit to shape me into what God wants me to be.

Paula Seales

Paula Seales

Madison was at the end of a series of church homes for me: Anglican, non-denominational, Pentecostal, and now Reformed. I was attracted to Madison because of its diversity and solid, biblical teaching. From my first visit in January 2005, I felt welcomed.

Although I came to the United States with a master's in business administration and had worked as a junior economist for a bank in Trinidad, any prior church and ministry experience was limited to relatively small, monocultural churches.

Serving at Madison, a large multicultural church, I have learned to love and serve those who think and look different from myself. I have learned to seek first to understand and then to be understood. I have learned that humility sets us apart as Christian leaders, that it means denying ourselves for the sake of others, and that this too is the gift of God's grace.

I am particularly grateful to Pastor Dave, who mentored me and was very influential in my development as a ministry leader. For several years I served on Madison's staff as the director of volunteers, also supporting adult education, hospitality, prayer ministry, and Freedom in Christ. I served on the preaching team, learned to preach in the CRC, and preached periodically. As a volunteer, I served as coordinator of the evening services, as a logistics person on Sunday mornings, and led the neighborhood prayer team as a way to share the Good News with the lost.

Prompted by a desire "to present myself to God as one approved" (2 Tim. 2:15), I have completed my M. Div. degree at Calvin Theological Seminary. In June 2016, I was ordained as a CRC Minister of the Word to serve in a volunteer role as Madison's community ministry pastor.

I appreciate Madison's dependence on God and its Christ-centeredness in its teaching and preaching. I appreciate that Madison embraces the "broken" and gives much grace to one another. I have become more sensitive to cultural and racial dynamics, gaining a deeper love for God and his people.

I have also been blessed by loving relationships that healed past wounds.

I feel at home.

Multiplying Multicultural Leaders

In 2004, the council appointed a Vision 2014 team to help discern ministry direction for the decade culminating in Madison's centennial year. Chaired in year one by Victoria Gibbs and Al Mulder, and in year two by Victoria Gibbs and Pastor Dave Beelen, the final 2014 Vision Report articulated six priority themes and related strategies.

One of these priority themes was "Multiplying multicultural leaders for diverse leadership needs within Madison and related ministries locally and globally." And of several strategies suggested, the first was to "Develop a multicultural leadership institute" for growing holistic ministry leaders for local and global ministry.

In 2005, when Pastor Sam Reeves felt called to return to Providence Baptist Church in Liberia, Madison made two important decisions going forward. One was to shift from the longstanding co-pastor model to a single lead pastor model. The second was to develop and implement a preaching team approach as a way to ensure diversity in preaching.

Both the multiplying multicultural leaders theme and the preaching team strategy resonated with Beelen's gifting and passion. In November 2006, he launched the Antioch Leadership Development Network (LDN) and summarized its purposes this way:

> Train present leaders as coaches and mentors for the next set of leaders.
>
> Improve the leadership and preaching skills of mentors and mentees.
>
> Prepare those interested in being ordained as commissioned pastors in the CRC.
>
> Prepare potential leaders for church planting, multisite congregations, and staff ministry in the local church.

Antioch is a reference to the early church in the city by that name (Acts 11:19) and its culturally diverse leadership team (Acts 13:1–3). Leadership Development Networks (LDN) were a system of non-formal training programs supported by CRC Home Missions and local committees throughout the United States and Canada. Antioch was the first LDN program to be housed and resourced primarily by a single local congregation.

Commissioned Pastors

Ordinarily the roles and responsibilities of Commissioned Pastors are essentially the same as those of Ministers of the Word. The primary practical difference is that, while the ordination of Ministers of the Word can be transferred to other churches and ministries, the ordination of Commissioned Pastors is limited to the particular church or ministry for which they were ordained.

The first cycle of monthly LDN sessions included twenty students: preaching team members, staff ministry directors, and interested congregants from Madison and other neighboring churches. Utilizing an array of ministry leaders and resources, this innovative training program encouraged the participants in their leadership growth, both practically and spiritually. Notably, this program also had an important role in the development of Madison's first preaching team members: Joy Bonnema, Cisco Gonzalez, and Alton Hardy. (For more information about the preaching team, see chapter 11.)

Over the years God has provided Madison with servant-leaders who were gifted and passionate about developing other servant-leaders. Particularly in the last decade, God has equipped people for service in a variety of ways by means of the Antioch experience. In 2012, for example, the program's focus was shifted to worship leading, in keeping with a growing need for worship leaders in Madison's multiple congregations.

Pastor Alton Hardy

Alton Hardy

Truly I was brought to Madison by the Holy Spirit. In 2003, I was invited to a two-day church planting assessment sponsored by CRC Home Missions. I had begun reading Reformed books on my own and was falling in love with Reformed thought. I also knew God had a calling on my life for full-time ministry but didn't have any idea how or where to pursue it.

One day my wife, Sandra, shared with Laura Pritchard that I was called to ministry and we were seeking next steps for a church home. This was around the time Pastor Sam was preparing to return to Liberia and Madison was making decisions about a preaching team format. Providentially, I was in the right place at the right time, and Madison invited me to the preaching team. I needed some polishing as a pastor and preacher, but Pastor Dave and Madison gave me all of that and much more. From preaching team member in 2005 to campus pastor at the Ford from 2007 to 2011, my time at Madison was a glorious season.

Even when my time with Madison came to an abrupt end, I never allowed anger or bitterness to take root in my heart. God used every relationship, every hurt, every joy, and every sermon to grow me into the servant-leader I am today. My Madison time helped me see believers who were serious about addressing the plight of the poor and about confronting the insidious sin of racism—in themselves as well as society at large. The Spirit of the Lord also convicted me that the Gospel alone provides adequate theological undergirding for working with urban poor and racial issues.

For some reason, when my time at Madison was ending, I was acutely aware that God would use it to send me where I never would have gone on my own. It's no accident that God placed me in a more conservative theological camp of Reformed churches in Alabama. Today I am more patient with people who don't share my theological convictions. Today I also have this unquenchable desire to help Reformed conservatives and Reformed progressives minister together among the urban poor.

And it's no accident that God placed me in Birmingham, with its racial bigotry and deep segregation. I experienced much racial healing at Madison. Plus, my sermons at Madison laid the foundation for my work here. Goliath, the sin of racism, is real. But Jesus is even more real. He is serious about His church being one. And He is serious about making known His manifold wisdom to the powers and authorities in the heavenly realms (Eph. 3:10).

Steve Agler

In 2011, when I first came to Madison, I was married, a father, and a chiropractor. I also was a hopeless alcoholic. I had been dropped off at Mel Trotter Mission, and the mission required us to attend Madison on Sunday mornings.

I was a blank slate. I didn't know anything. It was the pastors and people at Madison who demonstrated the love of Christ that allowed me to heal. It takes a congregation to raise up a child in the Lord. That is what I was and that is what they did. God used people to save my life and teach me how to live.

Soon after Pastor Dave started meeting with me, he invited me

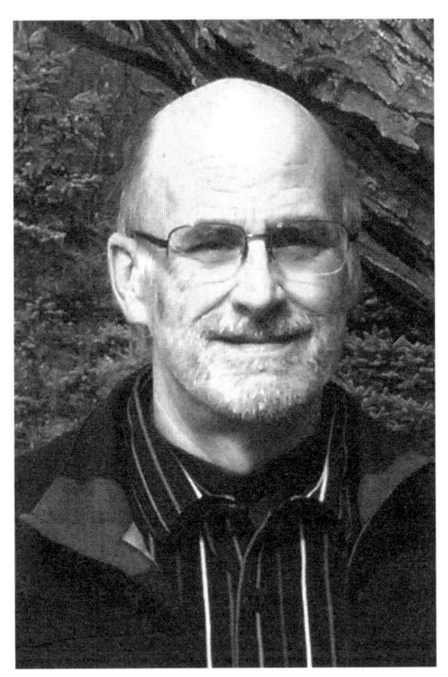

Steve Agler

along on a trip up north. I didn't realize it then, but he was giving me pastoral care. He became my mentor and met with me regularly. He identified gifts in me and invited me to practice them. He directed me to other people and programs.

Jay Laninga taught me to be an usher. Pastor Joy taught me how to treat women. I attended classes on prayer ministry and gifts of the Spirit. I learned about racial reconciliation. I was introduced to Christian Community Development. I attended Pastor Dave's Wednesday evening preaching class about Christo-centric preaching, including the four pages of a sermon and the works of Pastor Tim Keller. I served as a pastoral care elder, healing-prayer partner, and assistant worship coordinator. Victoria Gibbs mentored Ernie Long and myself as co-leaders of the recovery ministry. Pastor Amanda Roozeboom of a neighboring church tutored me for my examination for ordination as a commissioned pastor.

I have been a student at Calvin Theological Seminary and have served an internship as a congregational pastor with one of Celebration Fellowship's congregations at the Ionia Correctional Facility. This was such an exciting ministry opportunity, and I am trusting the Lord for what comes next.

God in His providence brought me to Madison. With the loving guidance of people, the reconciling power of Christ, and the comfort of the Holy Spirit, God's salvation will be present in future generations of my family.

Equipped and Equipping

Paul instructed his intern, Timothy, to "entrust (God's grace in Christ) to reliable people who will also be qualified to teach others" (2 Tim. 2:2). In keeping with this instruction, God used Pastors Sieplinga and Venegas to equip Pastor David Beelen; and Beelen to equip Pastor Alton Hardy; and Beelen and Hardy to equip Pastor Brad Knetsch. In turn, God has been using Knetsch to equip a *new* generation of leaders at the Ford—including Jermale Eddie (also see page 204).

Pastor Brad Knesch

I saw the equipping of others for leadership modeled right in front of me. Pastor Dave always made room to mentor seminary students on Wednesdays at 4:00 pm. For as long as I've known him, he's been doing that. Probably most important, he has helped me discover the importance of ministry rhythm: daily prayer, weekly date night, and monthly and annual prayer retreats.

Pastor Alton was the Ford Campus pastor when that congregation first began. He coached me on many areas—from urban ministry to leading teams to preaching. He always encouraged me by saying that ministry must flow from the heart. He would often say, "Brad, when you preach from the heart, you connect with the heart of the people."

Jermale D. Eddie

I grew up in a small town in southwest Michigan, received my college degree at Grand Valley State University, and worked at Calvin College in their multicultural office of student development from 2004 to 2007. During that time an African student died unexpectedly, and while some of us were at the hospital praying for her life, Pastor Dave came in to pray with us. God used this brief encounter to open me up to something I otherwise would not have considered—attending a Christian Reformed church.

We went to Texas for a while to help start a church plant. When we returned to Grand Rapids, we started a small downtown business. I was becoming a leader in the community and wanted to see change in the inner city. We also wanted to worship in the community and checked out quite a few churches, including Madison's Ford Campus.

What drew us initially was its smallness, and how much the kids were learning in children's church. Over time, my wife, Anissa, and I were invited to people's homes for dinner and genuine relationship building. I gradually began connecting with Pastor Brad. We liked the talk at Ford: Simplicity, community concerns, loving people where they are at, and racial reconciliation. I knew we could invite friends and not be nervous about what might be said by the people or from the pulpit.

When the Reaching-In Director position was posted in early 2014, at first I didn't give it serious thought. We were tired from our

Jermale D. Eddie

Texas experience. I didn't want to be carrying keys or giving out my phone number. However, Madison had a flavor and a history that attracted me, and I began to notice where I might fit. Then Anissa encouraged me to think about it. So did Christy Knetsch. At the last minute, I submitted my application.

In this position, God has continued to work on me and on my family. He led us to move into the community recently. God increased my desire for community engagement: Meeting people, encouraging others, and community advocacy. God has blessed me through Pastor Brad's friendship and his helpfulness toward me. And I believe God has blessed Pastor Brad through my helping him protect his time within ministry, and more recently through leading a pastoral care team.

Like two other significant local churches we experienced, Madison has a way of making a deep imprint on you. I am grateful for this season in my life. Each season is for a reason.

Equipping Youth for Ministry

Since 2003, under the leadership of Christy Carlin Knetsch, the vision of Madison's youth ministry is for young people to become lifelong followers of Jesus. All teens, regardless of race, class, or family situations, are provided safe space where they can be themselves and find open doors to hear God's voice, explore their gifts, and become leaders. Each meeting offers opportunities to learn about God, have fun, and be part of a community of believers who strive to live authentic lives for Christ.

Unique Ministry Markers

Here are some unique markers that have proven to be especially important for effective ministry with the youth.

Intentionally Developing Adult Leaders

A foundational marker is to recruit passionate leaders who are eager to use their gifts in the right place for the right reason, and the VIP method helps lay this foundation. Potential leaders are presented

Civil Rights Museum in Atlanta, College and Justice Tour 2015

a *Vision* that is worth following. Potential leaders are *Informed* of exactly what is expected of them, including a detailed job description. And their involvement also needs to be *Personal*, aligned with their giftedness and passion. Youth ministry volunteers also are provided initial and ongoing training, such as spiritual retreats to the Hermitage, Reload, the Urban Youth Workers Institute, and Christian Community Development conferences.

Where U At Urban Youth Conference

One of Madison's unique challenges has been finding conferences where its diverse young people can see themselves and their cultures reflected in the conference leadership, speakers, and worship teams. For eleven years running, Madison has collaborated with other local youth leaders in convening a conference called "Where U At," which is *for youth, by youth,* is intentionally multiethnic, and speaks to the issues our young people face in a language they understand. Empowering teens to lead and serve in prayer, worship, drama, and hospitality is a core value resulting in community growth, trust, and collaboration.

College and Justice Tours

Each spring break, Madison offers a College and Justice Tour that exposes teens to public, private, historically Black and Christian colleges and universities. The tour also explores justice issues by visiting historical sites where major movements of justice and resistance have taken place. Many local teens have gone on to enroll at these outstanding educational institutions.

Summer Mission Experiences

Madison's youth ministry has worked hard to introduce teens to missions that embody justice. Middle schoolers serve first in their own backyard, such as mission trips to the Grand Rapids Area Service Project and serving at local community organizations such as New City Farm. Every summer since 2003, older youth have visited the Pittsburgh Project, a CCDA organization whose mission is to restore the dignity of vulnerable homeowners. The visiting group joins the year-round Pittsburgh Project staff in providing home repairs, returning home with a roadmap for making a difference in their home communities. In summer 2016, a Madison group spent nine days in a Listen and Learn Cross-Cultural Engagement in Nicaragua—visiting missionaries, churches, and businesses; learning how God was already at work in Nicaragua; and listening for God to lead them in the next steps for living justly in their everyday lives.

Nicaragua Listen and Learn, 2016

Youth Leadership Development

The emphasis on developing multicultural leaders starts with youth as early as age eleven, in collaboration with other local ministries such as Camp Tall Turf, The Other Way, and Oakdale Park Church. During summer months, teens may be eligible for paid internship programs that allows them to gain experience in seeing how the Gospel holistically applies to their lives. Since 2006, Madison also has partnered in a major way with the Grand Rapids Initiative for Leaders (GRIL), whose mission of raising up Christ-like, cross-cultural, servant leaders aligns perfectly with Madison's vision for engaging young people in leadership, service, and social justice advocacy. Founded by Madison member Denise Fase, GRIL U—specifically for growing teens—has empowered over two hundred teens to be the change they wish to see in the world. In 2009, Madison and

Oakdale Park Church were awarded a $20,000 leadership development grant through the Fund for Theological Education, which also deepened the impact of GRIL for local urban youth leaders.

Stories of Transformed Lives

Terisa Bennett

In 2006, Jasmine Bennett was an active member of Madison's youth ministry. However, her mother Terisa, known to most as Momma T, was far from the Lord. Over the next decade, God would use Terisa's children to bring her into a vibrant relationship with Jesus. As Terisa began to serve behind the scenes in youth activities, God captured her heart with a passion for prayer and a new confidence in Christ. After her son Anthony completed GRIL U, Terisa joined the adult GRIL program. This led to a breakthrough plan that would change her life—and Madison's youth group. She not only is a foster parent and grandparent but also has become a key force in helping young people see that they belong, no matter where they've come from. Momma T led the Listen and Learn team trip to Nicaragua in 2016 and is key to the impact of the youth ministry at Madison. Her son Jamar will graduate in 2017, but she plans to continue serving teens for life.

Margarita Cavazos Chappell

When she started attending Madison's youth group as a fifteen-year old, Margarita was heading in the wrong direction. She had leadership written all over her but she didn't have a vision for life beyond her block. In youth group, Margarita met caring mentors who inspired her *to be* the change she wished *to see* in the world; they provided opportunities for her to live it out through the GRIL U program, College and Justice Tours, and trips to the Pittsburgh Project. With the support of her family and youth leaders, Margarita earned a BA from Western Michigan University and an MSW from the University of Michigan. In 2014, Margarita chose to move back to Grand Rapids and invest in her community. She now works for the Upward Bound program in the Grand Rapids Public Schools and worships with her husband, Jeffrie, at the Ford Campus.

Christy Carlin Knetsch

Knetsch became a Christian late in high school and was attracted to Calvin College by their offer of free laundry. Coming from Pittsburgh, Pennsylvania, she found the CRC to be a bit of a culture shock. But in 2001, Andy Schrier welcomed her at Madison and she soon became

Christy Carlin Knetsch

a youth ministry leader under Laura Carpenter Pritchard. When Pritchard transitioned to a new position in 2003, Knetsch left Wedgwood to become Madison's next youth ministry director. Trained in social work, and further impacted by the Antioch Leadership Training Network, Understanding Racism training, the GRIL program for adults, and a seminary Urban Cohort Program, Knetsch is passionate about developing Christlike, cross-cultural, servant leaders through whom God makes the Gospel accessible and relevant to others. In 2008, she married her Madison intern, Brad Knetsch. They have three amazing kids and worship together at Madison's Ford campus.

God blesses and empowers His church through willing and loving service. As the apostle Paul wrote so eloquently:

> To each one of us grace has been given as Christ apportioned it . . . to equip his people for works of service, so that the body of Christ may be built up until we all reach unity in the faith and in the knowledge of the Son of God and become mature, attaining to the whole measure of the fullness of Christ. . . . From him the whole body, joined and held together by every supporting ligament, grows and builds itself up in love, as each part does its work. (Eph. 4:7, 12–13, 16)

Madison Staff Members, Christmas 2014

From left to right: name, campus/site, full-time or part-time, start date

Front Row

1) Sean Johnson-Moore, Ford, PT, 2013
2) Kristen Lewis, Square, FT, 2011
3) Allen Pontarelli, Ford, PT, 2014
4) Jermale Eddie, Ford, PT, 2014
5) Dawn Flowers, Square, PT, 2014

Second Row

6) Christy Knetsch, All Sites, FT, 2003
7) Terisa Bennett, All Sites, PT, 2014
8) Shelli Fynewever, Square, PT, 2014
9) Laura Pritchard, Square, FT, 1996
10) Victoria Gibbs, Square, FT, 2012
11) Patty Hogan, Square, PT, 2012

Back Row

12) Hank Potts, Square, PT, 2009
13) Joy Bonnema, North, FT, 2008
14) Tino Scott, Square, PT, 2012
15) Eric Nykamp, North, PT, 2014
16) Jen Gebhardt, Square, PT, 2014
17) Susie Dixon, Square, PT, 2014
18) Missy Flockhardt, Square, PT, 2010
19) Joanne DeMoor-Tannor, Ford, PT, 2014
20) Ken Schripsema, Square, FT, 2006
21) Lori Robbins, All Sites, FT, 2003
22) Darrell Delaney, Square, FT, 2012
23) David Beelen, All Sites, FT, 1982
24) Marjorie Boerema, Square, PT, 2012
25) Don Bryant, Square, FT, 2010
26) James Abney (and child), Square, PT, 2013
27) Tim Jen, Square, PT, 2014
28) Brad Knetsch, Ford, FT, 2006
29) William Wiarda, Square, FT, 2003

Not Pictured: Mark Nieboer, Square, FT, 1996

9

Full Partners: *Promise, Pain, and Progress*

BY ANDREA BULT

> Even on my servants, both men and women,
> I will pour out my Spirit in those days,
> and they will prophesy.
>
> Acts 2:18

The seed of this bold promise—that both men and women would have the Spirit poured out on them—found fertile ground at Madison Square Church throughout its history. Even so, the faithful progress toward women in office included painful times as well. Presently, the Christian Reformed Church of North America allows all congregations to open the offices of deacon, elder, and Minister of the Word to women. Not that long ago, however, the denominational soil was not always hospitable to the seed of this promise, and Madison repeatedly positioned itself on the leading edge of this discussion. Standing where it is today, Madison is no longer swimming upstream on this issue and can boldly proclaim that this seed has indeed produced good fruit for this church, this neighborhood, and the wider body of Christ.

From the Beginning

Looking back in reflection helps to look forward with clarity. Much of Madison's history was characterized by reaching across seemingly impenetrable barriers with the power of the Gospel. This was certainly on display in the way that women were invited and empowered to use their gifts. Many church members, past and present, have played key roles in pushing doors open to official roles of ministry typically reserved for men. These pioneer advocates believed that when each part of the body works as it should and does what it is designed for, the body as a whole thrives. While this chapter names only a few of the many people who advocated prayerfully and passionately for utilizing women's gifts for ministry, the Holy Spirit used these advocates mightily to break

Andrea Bult

up hardened soil for planting this seed of promise in the hearts of others. Even as Madison recalls the moments of careful tending, fertilizing, and painful pruning that has happened over the years, it recognizes how Christ breaks down the walls that divide the church and builds unity in its place. And even in celebrating the fruit experienced today, Madison gives God the glory for the increase. Many men and women might plant and water, but it is the Lord who makes the seed grow.

Throughout Madison's history, women have always played a large role in the ministry of this church. Early on, evangelists like Elizabeth Smitter (1914) and Gertrude Holkeboer (1943) were brought on staff to help spearhead the mission of the church and to lead various Bible study sessions for adults. In the 1970s and 1980s, African American women such as Mary Cancler, Maggie Hollis, and Rosie Hair became leaders in the church—each in their own way—during a pivotal time for Madison.

They saw what was needed and made themselves available. During the leadership of Pastor Dante Venegas, well before church offices had opened up to women in the denomination, capable women such as these were encouraged to exercise leadership and influence in ways that an elder might have done in other churches. Because of their ability and passion, the level of women's leadership and influence was on the rise at Madison. In the late 1970s, the council allowed Hollis and the Missionary Band to host a Mother's Day worship service that was led entirely by women. Even though this service had to be reviewed by council before it could take place, God's promise indeed began to take root. The women showed their Spirit-led capabilities. As a result, Madison grew as a church presence in the neighborhood and as a forerunner in the denomination.

Think about This, My Dear Brothers

But there were certainly times when there was difficult soil to contend with. In her letter to the

Maggie Hollis

council in 1979, Maggie Hollis challenged them to consider all the women in the neighborhood when they had thoughts about opposing women in office at Madison: "Think about this, my dear brothers, when you oppose women in office. This area has more homes with women as the head of the house than men. What are you saying to these women? That they may come, but we (and I am talking about you white men) are the boss."[1]

Even as women's influence had grown, Maggie and many other women recognized that they were still only able to exercise those gifts outside of the official offices of the CRC. The church had more ground-breaking work to do in order to become truly hospitable soil for that seed of the promise in Acts 2:18. As a case in point, in the Public Profession of Faith form, for generations the church had promised to both men *and women* that "all the privileges" accorded to professing members were theirs. Yet, in reality, the privilege of serving in church office was restricted to men only.

1. Maggie Hollis, "Letter to Madison Council," December 1979.

A Denominational Debate

At Synod in 1978, male headship was an overriding issue during discussions about women serving as deacons. But some maintained that gifting, not gender, should be the guiding principle, and it was

"All the Privileges . . ."

Public Profession of Faith is the historic rite of passage to full membership in the CRC. People who come to faith in Jesus profess before the congregation that they believe in Jesus as their Savior and Lord. Madison calls it "Stand Up." Once people profess that they believe—whether baptized as children or newly baptized—they become *professing members* and are welcomed into *full* communion. Listen to this official welcome by the pastor:

> I charge you, then, beloved, that you, by the diligent use of the means of grace, and with the assistance of your God, continue in the profession you have just made. In the Name of Christ Jesus our Lord, I now welcome you to full communion with the people of God. Rest assured that all the privileges of such communion are now yours.*

What are "all the privileges of such communion"? Ordinarily these privileges include participation in the Lord's Supper, Christian baptism for their children, serving in the church's teaching ministry, voting at congregational meetings, and serving as an elder or deacon. For generations, however, *all* did not necessarily mean *all*. Specifically, the privilege of serving in church office was withheld from women until late in the twentieth century.†

**Psalter Hymnal*, (CRC Publications: 1987), 963.
†This sidebar was written by Al Mulder.

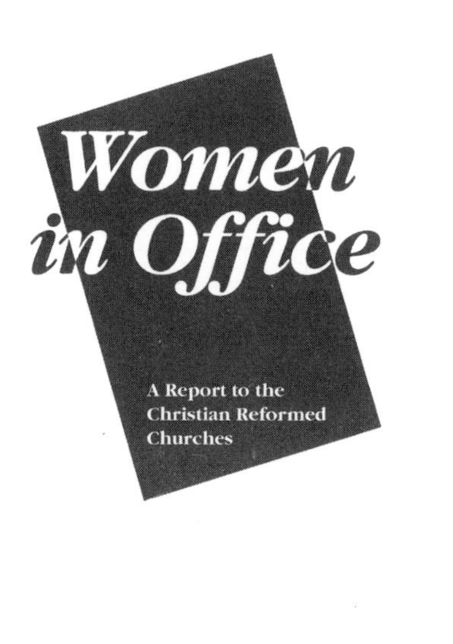

CRC Report on Women in Office

approved that women could serve the church as deacons. However, any decision made by Synod must be ratified the following year. In 1979, numerous overtures were presented to defer, further study, or overturn the decision of 1978. Some concluded that there should be more distinction between the offices of elder and deacon, stating concerns about women serving on council. Classis Grand Rapids East, however, stated that if such clarification meant that women could not vote on council, "then they are not deacons."[2]

When the denomination approved women to serve as deacons, the congregation elected Marian Takens to be the first deacon at Madison. This was fitting, as she served on the denominational committee advocating for women to be allowed to fully use their gifts in official church offices. This committee was a persistent advocate in the denomination until all offices became open, and Takens was at the forefront, serving at different points as its chairwoman, treasurer, and convention planner.

Not everyone at Madison was in agreement with the decision to elect her as a deacon. Even the church council itself was divided on the issue. While a number of men were opposed at the time, Takens recalled how people like Rod Mulder, Marty Meyne, and

Marian Takens

2. "Article 31," *Classis Grand Rapids East Minutes,* January 18, 1979.

Don Huizinga lent their supportive voices to this new direction. Don Huizinga, a Bible teacher, had read books on both sides of the issue as preparation for allowing his students to wrestle with the issue. "I saw the open position as best fitting the trajectory of Scripture," he noted. As an elder, Huizinga encouraged the council to boldly move forward based on their convictions. He recalls having to go by himself to a more conservative church in Hudsonville in order to defend Madison's actions because they believed Madison was an agent for disunity in the denomination. "We did not lead the way without cost," he concluded. "During our discussions and deliberations, we lost members on both sides of the issue."[3]

Even when Synod reversed its approval of female deacons the very next year, 1979, the council allowed Takens to continue to serve as she was already ordained to do so.

Men walking alongside of and encouraging women to use their gifts has been a big part of Madison's history. Pastor David Beelen, reflecting on the increased role of women in leadership, said, "Men really championed women using their gifts more than women forced their own way in."[4] He recalled men like Pastor David Sieplinga, Jim Haveman, Joel Huyser, and Earl James as those who helped do important ground work so this seed could take root more fully and women could move forward at Madison—even while the denomination was dragging its feet. While some saw this as a sort of rebellion, Madison leaders saw this as doing what they believed to be right.

Madison Takes a Stand

In a 1981 congregational meeting, discussion centered on allowing all professing members of the church to be eligible for all church offices. The congregation was presented with the rationale that the systematic exclusion of certain groups of the body from serving as council members, regardless of their gifts, was simply poor stewardship of the gifts the Spirit had given to the body of Christ. This was approved by the congregation with a 42 to 32 vote, and it was immediately followed by a vote to *not* inform Classis of the decision.

The denomination as a whole was still nearly ten years away from this kind of openness. In

3. Don Huizinga, telephone interview, March 28, 2015.

4. David Beelen, personal interview, June 10, 2015.

Elaine Smeelink

1988, Elaine Smeelink was the first woman at Madison to be elected as an elder, two years before the denomination voted to open all offices to women. Synod actually wanted churches who were ordaining women to cease doing so. Yet when Madison informed the denominational office of their decision, the office simply received it as information.

All this time, God had been doing His work behind the scenes. In 1982, when David Sieplinga took a call to Chicago, Madison called David Beelen to serve as co-pastor with Pastor Dante Venegas. God had already been working on Beelen throughout his own formation for ministry, slowly growing him in his conviction that women should be allowed to make full use of their gifts in the church and work alongside men in furthering the reach of the Gospel. As a sophomore at Calvin College, Beelen heard a sermon on women in the Bible using their gifts and was persuaded that an opposing view of women in church leadership was scripturally more difficult to maintain than an affirming one. A few years later he experienced a sermon preached by a woman from South Africa that confirmed in his mind God was speaking to him, clearly and powerfully, through a woman. This gradual changeover in his position was more than just anecdotal; for him it was biblically defensible. The more he studied it, the more he became convinced that the traditional application was more difficult to maintain. In fact, he felt that some arguments used for closing offices to women were applying Scripture in ways that were not consistent with its intent.

All this meant that by the time Beelen arrived at Madison, his conviction had grown to the point where he continued the support for women using their gifts in official church offices. “Initially, men opened doors to be sure,” he reflected. “But women in this church have also served faithfully without a chip on their shoulder about their right to lead. They led out of their competence and not their ‘comeuppance’.” Reflecting on the women who had served in different capacities throughout Madison's history, Beelen, an avid kayaker, added, "Their bow in the water, their cutting edge, was never feminism—it was the Spirit's call on their life."[5]

More Progress, More Pain

Having a pastor with this conviction opened even more doors for women to use their gifts. But even as Madison sought to be clear, consistent, and intentional in their vision for what the bold promise of Acts 2:18 meant, the progress made in this journey was not achieved without pain. As in many churches, some decisions regarding the role of women were met with uncertainty and outright opposition. One such recurring wave hit in connection with Madison appointing and ordaining Joy Bonnema to serve on its preaching team and be part of the *regular* preaching schedule.

Beginning to teach and preach at Madison was an eye-opening and heart-opening experience for Bonnema. In obedience, she moved more fully in the direction of ministry rather than biology, preaching rather than teaching, and being

5. David Beelen, personal interview, June 10, 2015.

Bonny Mulder-Behnia

Bonny Mulder-Behnia served as Madison's director of children and youth ministries from 1994–1999. Ordained as a Commissioned Pastor in 2002 and a Minister of the Word in 2009, she serves as executive pastor at Rosewood CRC, Bellflower, California.

I Watched in Awe

By Bonny Mulder-Behnia

When Maggie Hollis preached at Madison on Mother's Day in 1986, I watched in awe and my eyes teared up. She was the first woman to ever preach in my presence. While I don't remember a thing she said, I remember the feeling that God was opening a door I would someday walk through. She personified the possibility of women in church leadership, something I had always longed to see.

Little did I know that just six years later I would be preaching from the Madison pulpit as a seminary student and bringing God's Word some twenty times from then until 1999 while serving on staff. God confirmed his call on my life through Maggie Hollis and the welcoming pulpit at Madison.

Pastor Joy Bonnema

First Female Pastor at Madison

By Joy Bonnema, as told to Lorilee Craker

When Joy was at a crossroads, trying to decide whether to leave her career as a biology professor to pursue ministry, key counsel came from an unexpected source: her "wise, uneducated, Jesus-loving, Bible-saturated farmer" grandpa, John Asche. "I've been saying for a long time it would be better if women and men served together," he said.

When she looks back, Pastor Joy sees God's hand directing her on a path that few had traveled at that time, eventually guiding her to become the first female pastor at Madison.

At the age of twenty Joy married Chad Bonnema. Chad, a builder, followed Joy to Calvin College and then graduate school. She received a PhD in immunology in 1996, and in 1997 she came back to Calvin, this time as a professor.

In 1997, Joy and Chad began attending Madison. She began to serve by leading the church's college ministry, a role that gave her joy and allowed her to use her gifts more fully. Daughter Meikea came in 1999, and Pastor Dave Beelen gave Joy the chance to speak at her daughter's baptism about the foundations of the sacrament. Then in 2003 Pastor Dave invited Joy to co-preach with him on creation. "He sent me a note afterward of great encouragement and affirmation," she said. "He wanted me to lean in and listen to what the Spirit was saying."

When Pastor Dave gave a sermon not long afterward on Ephesians 5, the hotly debated "submission" passage, "It was an eye-opening and stirring sermon," she said. "We are called to mutually serve one another."

This pull on her life increased as she studied the Bible. "I began to see threads throughout Scripture of how God had called men and women to speak and proclaim together," she said. "Gifting is not gender-specific, but Spirit-specific."

From 2005–2008, Joy worked part-time at Calvin and part-time on the newly formed preaching team at Madison (Cisco Gonzalez and Alton Hardy rounded out the team). Though she faced some resistance from those "who didn't interpret Scripture the same way I had come to," overall Joy felt the blessing of the congregation.

In May 2008, she became pastor of congregational life at Madison and was ordained as a Commissioned Pastor in the CRC. Her heart sang, and she knew she had been brought to this place by a loving Shepherd's staff.

a pastor rather than a professor.[6] Even with Madison's healthy history of opening doors for women, this new normal broke more new ground at Madison. As Bonnema worked through her inner questions and concerns about God's direction, questions and concerns were also coming from the outside. Despite the fact that the elders had approved women exhorters for services back in 1993, not everyone at

6. Joy Bonnema, personal interview, July 24, 2015.

Madison was hospitable to the idea of a woman regularly preaching from the pulpit.

This was not the first time people felt uncomfortable enough to go elsewhere. When Elaine Smeelink was first elected as an elder in 1988, a few members left Madison despite the fact that she was well-liked and well-respected among those in the congregation. When Bonnema was appointed to the preaching team in January 2005 and began to preach regularly, again some members left despite the fact that she too was well-liked and well-respected in the congregation. By 2008, when Bonnema transitioned from the preaching team to pastor of congregational life, Madison saw even more members seek out other church homes, although many were hesitant to admit that women in leadership was a key issue.

The council had not planned on revisiting this issue, but because of how this matter was now forced back on Madison to consider both as a council and as a congregation, Beelen noted that it actually solidified their position rather than dismantled it. Madison had already tasted and seen the good fruit produced by men and women working as full partners in the Gospel, and there was simply no going back. Madison had become a church where those in leadership were expected to share this value. It transitioned from a church that had wondered if the concept of women in leadership was even biblically permitted to being a congregation solidly rooted in the conviction that it was more than just permissible. That conviction reflected what it meant to fully live out the Gospel.

Another Wave of Resistance

Out of the blue, another wave of resistance struck. In 2011, Pastor Alton Hardy had been planting and leading the Ford Campus, a multisite congregation of Madison worshiping at the Gerald R. Ford Academic Center about a half mile north of the Madison Square campus. Hardy was gifted and passionate about urban ministry, and the Ford congregation was beginning to grow solid legs under his leadership. Hardy, however, based on his personal study of Scripture, was never fully convinced of Madison's position on women in church leadership. As he was faced with appointing leaders at the Ford site, he began questioning whether he could take a public stand against women holding authority in the leadership offices of the church and still maintain a working relationship with Madison.

Hardy's concerns caught the council by surprise. The council thought this problem had been resolved as early as the 1990s and was not expecting it to come back with such force some twenty years later. Interestingly, while the earlier history of Madison saw men advocating for the role of women in church leadership, now the council included women leaders whom God had raised up to advocate for themselves.

For a number of years, Hardy had been sitting at the table with women who were diligently and competently serving on council as elders and deacons. Now, the council wondered how they might proceed with these conflicting positions. Was there a way to honor Hardy's passion and obvious gifting while also remaining consistent with Madison's value of encouraging women to use their gifts fully? The council found clear guidance and support in Madison's governance policy regarding multisite leadership.

The policy clearly stated that one of Madison's shared values was gift-based serving, which meant that people were to use their Spirit-conferred gifts regardless of ability, age, gender, or race. Further, it stated that every multisite congregation must maintain the same vision, mission, and shared values. In other words, every pastor and leader at each multisite congregation must affirm, claim, and live out the values of the church as a whole, not only in regard to race but gender as well. In addition, these understandings were stated clearly in Hardy's Letter of Call. This guided the council as they considered Hardy's question about whether he was required to submit to church authority as expressed through women in church leadership. And so the council answered with a decisive "Yes."

This new leadership model was now signed and sealed. Earlier in Madison's history, the care of the seed of God's promise was left primarily to men as the decision makers and advocates. But now an obvious shift had occurred. The council included many women also serving in leadership positions and working side-by-side with men to guard and guide all that had been taking root at Madison. They provided direction and leadership as this multisite church worked through a difficult year of questions centering on gender and leadership.

With overall appreciation for Hardy and his passion for the surrounding community, the council leadership even expressed willingness to explore the option of Ford

Victoria Gibbs

Linda Naranjo-Huebl succeeded Gibbs as council chair and served into 2014.

Kris Vander Stelt served as elder from 2005–12 and was serving as elder chair during this difficult time.

redefining itself as a church plant. In distinction from a multisite relationship, which required the campus pastor and congregation to embrace Madison's core values such as affirming women in official leadership, a CRC church plant—even with Madison as its calling church—would be free to adopt its own core values. This would offer only a partial solution, however, in that Hardy would still be accountable to Madison's council for matters of personal Christian living and Reformed doctrine until the church plant became an organized CRC church. In addition, the members at Ford would have to agree to this change in status. In the end, after much discussion and prayer, Hardy held to his convictions and concluded that God was leading him to leave both Madison and the CRC.

Council chair Victoria Gibbs facilitated a number of painful town hall–style meetings during which members of the Square and Ford congregations could ask questions and raise concerns. As an African American and as a woman, with Beelen on sabbatical part of that time, and notwithstanding her years of experience in a council leadership role, this was by far the most difficult and emotionally demanding leadership experience in her tenure as elder and as council chair. Drained from the process of Hardy's departure and its attending dynamics, Gibbs stepped down from both positions.[7]

Gibbs' female co-elders Kris Vander Stelt, Cherith Nordling, and Linda Naranjo-Huebl also played important leadership roles in working through the governance and theological issues associated with this difficult situation. Naranjo-Huebl was a founding member of the Ford campus and served as one of its two elder representatives. Despite not growing up in the denomination, she brought valuable leadership and effective

7. For more information regarding Victoria Gibbs, see chapters 1 and 10.

communication skills to the discussions during this turbulent time, especially with helping to bridge the two congregations.

Vander Stelt, chair of the elders during that year, was grateful the council could rely on Madison's clearly stated governance documents. Frankly, they were not prepared for the heightened emotions all around as the church revisited this issue. But the council, and the women on council in particular, would not be turned back and were strengthened by those who had come before them. Women like Maggie Hollis, Marian Takens, Rosie Hair, Elaine Smeelink, Marian Van Spronsen, Mary Robinson, Ida Reid, Jo-Anne Swart, Mary Hollebeek, Stacia Hoeksema, Janice Turnbull, and others had made a way, walking difficult yet helpful paths for those who took leadership roles after them. The importance of having women at the table was not lost on Kris Vander Stelt. "Any time you diversify the viewpoint, in terms of race, age, ability, gender, ethnicity . . . you make better decisions. That is not just a gender consideration; it's a leadership issue." She added, Vander Stelt reflected honestly, "It was a painful time and a painful loss. Madison lost a great pastor, and a great pastor lost his job. But we remained united as a council regarding our vision, mission, and shared values."[8]

Good Fruit and Steady Multiplication

Throughout this time of upheaval and transition, Madison stood firm in its commitment to move forward within its vision and values. It continued to hold doors open for women in ministry leadership, and many faithful and competent women have been walking through them into key council and staff leadership roles. The result has been very good fruit and a steady multiplication of Spirit-gifted women who have made rich contributions to worship, preaching, pastoral care, and community relations. Madison has continued to advance God's kingdom through the diversity of its leadership.

Continuing on this path at Madison Square are women such as Laura Pritchard, Christy Knetsch, Paula Seales, Patty Hogan, and Kristen Lewis, to name only some of the long list of women who have given Madison's vision and mission real feet in the church and in the community.

8. Kris Vander Stelt, telephone interview, August 25, 2015.

Kristen Buurma Lewis

Kristen Buurma Lewis graduated from Calvin Seminary in May 2011 and became Madison's director of children's ministry in June 2011. She was ordained as a Commissioned Pastor on March 30, 2014.

Reflecting on her personal ordination experience in 2014, Lewis wrote:

> It was so powerful. It gave me such a clear sense that what I had been feeling God had called me to do was what my church also saw in me. It was beautiful to have the whole church affirming me and saying they saw these gifts in me and felt God wanted to use me in this way. I don't face any obstacles here. People I barely know call me Pastor. This was definitely not an option for me growing up; I am so thankful to be in a church that not only has allowed me to use the gifts God has given me but also helped me to grow in these gifts.[9]

Over the years, Madison has been blessed by many gifted women living fully into the Spirit's calling on their lives, in large part because of the way this has become such a strongly held value at Madison. "All these women have been disarming in their leadership," Beelen reflects. "And none of it was our own doing. It was God's gift to us that He gave us women throughout Madison's history for whom gender was not their issue, even when others tended to make it so."[10]

When asked what has been the fruit of Madison having opened doors to women in leadership, Beelen leaned back in his chair and thought for a moment. "Better decisions across the board," he concluded. "Better decisions were made because women were in the circle. They can understand those who are looked over and left out. Having women at the table means we are a better reflection of God's kingdom, because God's kingdom is unity in diversity. And the better you reflect that

9. Kristin Lewis, email interview, March 24, 2015.

10. David Beelen, personal interview, June 10, 2015.

diversity, the healthier you'll be as a congregation."[11]

Now that all Christian Reformed congregations have the local option of allowing women to serve in the offices of minister, elder, and deacon, the opposition and obstacles to such service might not seem all that difficult to overcome. Yet over the years, many Madison men and women bravely did exactly that, and in doing so fostered a church where God's work could be done more freely and His promises realized fully. It wasn't always done perfectly. And it wasn't always pain-free. But the progress was purposeful as people intentionally walked in obedience toward a promise that God made through His Word—the Acts 2:18 promise of pouring out His Spirit on both men and women.

About the Writer

Andrea Bult began attending Madison in 2004. Her husband, Michael, and their children, Eli and Annika, love the ways this church helps to build and encourage their faith. Andrea began preaching at Madison in 2012 and has recognized that the ways in which this church encourages women to use their gifts has had a direct impact on her own preaching journey. Andrea is now at Calvin Theological Seminary studying toward a Masters of Divinity degree.

11. Ibid.

10

Are We There Yet?

BY AL MULDER WITH LAURA PRITCHARD

So from now on we regard no one from a worldly point of view.
Though we once regarded Christ in this way, we do so no longer.
Therefore, if anyone is in Christ, the new creation has come:
The old has gone, the new is here!
All this is from God, who reconciled us to himself
through Christ and gave us the ministry of reconciliation.

2 Cor. 5:16–18

Christmas Eve, 1992

Laura Carpenter Pritchard grew up learning to love and follow Jesus. Discipled briefly by her mother and then her grandmother, and all the while by Bible-teaching pastors, she approached Christmas 1992 with no idea where her journey would be taking her. Her marriage had come to an end. The small African American church she attended was coming apart. She did guest singing in area churches, Black and White, but was starting to feel like she didn't have a church home.

Almost on impulse, Pritchard decided to attend the Christmas Eve service at Madison Square. She had sung at Madison and had led an exercise class there. She had also counseled with Dr. David May, an African American with an office at Madison. She also knew a few White people from Madison such as Tom Mockabee and Kris and Nate Vander Stelt. Yet, as she recalled, the only thing that consciously factored into her decision that evening was her prayer: "Lord, if I leave my church, what church would you have me go to?"

"There was so much chaos in my life," she mused, "but that night in that service *there was peace*." Allen Likkel, a White denominational leader and associate pastor at Madison, brought the message, and God used him to speak peace to Laura's spirit. When she went back the following Sunday, Pastor Dave Beelen was preaching; she liked his preaching too. Along the way

Laura Pritchard

Laura Carpenter Pritchard was born in Cook County Hospital, Chicago, and moved from Chicago's South Side to Muskegon Heights, Michigan, at age seven. As the only African American girl at Camp Pines and Dunes and the only African American teen at Campus Life, Laura was already being called by the Lord to be an antiracist bridge-builder. When she was fifteen, her mother led her to the Lord; four years later her mother died. Laura moved to Grand Rapids and worked at Zondervan for ten years. Before coming to Madison, she attended what she called a "Bapti-costal" church.

A Long Bus Ride

From time to time this chapter uses the metaphor of riding a bus—in recounting Laura Pritchard's lengthy journey with Madison Square Church and the even longer and more tedious journey of a congregation in pursuit of racial reconciliation with justice. The use of this metaphor intends no allusions to the Selma boycott or other historic and sacrificial resistance to racism.

Pritchard also had prayed, "Lord, let the music be right;" the worship that day was being led by African American musician and worship leader George Davis. Not so incidentally, she also was blessed to see a Black Puerto Rican pastor on the platform; Pastor Dante Venegas was "real" and soon became a healing presence in her life.

A Road Less Traveled

Pritchard had often been told that Whites were blue-eyed devils. However, based on a series of experiences in predominantly White places, she sensed that at least some Whites were not the devils she had been told they were. She continued singing at White churches—in Holland, Hudsonville, and Grand Rapids—and was warmly received. She interacted positively with White folks in her work, both at a local radio station and at Zondervan. And, inexplicably, a White Madison member had given her generous assistance for housing, no strings attached.

After a few months, Carla Tett, an African American volunteer, invited Pritchard to volunteer with Madison Girls.[1] Others invited her

1. Madison Girls is a midweek program for middle school girls from the church and the community.

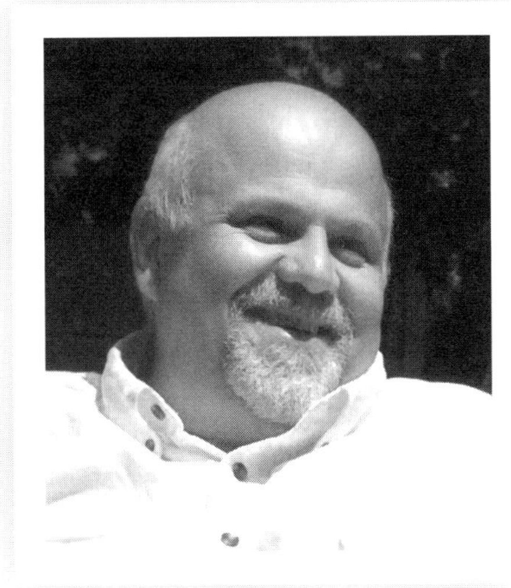
Bob Reed

to join the Gospel choir. Fairly soon she started hanging around Madison more and more. She attended the class for new members. Beelen had conversations with her about pursuing a leadership pathway. In a discussion about leading the Madison Girls ministry, Hope Bradley, a White volunteer, asked her, "Laura, what do you think?" It was a new experience for her to have a White person ask her what *she* thought. God touched her deeply through this question and emboldened her to accept larger responsibilities as a volunteer leader.

Several years after that 1992 Christmas Eve service, the youth ministry position at Madison came open. Mostly unaware of the rough stretch of road that had led to this staff vacancy, Pritchard was invited to apply. Earl James, Madison's executive director of ministries and communication, himself an African American, encouraged her to consider the position. So did Bonny Wynia (now Mulder-Behnia), a White staff member who would become Pritchard's immediate supervisor. There were more interviews and team meetings, with everyone saying "Yes!" Finally, she met with Madison's council. One memorable exchange was with council member Bob Reed, who asked her to describe her five-year goals. Pritchard said frankly, "I don't have five-year goals; I just follow where the Lord leads." She became Madison's youth ministry leader in July 1996. And Pritchard and Reed became precious friends.

When it became official that Pritchard got the job, another African American staff member at that time pulled her aside and said, "Laura, you're the golden child now. Don't mess up!" This staff member had been around long enough to observe a pattern of Black folks coming and going from staff positions. White folks would come and go too, but somehow that seemed different. White people boarding the staff bus and getting off again was considered fairly normal to both Blacks and Whites. By contrast, having Black persons come aboard as staff members seemed more significant somehow, and Black staff members leaving tended to be a bigger deal as well. When a Black person came on staff, at a certain level this person felt extra pressure from both Blacks and Whites to succeed! So . . . "Don't mess up, Miss Laura!"

From the Rearview Mirror

Before Pritchard came on board, Madison's story had already included lots of comings and goings of Black folks. The Rev. Virgil Patterson became Madison's first African-American pastor in 1974 only to resign in 1977 in the midst of pain and disappointment. And Mr. Tom Raysor, also an African American, had come aboard as youth leader in 1975 but left in frustration in 1978.

As frequently as leaders got on and off the bus, Madison's council can be commended for its strategic commitment to racially diverse ministry leadership. Rev. Patterson was succeeded by a White man, Pastor David Sieplinga, who was soon joined by Dante Venegas, a Black man. Serving initially as the minister of evangelism, Venegas broke the mold by staying around for many years! Yet unrest and challenge continued, even as Madison persevered in pursuing its elusive vision for deep racial unity.

In December 1979, the predominantly White council received a letter from an influential African American female leader, Maggie Hollis, challenging them to take Black members more seriously: "Your ways are always best. This is what the White man has been saying all the time to Black people: 'You may learn from us [Whites] but you [Blacks] have nothing for us. . . . We [Whites] will not change our way of doing anything at all, but we want you [Blacks] to change.'"

Council minutes from this time indicate both the struggle and the determination of mostly White leaders to see greater inclusiveness in congregational life and ministry. In June 1981, Sieplinga wrote, "If indeed reconciliation is the theme of our mission, then that ought to be reflected in the organizational structure, the composition of task groups, and our style of doing business."[2]

After five exhilarating and often exhausting years of almost continual growth and challenge, in the summer of 1982 Sieplinga accepted another great challenge: becoming the pastor of Garfield CRC, a predominantly African American church in urban Chicago.

Within months, the racially diverse pastoral team of Sieplinga and Venegas was succeeded by the racially diverse pastoral team of Venegas and Beelen. Surviving this partial pastoral transition, Madison included its 1981 Statement of Purpose in its 1984 Organizational

2. "Madison Council Minutes," June 1981.

Early Diversity and Inclusion

The Coalition for Minority Involvement included four African Americans, Rosie Hair, Ron Joseph, Lu Robinson, and Cindy Monroe Vander Kodde; one Hispanic, Jeannie Huyser; and two Whites, Joel Huyser and Jackie Venegas.

The *ad hoc study committee* consisted of Michael Traylor (Black); Pastor Dante (Hispanic); and Jack Brothers, Marty Meyne, and Sam Cooper (White).

Guide with the observation that "The biracial pastoral ministry team is an important dimension of our witness to the reconciling power of God."[3]

There were other forward-leaning initiatives as well. The May 1985 council minutes made mention of the Coalition for Minority Involvement, a group charged with developing a plan for training minority persons for leadership roles in the church. A series of similar efforts were noted in council minutes over several years: a revised leadership training team, a minority concerns committee, an *ad hoc* committee to study minority leadership and outreach, and a minority-majority breakfast meeting that highlighted a plea for more access, more training, and more involvement of minority members.

An Accident Waiting to Happen

The late Dr. Rod Mulder, a long-time Madison leader and a sociology professor at Grand Valley State

Dr. Rod Mulder

University, liked to describe Madison as a "sociological nightmare held together by the Holy Spirit." Not only was Madison multiracial; it was also diverse educationally, economically, and in terms of Christian traditions. Earl James,[4] Madison's director of ministries and communications from 1994 to 1998, recalled that at one point in his tenure the religious history of Madison attendees included African Methodist Episcopal, Baptist, Episcopal, Church of God in Christ, Methodist, Roman Catholic, Pentecostal, and other mainline and independent churches—along with CRC and other Reformed background folks making up only one-third of the whole.

James also expressed the opinion that in the early 1990s Madison was

3. "Madison Council Minutes," January 1984.

4. Earl James, personal interview, June 2014.

a "conflict pending, something that needed to occur." History has borne that out! In 1993, this conflict did occur when Madison hit an especially painful stretch of road. In the process of selecting a new leader for youth ministry, it experienced a multiple-person pile up.[5] In retrospect, James reflected on a number of warning signs that those in the driver's seat had failed to see. It was an accident waiting to happen!

Pastor Greg Cumberland

The Warning Signs

Warning Sign #1: Contrasting views on how to discern the will of God. A traditional *Reformed* mindset relies heavily on careful planning, official recommendations, prayer for guidance, and a congregational vote. A *charismatic* view relies more heavily on direct guidance from God, especially through words of wisdom and knowledge from respected leaders. In James's opinion, the leadership, including himself, had not sufficiently acknowledged these differing views. "The way we spoke about the Holy Spirit kept people from asking the hard questions, and this shut down our ability to discuss these tensions." Ultimately, the council decided to do things "the Reformed way," expecting the Holy Spirit to make things work out in keeping with God's will.

Warning Sign #2: The dual values of trained Black males with a sense of call to pastoral ministry and leaders with gifting and passion for ministry with youth. These two values are not necessarily incompatible but neither are they always complementary. James identified these three components: "The availability of Greg Cumberland as a seminary-trained Black male; a strong sentiment on the part of some that Madison should employ him; and Cumberland being named one of the candidates even though youth ministry was not his professed love."

Warning Sign #3: The youth of the church had been assured they would have a voice in determining the outcome. There were three candidates on the ballot: a Black male, a White male, and a White female. A number of the young people knew and

5. This difficult experience also is referenced in chapter 6.

strongly preferred the White male. The young people also had high expectations of deciding the outcome. Just exactly *how* that would work, however, was not clear.

The Collision

The time came for the congregation, including the young people, to cast their votes. Because the first vote was not decisive, the congregation voted again; the second time it was between the two male candidates. Congregants were given opportunity to comment before voting again, particularly if people believed they had a word from God. These "words" pointed in the direction of the Black male, and the second vote gave him the majority. When the results were announced, as James described it, "All hell broke loose. White young people cried. White parents walked out in anger and tears. Persons of Color expressed deep hurt. It was a spirituality fight, a race fight, and a fight over 'our youth.'"

In the days and weeks and months that followed, the pastors and council absorbed intense criticism. Some criticism was reasonable and constructive; other criticism was angry, judgmental, and deeply hurtful. Through intense prayer and difficult dialogue, the leaders came to recognize leadership failures and lessons to be learned. They also worked hard at responding pastorally to personal hurts and frustrations. But sadly, reconciliation and healing were never fully realized.

In February 1993, the council responded. Prompted by members who appeared before them to express their concerns, the council adopted the following statement:

1. As leaders we admit that we have made mistakes in the process of choosing a youth pastor, and that these mistakes have caused hurt. We ask your forgiveness. Among these mistakes are: (a) failure to clarify the vision of the position at the beginning of the process; (b) inadequate discussion at the congregational meeting; and (c) failure to follow up effectively after the congregational meeting with people who were hurting.
2. That the council take the lead in calling ourselves and the congregation to self-examination, confession, and forgiveness.
3. That the council commit ourselves anew to clarifying the vision or visions to which we believe God is calling us as a church, and that council involve the congregation in this

Joel and Jeannie Huyser

In 1993, Joel Huyser was a practicing attorney in Grand Rapids; Joel is White, his wife Jeannie is Latina. In 1995, they joined the staff of Christian Reformed World Missions (CRWM) in Central America. In 2016, Joel was serving as Regional Director for Transformational Networks with CRWM.

process. The issues may include cultural diversity, pastoral care, the role of leadership, etc. [6]

It is difficult to assess how well these commitments were communicated and how effectively they were carried out. We do know that pain and hurt endured. More than twenty years later, Joel Huyser, who was serving as Madison's council chair at the time of the collision, still was reluctant to discuss the matter. At all. The reason for his reluctance was his awareness of the indelible scars and debilitating pain of the Cumberland and Venegas families and others. Huyser did observe, however, that "the whole incident revealed that we had only made baby steps in learning how to live together as a multiracial congregation."

Learning to Travel Together

In the aftermath of the explosive vote, one response was to bring in Spencer Perkins and Chris Rice, co-authors of the book *More Than Equals: Racial Healing for the Sake of the Gospel.*[7] A racially diverse team with training and experience in cross-cultural ministry, Perkins (Black) and Rice (White) were flown in from Jackson, Mississippi, to lead a weekend retreat with about eighty Madison leaders. Perkins and Rice also led Sunday morning worship and conducted a discussion with adults between the two services.

One challenging strategy that outlasted the Perkins and Rice visit was their concept of *biblical yokefellows.* This term appears in the King James Version of Philippians 4:3 and is fleshed out in the final chapter of

6. "Madison Council Minutes," February 9, 1993. At this meeting, the council also ratified the congregational vote that had elected Greg Cumberland.

7. Spencer Perkins and Chris Rice, *More Than Equals: Racial Healing for the Sake of the Gospel* (InterVarsity Press, 1993).

Breakfast Club Partners Scipio Reid and Don Huizinga

More Than Equals. As yokefellows, Persons of Color and White persons agree to be in deep relationship with one another. Council members decided to practice and model this concept to the congregation. Pastors Venegas and Beelen took the pledge. So did nurse Judy Abedi-Smith and elder JoAnn Lieffers Swart, and elders Earl James and Don Huizinga.

Nearly twenty years later, reflecting on how this experience impacted him, James said this was when he became convicted that personal cross-racial relationships were critical to healthy multiracial congregations. Huizinga's experience was impactful as well. In a particular yokefellow conversation, James asked Huizinga, "Which is more important to you: Being Reformed or being in relationship with me?" To appreciate the force of this question, Huizinga was a teacher of Bible and Reformed doctrine in a local Christian high school! He knew what the right answer was, and this was a turning point for him. Teaching Bible and Reformed doctrine was his life, but so was the call to racial reconciliation. Love is equally as important as truth.

The *biblical yokefellows* concept eventually transitioned to the breakfast club, which was modeled after a program of the Chicago Urban Reconciliation Enterprise (CURE). Madison's breakfast club was enthusiastically supported by James and by Pastor Sam Reeves. February 1999 council minutes reported that Madison had forty-four breakfast club teams up and running, with the goal of one hundred participants in sight.

And Then There Was One

One of the most far-reaching repercussions of the collision was yet to be felt. Earl James became Madison's director of ministries and communications in 1994, bringing the number of Madison's Black male ministry leaders to four. Briefly. George Davis, a brother-in-law of Greg Cumberland, left Madison in August 1995. Cumberland, already on leave when Davis left, resigned in January 1996. Venegas moved on in August 1996. James, and James only, remained.

Another major response to the collision was the council's determination to become even more intentional about dealing openly and honestly with issues of race. Elders Ardie Burger and Don Huizinga, both on council at the time, framed the basic question this way: "Were we as leaders to simply acknowledge that we were all God's children, leaving the rest up to the Holy Spirit to work things out? Or were we being called to greater intentionality about openness and honesty? The council said 'Yes' to the latter, and there was no going back."[8]

In 1996, when Pastor Dante transitioned to Alternative Directions, once again Madison was faced with the need for another pastor. Council wrestled with the church's readiness—and its own readiness—to truly accept and support Leaders of Color. Were their voices being received with the same respect as White voices? Were White leaders equally willing to make sacrificial changes in their ways of listening and leading, instead of expecting only People of Color to make changes in their ways of listening and leading?[9]

In 1998, Pastor Samuel Reeves, a Princeton seminary graduate and native of Liberia, joined Beelen as co-pastor. The January 1999 council minutes illustrate Reeves's voice being heard by way of a committee report to council: "The elders are directing council to implement immediately, as policy, Pastor Sam's recommendations that all ministry leadership teams at Madison must reflect the racial make-up at Madison; this requires that elders and deacons reflect, at all times, the diversity within our congregation."

Directly or indirectly, the collision over the youth leader vote also had an impact on how Madison has made leadership selections ever since. Staff persons are now selected by the executive staff. And Madison's prevailing pattern for electing deacons, elders, and pastors has long been to present individual nominees to the congregation for affirmation.

Steering an Antiracism Bus

In 1996, the Synod of the Christian Reformed Church adopted a report

8. Ardie Burger and Don Huizinga, personal interview, June 2014.

9. "Madison Council Minutes," January 1997.

As defined by *United by Faith*, "a multiracial congregation (is) a congregation in which no one racial group accounts for 80% or more of the membership."*

*Curtis De Young, et al., *United by Faith: The Multiracial Congregation as an Answer to the Problem of Race* (Oxford University Press, 2003), 3

from its Committee to Articulate Biblical and Theological Principles for the Development of a Racially and Ethnically Diverse Family of God. Along with articulating these principles, Synod declared "that to be in Christ is in principle to be reconciled as a community of racially and ethnically diverse people and that to ignore Christ's calling to turn this principle into experienced reality is sinful according to God's Word and the Reformed confessions."[10]

Two years later, seeing little evidence of this principle becoming experienced reality in the CRC, a cluster of denominational ministries[11] embraced a partnership with Crossroads. Founded in 1986 with offices in Chicago, Crossroads was committed to helping churches and organizations dismantle systemic racism and build antiracist multicultural diversity within institutions and communities. Crossroads defined racism as *race prejudice plus the misuse of systemic or institutional power*.[12] White people tend to equate racism with race prejudice. People of Color, however, tend to experience racism as race prejudice *plus* the power of institutions and systems to protect privilege for Whites, most often at the expense of People of Color. The Crossroads approach was designed to help CRC ministries form and empower antiracism teams to dismantle racism within their respective organizations.

Earl James was included in the group of CRC leaders that recommended working with Crossroads. The actual work with the CRC ministries began in 1999. About a year later, these CRC ministries decided to work with congregations and invited Madison, Church of the Servant, and Coit Community Church to join the initiative.

The first reference in council minutes to either Crossroads or antiracism work appeared in December 2001 under the heading of "Crossroads Update." Laura Pritchard and Chris Schoon[13] reported to the council that Madison's "six-member task force is in the process of working with Church of the Servant and Coit Community Church to form a common vision of how to do this work with the other

10. *God's Diverse and Unified Family* (CRC Publishing, 1996), 30–31.

11. Participants included the denominational office, CRC publications (later *Faith Alive*), Calvin College, Home Missions, World Missions, and World Renew.

12. *Crossroads Antiracism Training Manual*, 2002.

13. This is the same Chris Schoon whose profile appeared in Chapter 8.

churches, and to finalize the proposal by the end of January 2002."

In March 2002, Crossroads director Joe Barndt and CRC advocates Art Hoekstra and Peter Szto met with the council. Pritchard, Schoon, and Bob Reed were present on behalf of Madison's antiracism task force. Council minutes reported that "By a vote of 15 in favor and 3 abstentions, it was decided that Madison Square CRC will proceed in our relationship with Crossroads." This officially opened the way for dozens of Madison folks, including a number of council members, to participate in intensive training by Crossroads. Church of the Servant and Coit Community Church also agreed to participate.

This training led to the formation of antiracism teams within all three congregations. In June 2002, the three councils each approved the following mandate for their respective teams: "To design, implement, and oversee a long-term strategy to combat the sin of racism and lead our congregation toward becoming an antiracism institution."[14] With organizing help from Crossroads, and on a parallel track with the CRC ministries, the three congregational teams also developed vision statements, goals, and objectives for antiracism work in ensuing years.

14. "Madison Council Minutes," June 2002.

Madison's Antiracism Team

In October 2002, Bob Reed reported to the council on behalf of Madison's Antiracism Team (MART). The council recommended that MART be officially commissioned before the congregation as a demonstration of Madison's commitment to its work, with the goal that it would become everybody's work. In 2009, the council expanded the role of MART by positioning it as a sub-team of the council with this enhanced mandate: "To serve as an antiracist advocacy resource and advisory voice to council in implementing and assessing progress toward combating the sin of racism and becoming an antiracist congregation transformed by Christ."[15]

Since the early 2000s, MART has given leadership in several important ways, including helping Madison leaders better articulate their commitment to an antiracism approach and espousing the core value of "Celebrating Diversity." This became one of Madison's four ministry themes: "Pursuing racial reconciliation with justice in our personal relationships and congregational ministry structures." In 2013, the core value was renamed "Diversity with Justice" and was articulated in a more balanced way:

15. "Madison Governance-Ministry Guidelines," October 2013, 12–13.

Madison members accept PRFC Award in 2013. From left to right: Al Mulder, Jody Smith, Stacia Hoeksema, Laura Pritchard, Linda Naranjo-Huebl, Victoria Gibbs, Lorraine Woodward, Dorwin Gray, Cherith Fee Nordling, Audrey Laninga, Nalini Suganandam Vanden Bosch, Pastor Joy Bonnema, Pastor Cisco Gonzales, Mary Bowers

"We celebrate diversity in community as God's gift to us and pursue reconciliation with justice among ourselves and in our society and systems as our response to God."

The primary role of MART has been to lift up this core value. It has regularly reminded the council of the importance of being trained in and affirming of its commitment to be antiracist. In September 2004, when the council endorsed the transition from a diverse co-pastorate to a diverse preaching team, it observed that "people on the preaching team would need to be antiracist." MART urged Madison's leadership to expect all its ministry directors to incorporate antiracist goals and plans for implementation. In 2012, it helped the council draft a position statement regarding multicultural leadership.[16] In 2013, MART led the charge in helping Madison qualify as an official partner with the Grand Rapids Partners for a Racism Free Community (PRFC) initiative, with Madison being the first local church to be recognized as meeting the standards for this designation.

Further, MART consistently collaborated with Pritchard, then Madison's director of multicultural living, in helping congregants pursue reconciliation with justice. Initially Crossroads provided all of the training for Madison leaders and members, but eventually MART began augmenting this training with storytelling, field trips, book discussion groups, multicultural fellowship meals, town hall meetings to address race issues, and New Community Living conversations. This multi-strategy approach was designed to help folks recognize the many faces of racism and gain a deepening consciousness of our own racialization.

New insight is critically important to reconciling across racial

16. Ibid., 31–32.

Differing Realities

White member Jim Ippel is a father of four sons and four daughters, all of them now adults. At a 2015 town hall meeting about a police shooting of a Black man, Ippel heard story after story of Black parents warning their children about how to behave when stopped by police. God opened his eyes to the fact that he never felt the need to warn his children about this. It was a new insight for Ippel: "My reality is different from the reality of African American parents."

differences. Antiracism advocate Victoria Gibbs put it this way:

> A willingness to accept that my reality as a Person of Color is different from your reality as a White person is essential; and to accept that my reality is real also is essential. You may never have enough evidence to prove that what I say is true. But you have to come to the point where you believe me, where you accept my reality—the reality that this is life according to me.

Congregations Organizing for Racial Reconciliation

In God's good providence, there was one particular dimension of the three-church (Madison, Coit, and Church of the Servant) agreement with Crossroads that proved especially strategic. Pritchard and Janice McWhertor, a White ministry leader from Church of the Servant, were granted staff time to apprentice with Crossroads. After extensive observation and experience, they were certified by Crossroads as antiracism trainers and organizers.

Early in 2004, as the three-church collaboration was more fully embracing the antiracism analysis and organizing strategies, the CRC Ministry Council concluded its contractual arrangement with Crossroads in favor of developing its own training and organizing pathway. By the end of 2004, Pritchard and McWhertor were released from their trainer and organizer roles with the CRC's Office of Race Relations. In effect, this congregational pilot was "cut loose" from the denominational initiative.[17]

What would they do now? After careful discussion and prayer, the decision was made to "keep on keeping on" with their recently adopted antiracism pathway. The already-certified trainers and organizers, in collaboration with their pastors and others, continued to revise and adapt their strategies and materials in alignment with a biblical and Reformed perspective. In 2006, the three churches formally organized their continuing initiative under the name Congregations Organizing for Racial Reconciliation—CORR for short.

From its inception, CORR consisted of a small representative board, a shoestring budget, two

17. "Madison Council Minutes," June 19, 2007.

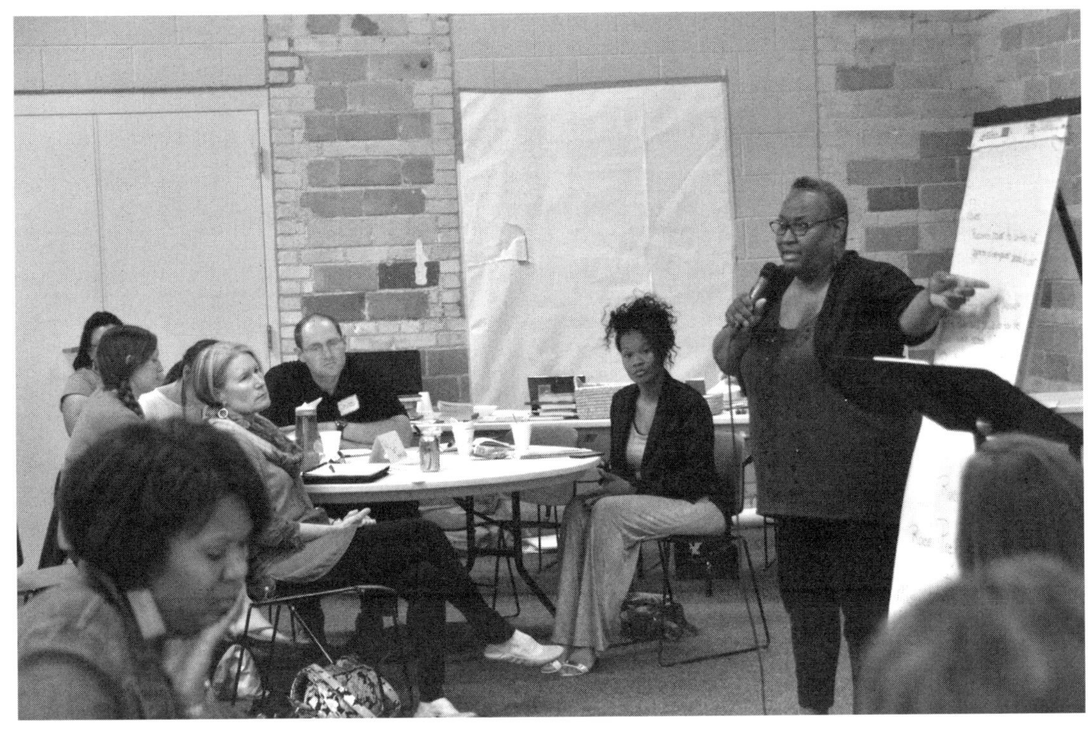

Laura Pritchard leading an Understanding Racism workshop

certified trainers, a part-time coach/team developer, and several high-capacity apprentice trainers. Their "bread and butter" has been the two-and-a-half day "Understanding Racism" workshop, which has been offered two to three times a year and has enjoyed total attendance of more than a thousand people from dozens of churches and Christian organizations in and around the Grand Rapids metro area.

Kris Vander Stelt, CORR co-chair, commented on the significance of multiple churches deciding to wrestle the issue of race together. "It provided accountability," said Vander Stelt, "and in a real way was a support group for our respective antiracism teams and leaders." Co-chair Victoria Gibbs emphasized the importance of feeling called to this work: "It is clear to me that my call before God is to be about the ministry of reconciliation: Reconciling people to God, and then to one another. This is why I am on this planet." Pritchard described a similar call and conviction: "The Word keeps me in the work. I still truly enjoy this work."

As the Madison bus reached the 2016 mile-marker, Pritchard marked twenty-four years on this ride, twenty of those years in Madison's employ! In her journey, she has traveled many roads: From a volunteer with Madison Girls to youth ministry staff; from joining a worship team to leading worship teams; from a regular hearer of the

The Work refers to antiracism work, racial reconciliation work, and reconciliation with justice work. It is transitioning from paternalism to equality. It is personal and it is organizational. It is mental and emotional and practical, all with a spiritual emphasis. It is sharing power and privilege and resources. It is rejecting internalized racial oppression and internalized racial superiority. It is clinging to continuing renewal in Christ.

Word to a periodic preacher of the Word; from a student of antiracism to an antiracism trainer and organizer; from the director of youth ministry to the director of multicultural living; and from Miss Laura Carpenter to Mrs. Henry Pritchard.

Recalling the caution of twenty years ago, her African American colleague would agree, "You didn't mess up, Miss Laura!" This is not to say the journey is complete. We've come a long way by faith. Every once in a while we get a glimpse of the goal, but still only dimly.

Henry and Laura Pritchard

Here We Go Again

Victoria Proctor Gibbs was one of Madison's more prominent lay leaders in recent years. She co-chaired Madison's Vision Team 2004–05, was elected an elder in 2005, and co-chaired or chaired the council from 2005–11. She also co-chaired MART and CORR. Gibbs was a key force, along with Pritchard, in Madison's gaining the recognition of Partners for a Racism Free Community. In 2012, with much excitement, Gibbs joined the Madison staff as co-director for Reaching In; in this role she also championed and supported Recovery Ministries at Madison. In 2013 she co-chaired Madison's Centennial Committee with Don Huizinga; in 2014 she partnered with Al Mulder and Ann Spangler in drafting the guiding proposal for *This Far by Faith*.

But here we go again! In 2015, three years after joining Madison's staff, Gibbs was released from her ministry position. Madison's leadership agonized over it. Gibbs was crushed by it. Friends and colleagues made waves over it. Relationships were fractured. Why can impasses like these not be resolved in a Christian organization? What is it about being racialized that only adds to the complexity? In the course of the past year, Madison's staff leadership, with the endorsement of the council and the help of outside expertise, has been delving more deeply into these vexing questions.

The Ministry of Reconciliation

Notwithstanding stumbles and missteps, there is reason for hopefulness in Madison's commitment to reconciliation with justice. Jevon Willis, a biracial African American leader, said of Madison's diverse leaders: "Our journeys are different but our destination is similar." He added, "What gives us courage to keep on going is this brilliant commitment of White leaders and Leaders of Color working *together.* It is this *collective* wisdom that gives us hope."

Ultimately, of course, reconciliation is God's idea. As the apostle Paul wrote so eloquently in 2 Cor. 5:18: "All this is from God, who reconciled us to himself through Christ and gave us the ministry of reconciliation." There is no greater

Jevon Willis

reason for hopefulness than being in the center of God's will. Leaders and members alike are propelled and preserved in their commitment to this lifelong journey by God's empowering grace.

> God, the Father of Your people,
> You have called us to be one;
> Grant us grace to walk together
> In the joy of Christ, Your Son.
> Challenged by Your Word and
>   Spirit,
> Blest with gifts from heaven
>   above,
> As one body we will serve You,
> And bear witness to Your love.[18]

18. "God, the Father of Your People," lyrics by Alfred E. Mulder, 1978 (Faith Alive Christian Resources, 1987).

CORR Leaders from left to right: Laura Pritchard, Albert Hamstra, Victoria Gibbs, Kris Vander Stelt, Lorraine Woodward, Willie Mae Rayburn, Janice McWhertor. Not pictured: Pastor Jerome Burton, Kafi Carrasco, Al Mulder, Ellen Westrate

CORR

The vision of CORR is to empower and equip churches and other Christian organizations in West Michigan to organize and disciple their members and constituents to become agents of institutional and individual racial reconciliation.*

*See CORR website, http://www.corrnow.org.

11

Learning to Love Our Neighbors

BY AL MULDER WITH EARL JAMES

Jesus replied: "'*Love the Lord your God with all your heart and with all your soul and with all your mind.' This is the first and greatest commandment. And the second is like it: 'Love your neighbor as yourself.'*"

Matt. 22:37–39

Therefore go and make disciples of all nations,
baptizing them in the name of the Father
and of the Son and of the Holy Spirit,
and teaching them to obey
everything I have commanded you.

Matt. 28:19–20a

Madison has been about learning to love our neighbors in contextual ways for more than one hundred years, as earlier chapters recognize and affirm. This concluding chapter, which spans only the last few decades, limits its focus specifically on Madison's commitment to Christian Community Development, planting new churches, and becoming a multisite church.

In October 1978, about a year after Pastor David Sieplinga arrived at Madison, and hardly a month after Minister of Evangelism Dante Venegas arrived, the council authorized them "to visit Mendenhall, Mississippi, John Perkins and Voice of Calvary to learn about this ministry and its relevance for Madison Square."[1] Dr. Perkins's unique philosophy and practice had been taking shape for some time, although it would take another several years for his ministry approach to become known as Christian Community Development.

1. "Madison Council Minutes," October 10, 1978.

Christian Community Development

The 1980s was an active and demanding decade for Madison with its many challenges: Settling into the much larger facility at 1441 Madison; defending and implementing Madison's commitment to the full use of women's gifts; shifting from one racially diverse co-pastor team to a second racially diverse co-pastor team; transitioning from one morning service to two and then from two to three; and by the early 1990s, planning and funding two phases of enlarging the facilities at 1441 Madison.

Around the country, a movement was taking root and sprouting. The John M. Perkins Foundation for Reconciliation and Development formed in 1983, and the Christian Community Development Association (CCDA) was formed in 1989 with its first annual conference held the same year. Community development seeds were breaking ground at Madison as well. Earl James, on a career path with the Michigan Department of Corrections and an elder at Madison, credits Rosie Hair with introducing him to Perkins and his work. When Perkins came to town, James arranged a couple of gatherings for local Black pastors, in part so that he could personally get time with Perkins. James recalls reading Perkins's now classic book *Beyond Charity*.[2] "The book changed my life. It helped me focus with Vinedressers and gave me a sense that I should leave my Corrections career and join Madison's staff."[3] In August 1994 he did just that, and in November, along with staff

Earl James

Earl James is a former Madison member and elder, and in 1994 became its first director of ministries and communications. From 1998 to 2007 he served as executive director of City Vision, a faith-rooted consulting and collaboration group. Since 2007, James has provided denominational leadership with the Reformed Church in America, assisting congregations to increase their cultural agility, address public policy through advocacy, and respond to the global refugee emergency. He and his wife, Norma, live in New Jersey.

2. John M. Perkins, *Beyond Charity: The Call to Christian Community Development* (Baker Books, 1993).

3. Earl James, email interview, May 2, 2016.

colleagues Greg Cumberland and Bonny Mulder-Behnia, James attended his first CCDA conference in Baltimore.

Three Strategic Ministry Shifts

The pages in this section, which are based primarily on the memory and materials of Earl James, recount three strategic ministry shifts that leveraged great change in Madison's outreach to its neighbors in the mid to late 1990s: Vinedresser Ministry, the transition in the role of deacons, and the establishing of Restorers. [4]

Vinedresser Ministry, Inc.

For most of 1993, while serving as an elder, James met with six other Madison folks almost every other week for three to four hours. The group represented a rich array of professions: Pastors Dante Venegas and David Beelen, clergy and churches; Rosie Hair, medical; Mary Stamps, social work; Joel Huyser, law; Cisco Gonzalez, community corrections; and Earl James, adult corrections and judiciary.

They lamented that many in Grand Rapids seemed unable to manage their lives and live abundantly as Jesus wanted, despite the active presence of volunteers and professionals. They dreamed of ministry models that might bring hope and increased capacities for under-resourced people and communities.

Gonzalez led the group in a study of John 15:1–11 on the subject of God the Vinedresser. The inevitable pain in everyday life can be redeemed, but what does that look like? How are vines pruned to bear more fruit? That question consumed the group. CCDA's principles[5] provided inspiration and clarity, especially regarding redistribution of knowledge, skills, and relationships as well as indigenous leadership development and holistic approaches to ministry. The group developed a basic ministry model around these principles and formed Vinedresser Ministry, Inc. Over the next five years, Vinedresser incubated and launched numerous innovative approaches to help people achieve greater charge of their lives:

- Moms in Unity, a single mothers' support group, later transferred to the Pregnancy Resource Center.

4. Earl James, personal correspondence, September 5, 2015.

5. See website, www.ccda.org.

- Young Dads, for fathers who were not parenting their children.
- Madison Cubs, an entrepreneurial club for junior high pre-gang boys.
- Professional assistance for people who desired to become writers.
- Consultations on racial reconciliation and church-based community development.

Although Vinedresser and its initiatives were officially independent of Madison, a number of Madison members joined the founding group, adding great value to Vinedresser's overall impact.

Transition of the Deacons

Concurrently, James's staff role was to provide strategic ministry support for the deacons. Three successive deacon chairpersons—Mary Vermeer, David Wynia, and Renita Reed—partnered with James for a specific outcome: To relieve the deacons from property management and budget oversight and also release them to design and bless the diaconal ministry of the church. With this goal in mind, the deacons initiated the practice of starting their monthly meetings with Bible study, exploring their unique callings and the ministry principles of community development. Early in 1997, the deacons initiated their first transition. While a few of them continued in traditional diaconal roles, the rest of them began leading and doing church-based community development. Several important diaconal ministries were designed and blessed, including parish nursing and a host of outreach ministries to which God was calling ordinary members in their everyday lives.

Restorers, Inc.

The deacons were eager to radically increase Madison's impact in the surrounding community. Using CCDA principles, the deacons, James, and an elder hosted an ongoing series of gatherings in nearby homes to listen to the community. About a dozen neighbors who did not attend Madison, some unchurched, joined them to explore the potential of church folks and neighbors agreeing to do mutually meaningful work together. After nine months of discussion and some small pilot projects, the participants committed to each other and began seeking long-term, sustainable changes that benefited the community—all in the name of Jesus!

Restorers was launched in 1997 with Isaiah 58:9–12 as its

By Steven Colthorp

Andy Schrier

"Don't Let Anyone Look Down on You Because You Are Young . . ." (1 Tim. 4:12)

Andy Schrier passed away on May 31, 2003, which was only a month and a half before his twenty-sixth birthday. Yet he was able to accomplish a great deal for the Kingdom before he met his beloved Jesus. Andy had a heart for the Madison Square neighborhood and specifically for its young people. Never one to sit around and only talk about doing something, Andy worked with a few community leaders and soon had the Hattie Beverly Tutoring Center up and running through Restorers, Inc. The tutoring center continues to assist students today.

Andy inspired many young people to learn and to seek to go beyond even the high school diploma they were working to earn in the present in order to reach their potential and a brighter future. Andy also encouraged church members and neighbors to learn from one another about their cultural, racial, and economic differences. Friends and family set up a scholarship in Andy's name, and it continues his legacy of assisting those in and around Madison Square Church with financial assistance to reach their educational goals.*

Though no longer present in the flesh, Andy's huge heart for the neighborhood lives on—inspiring and encouraging friends, family, and young minds throughout Madison, the surrounding Madison/Hall neighborhood, and beyond.

*More information can be found at asmsf.org.

motivating Scripture. It was incorporated in 1998 by founding representatives from the neighborhood, three nearby African American churches, and Madison. While legally independent from Madison, Restorers has consistently partnered with Madison to leverage its impact among neighbors and neighboring churches in ways that Madison could not have accomplished by itself.

As Restorers was founded, Vinedresser was ended. Its ministries either continued on their own, were transferred to other ministries, or also ended. By this time, James had left Madison's employ to launch a new ministry, City Vision.[6]

Renita Reed ably led Restorers through its early years as its first director (1997–2005), introducing and sustaining a wide area of neighborly initiatives: innovations to Madison's food pantry, employment services, Financial Freedom classes, car ministry, young women's ministry, developing accounts for home ownership, renovating and selling houses, business startups, marriage support programs, English as a second language (ESL)

6. Earl James, email interview, June 27, 2016.

Renita Reed-Thomson

Sandra Hardy

Kafi Carrasco

classes, and—guided by the creative leadership of Andy Schrier—tutoring for students.

Sandra Hardy was Restorers' second director from 2005–12. During her tenure, Restorers continued various programs. These included the Hattie Beverly Tutoring Center, the Andy Schrier Memorial Scholarship Fund for High School Seniors, ESL training, and Financial Freedom classes. She added the Summer Learning Academy program.

Kafi Carrasco, who started in 2012 as Restorers' third director, reported in 2016 that Restorers has remained a CCDA organization and continues to offer assistance for emergencies, employment, and education. Additional innovations have included Long-Term Investment (mentoring for women) and Restorers' Business Partnership, which is designed to help build businesses and create jobs in Madison's high-unemployment community.[7]

Madison Planted a Church

In February 1990, Madison established its first church planting committee, with a view to planting a new church "that reflected the values and expectations of Madison Square Church."[8] Simultaneous with moving into the new and larger sanctuary, the elders approved starting a new church in the Eastown neighborhood of Grand Rapids but later decided not to proceed.

Some years later, still embracing its planting vision, the council boldly agreed "to plant and parent a multiethnic daughter church in Kentwood."[9] Around a dozen families and individuals from Madison committed to the new plant called CentrePointe. Glandion Carney, an African American originally from

7. Kafi Carrasco, email interview, May 25, 2016.

8. "Madison Council Minutes," May 9, 1990.

9. "Madison Council Minutes," June 14, 1994.

Alabama, became CentrePointe's first pastor in July 1995, and CentrePointe soon appeared to be thriving. By the spring of 1997, worship attendance had surpassed the two hundred mark with some regularity.[10] But only a few months later, Carney left rather abruptly for a new position in Alabama and CentrePointe was left reeling.

Andre Daley was CentrePointe's next pastor. An ordained minister in the Reformed Church in America, originally from Kingston, Jamaica, Daley pastored from July 1998 until his sudden resignation in April 2002. He was succeeded in 2003 by Pastor Mark Mayor, who moved to Florida in 2006 for family health reasons. After prayer and discernment, the members decided to not continue, and CentrePointe held its final service on January 14, 2007.[11]

One Church, Multiple Locations

In 2004, ten years after the council decided to plant a church in Kentwood, council chair Gary Mulder gave Pastor Dave Beelen a copy of *Beyond the Box*[12] that introduced several innovative church concepts, including that of preaching teams. The timing was remarkable. Pastor Sam Reeves had just declared his desire to return to Liberia, which raised questions about the wisdom of pursuing another co-pastorate. Beelen had been a co-pastor at Madison for twenty-two years at this point, and key leaders seriously questioned whether another authentic "co" relationship could be developed under these circumstances.[13] Subsequently, the council adopted the "preaching team" model as an alternative approach to ensuring diversity in worship and preaching leadership. In early 2005, the council approved a two-year plan with Beelen serving as solo pastor, assisted by a preaching team under his tutelage and supervision.

Madison's first team of apprentice preachers consisted of Alton Hardy, Cisco Gonzalez, and Joy Bonnema. Beelen immediately implemented a non-formal training with them, including weekly meetings and periodic retreats. In May 2008, after three years of preaching experience, all three were examined by Classis Grand Rapids East and heartily approved for ordination. Soon afterward, they were ordained by Madison as commissioned pastors. Within the next

10. Rachel Hyde, *CentrePointe Church: A Brief History* (self-published booklet, 2007), 6.

11. Ibid., 7–13.

12. William Easum and Dave Travis, *Beyond the Box: Innovative Churches That Work* (Group Publishing, Inc., 2003).

13. David Beelen, email interview, May 14, 2016.

The Preaching Team: Alton Hardy, Cisco Gonzalez, David Beelen, and Joy Bonnema, 2006

five years God would use them to launch Madison's first three multisite congregations.

In January 2006, the council approved the first steps toward purchasing and renovating the vacant building at 1401 Madison, now named Madison Place, to enhance its ministry to the community. Meanwhile, Beelen had developed a sabbatical plan for that summer in order to further study a second concept in the book *Beyond the Box*—the concept of multisite churches. Council granted permission for the sabbatical and for him to attend a church conference in South Carolina with Tom Mockabee, Madison's executive director of ministries. Beelen returned with considerable enthusiasm for this new way of making disciples.

In November 2006, along with ongoing consideration of renovating 1401 Madison, the vision for becoming a multisite church was formally presented to the council. By a unanimous vote, the council decided "to approve in concept the multisite expansion proposal that we expand and make room by becoming a church in more than one location."[14] In December, the elders made two additional decisions: 1) "That for the first multisite, we will have *in-person preaching* only (not video) for at least the first year," and 2) To approve steps for drafting a campus pastor job description and authorize Beelen to begin soliciting names of potential candidates for the position.[15]

The year 2007 involved more planning: refining guidelines for the preaching team, honing job descriptions, evaluating multisite locations, and considering applicants. Selecting the location—the Gerald R. Ford Academic Center—was a comparatively simple process. Selecting a campus pastor took longer. Early on, some eyes were on Alton Hardy, although as he put it, "I was 'No' from the git-go! I was like Moses. I wasn't even interested. I was working at Restorers. I didn't think I was called to pastoring—just to preaching. But the elders wanted me, Pastor Dave encouraged me, and Sandra said, 'Okay.' So I went to the interview; somehow I got thrown into the mix, and the doors opened."[16] Hardy was affirmed by the elders in August and by the

14. "Madison Council Minutes," November 21, 2006.

15. *Madison Elder Minutes*, December 19, 2006.

16. Alton Hardy, telephone interview, September 2015.

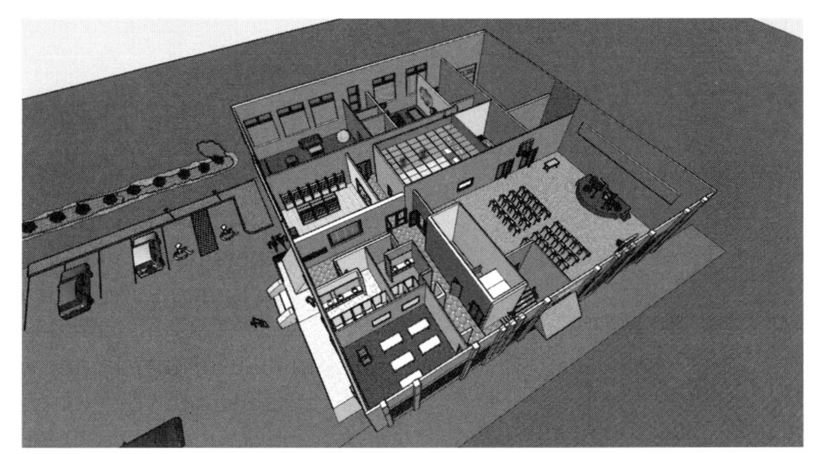

Birds' Eye View: 3D Rendering of Madison Place by Rick Bengelink

council in September for recommendation to the congregation as campus pastor-elect. At that meeting, along with approving a fund-raising plan for Madison Place, the council designated $100,000 for assisting with the multisite outreach.[17]

Ford Campus: Stanza One

In fall 2007, prayerful planning shifted to prayerful action. Madison Square put out sign-up sheets for volunteers to commit to doing setup, hospitality, nursery, and children's ministry at the new Ford campus. A logistics group was formed (Bill and Deb DeJong, Dave and Sally Jeltema, Ernie Long, Brian Seifert, and John and Janice Turnbull) to assist Hardy in leading the volunteers and the worship service. Several gatherings were scheduled during the fall and winter months to prepare for the Ford's launch on Easter Sunday, March 28, 2008. More than one hundred people attended that worship service.

In fall 2009, Hardy was invited onto Kuyper College's board of directors. At his first meeting, he met outgoing board member Ed DeVries, which led to animated discussion about the Ford and Hardy's passion for inner city youth, racial reconciliation, and community development. DeVries, a local developer, had just recently acquired the vacant facility at 415 Franklin (formerly Grand Rapids Christian High School). DeVries and Hardy envisioned how the Ford could potentially be an "anchor" church that attracted other ministries for 24/7 outreach to the community. Prayerful walks through the building reignited a vision Hardy had written up years earlier, entitled *Urban Hope.* Teaming up with Asha Emmerson, a Ford member, worship team leader, and experienced international economic developer from Zimbabwe, they began negotiations and dialogue with potential partners. Asha assisted in creating architectural

17. *Madison Elder Minutes*, August 28, 2007.

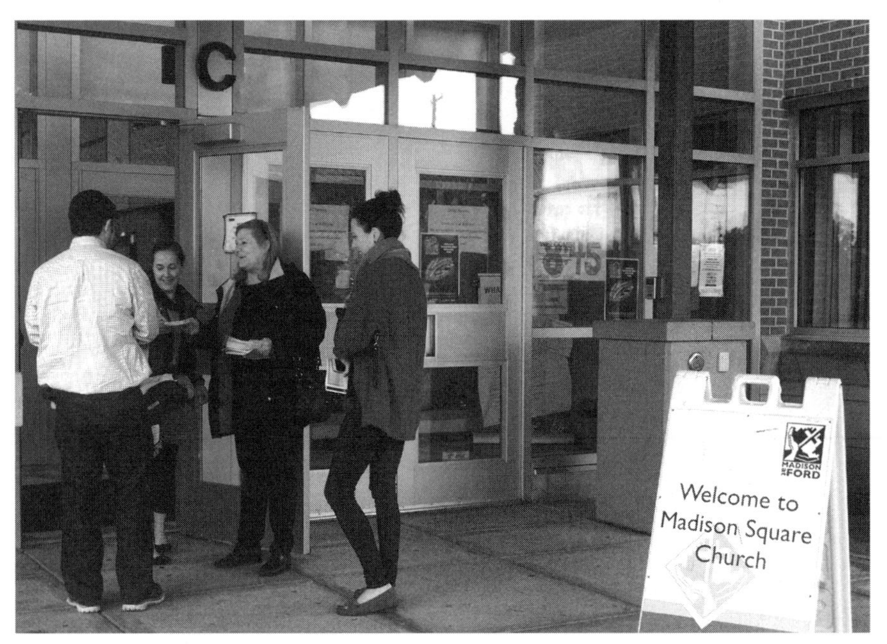

Gerald R. Ford Academic Center, Cafeteria/Gymnasium Entrance

drawings for the DeVries company to use for renovation; they also further developed Hardy's *Urban Hope* into a development plan (completed in July 2010).

By fall 2010, Hardy was increasingly busy with 1) managing rapid church growth and ministries, 2) questioning how to integrate the Ford and the Urban Hope plans into 415 Franklin, and 3) juggling invitations into widening circles of influential community developers and well-funded foundations. As Betsy Bascom observed, "There was an acute need for visionary leadership who would listen to the Lord for direction, and pray for wisdom and protection as the church sought to step into the spiritual battle of transformational community ministry."[18]

Some of Ford's prayer servants, sensing Hardy's anxiety over the next steps, urged him to bring other leaders around him for prayer and guidance. Eventually he invited five couples to meet for prayer: Johnathan and Betsy Bascom, Bill and Deb DeJong, Derek and Karyn Perkins, Tim and Patty Stoner, and John and Janice Turnbull. At the heart of his hesitancy was Hardy's preference for a males-only leadership model. Initially he argued for this as a cultural, contextual necessity, but over time he voiced biblical objections as well. And just a few months after this team started meeting, Hardy dismissed the women

18. Betsy Bascom, personal correspondence, fall 2015.

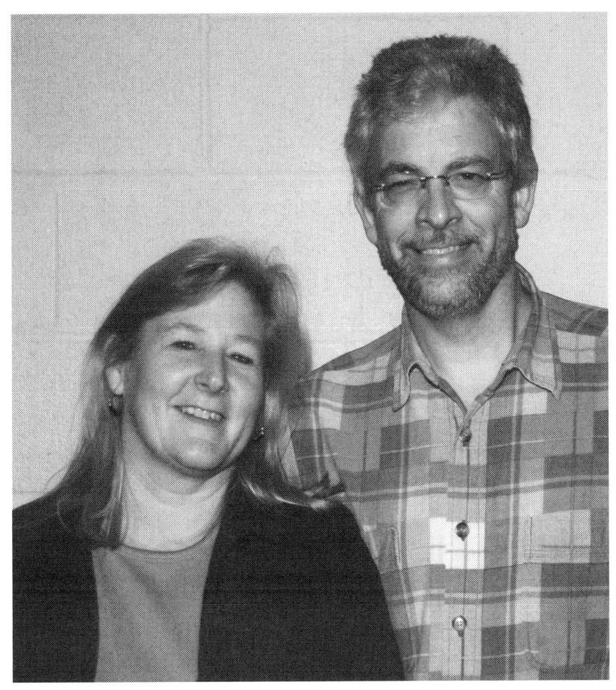

Betsy and Johnathan Bascom

Betsy Bascom assembled extensive research and interview notes for Madison's multisite story, particularly the launching and development of Madison's first new site at the Ford school. Betsy and her husband, Johnathan, also were founding members of Madison Church: Ford Campus. Thank you, Betsy!

without discussion. The group was now male only, but conflicted.[19]

The private struggle became public. Hardy shared his views with his supervisor, Pastor Dave Beelen. Being in conflict with Madison's stated values, Hardy found himself on the defensive with several groups: the Multisite Leadership Team (MLT), the elders, the council, and both the Square and Ford congregations. Madison's council met frequently over the next months, exploring possible alternatives for resolving the issue within the framework of its stated values. The Ford congregation also debated the matter and voted to affirm women in church leadership. Hardy clung to his convictions, even while realizing his role as campus pastor would end. With mutual appreciation and shared pain, Hardy conducted his final service on August 7, 2011.[20]

A Hardy After-Word

When given opportunity to comment on how his journey with Madison would be presented in this book, Hardy wanted folks to understand that his burning passion for reaching Black men affected his relationship with Madison in ways he did not anticipate or intend. At the same time, his explanation underscores how his ministry philosophy came into conflict with Madison's commitment to the full use of women's gifts:

> For me, the core issue was not about women in ministry or men-only as elders. My driving concern was about reaching men, and especially Black men who are at the bottom of the social and economic ladder. I was trying to preach and teach male responsibility from the pulpit. I was trying to reach young men by giving

19. Ibid.
20. For more information on this transition, see chapters 8 and 9.

them the truth about what God was calling them to be and do.

Out of naïveté, I was not prepared to deal with the implications of egalitarian versus complementarian views on marriage and gender roles and the like. My primary concern was and still is to bring a Gospel of transformation and restoration to the hood. Nothing less and nothing more. As I see it, leaving Madison was less about female elders and more about preaching the message of male responsibility and empowering men to serve and lead as Jesus served and led.

It's what I'm doing now in Birmingham: A strong message bent toward men that attracts young men back into the church. Men attract men, and our communities need men to know their God-given role and responsibilities in the home and in the church. I can't speak for White communities, but the egalitarian viewpoint doesn't help the Black urban poor community. We need men to be men.[21]

Pastor Brad Knetsch

Ford Campus: Stanza Two

Disheartened but not despairing, the wounded Ford congregation moved forward, trusting the One who holds the future. In consultation with Beelen, a team was formed to assist in the search for new pastoral leadership. Pastor Brad Knetsch, who by then had been ordained as a minister of the Word and serving as Hardy's assistant pastor, was named Ford's interim campus pastor. In turn, Knetsch was assisted by Gina Dick, a seminary intern. Knetsch gave priority to visiting Ford members—listening to their concerns, praying for healing, and encouraging all to move forward together. In January 2012, the Ford congregation affirmed Knetsch as Ford's second campus pastor.

Fairly soon, establishing a Congregational Leadership Team (CLT) was discussed. But what exactly is a CLT? It's not council governance as such but rather is an advisory and support team for assisting the pastor in fulfilling the ministries specific to the site. According to newly adopted Madison Guidelines, the CLT was to be formed initially at the discretion of the campus pastor, in consultation with the Multisite

21. Alton Hardy, email interview, July 2016.

Pastor Jason Botbyl

Leadership Team.[22] However, given its three-year history, Knetsch invited the Ford congregation to join him in a period of prayerful discernment for naming CLT nominees.

Before the team was determined, God seemed to run ahead by orchestrating a "chance meeting" between developer Ed DeVries and a Ford lay leader named Jason Botbyl.[23] The 415 Franklin Project had gone dormant with Hardy's departure. So when DeVries recognized Botbyl, he was curious as to "what the Ford is thinking about the building." DeVries suggested a meeting with the new pastor and leaders. Knetsch shared this opportunity with the former pastoral search committee, saying, "Pretty cool how Jason crossed paths with Ed last week and he is asking to meet with me and 'my people.' Problem is, I don't have a leadership team in place!"[24]

22. "Madison Governance-Ministry Guidelines," October 18, 2013.

23. Jason Botbyl was an emerging leader at the Ford in 2012. In 2015 he was ordained as a Commissioned Pastor and preaches monthly at the Ford.

24. Brad Knetsch, email correspondence, March 20, 2012.

Ford's Ministry Staff from left to right: Jason Botbyl, Jermale Eddie, Joanna DeMoor-Tannor, Sean Johnson-Moore, and Pastor Brad Knetsch

This led to a flurry of emails between Knetsch, Botbyl, Scott Huebl, Jonathan Quist, and Joanna DeMoor-Tannor about a whole series of pressing questions. Nevertheless, the group agreed to meet DeVries with an open mind. As Huebl articulated and prophesied, "I think we can hear what he has to say. This opportunity, especially if it's from the Lord, will not go away any time soon."[25]

The Ford then affirmed its first CLT—Joanna DeMoor-Tannor, Jonathan Quist, Jackie Baber-Bey, Derek Perkins, Eric Taylor, and Wendy Davis—and prayed for guidance on whether to resume a potential partnership with DeVries. In time, they felt led to continue building the Ford congregation and refresh its commitment to ministry at the school. If the Franklin building was to be part of the Ford's future, the

25. Scott Huebl, email correspondence, March 20, 2012.

leadership was trusting God to show them.

Shortly after this decision, in May 2012 the church hired Doug Roede as Reach In director and named Jason Botbyl as an apprentice preacher; a few months later, Sean Johnson-Moore was hired as Reach Out director. In March 2013, Jermale Eddie replaced Roede, who had decided to pursue seminary; five months later Joanna DeMoor-Tannor was named children's ministry director. All these leaders were from within the Ford congregation.

Sean Johnson-Moore

Sean Johnson-Moore grew up in Madison's neighborhood and felt welcomed at youth group. Years later, reconnecting with former youth leader Brad Knetsch (now pastor at Ford), he was "hungry to do what was right." Knetsch met with Sean regularly to mentor him and nurture the leadership gifts God had given him. Sean served as Ford's Reach Out director from 2013-2016. He is married to Shardaira. They both perform Christian rap, are certified fitness trainers, and are blessed with eight children.

Reach Out

By Sean Johnson-Moore

Reach Out Reach Out Reach Out
It's understanding and advancing the people
Fighting the evil
By living free as a diverse community of people who
Reach Out

Collaborations, partnerships, growing relations
God's will in practical demonstration
Locking arms with different organizations
Making disciples of all nations
Via creative communication
Reach Out

Evangelism, community, education
Your life don't waste it, your gifts just take it and
Reach Out

Extending your hand, playing your part, placing others in our plans
Not being a religious group who dawns
But a people sent to equip and empower, showing hope in the dying land
It's all found in the God-Man who
Reached Out

To infect causing an effect
See God sent us to connect the people

Stretch the people to collaborate, come together to invest in people
Watch the cycles continue as invested people invest in people
Reach Out

This is not only opportunity to teach but it's our lesson people
Reach Out

See me, I grew up in a generation of men steeped in prison
No hope for new living
School was detention, church was tradition and religion
And love was conditioned, my inspiration was my self-ambition
But God placed me here on this mission to
Reach Out

To a fallen world with the hope of redemption
Via our life experiences, pains, failures
Conditions, traditions, passions, inflictions
Gifts and wisdom
Can now be used to show we are enlisted to
Reach Out

Third Time's a Charm

By spring 2014, the Ford was restless for a permanent home. This was provoked in part by the changes in their rental agreement with Grand Rapids Public Schools, who closed off classrooms for church use, eliminated Ford's access to on-site storage, and raised the rent. As a result, Knetsch and the CLT determined that "after 6 incredible years of renting from GRPS, we desire to put down roots. By God's grace we hope to land a worship space that better serves the growing church family as well as a ministry house that empowers the Ford staff and congregation to be an intentional presence within the community."[26]

Within months of committing to this goal, a Ford task force searched for a suitable space and was led to the old Christian High chapel at the 415 Franklin building, convinced that it was the best and only reasonable option. Quoting Knetsch, "For years we prayed for space, and God answered in ways far beyond what we could possibly imagine by providing us with a home at 415 Franklin." More specifically, 65,000 square feet of space. In September 2014 the DeVries family offered to *donate* the building to Madison; in November 2014 an anonymous donor offered to cover all holding costs up to $20,000 annually for up to two years. And the Ford

26. "Following God's Thread," *Madison Annual Report, 2014–2015*, 10.

415 Franklin, future home of Madison Church: Ford Campus

congregation voted overwhelmingly to accept the gift in December 2014, with the council affirming the decision. In February 2015, the DeVries family transferred official ownership to Madison for 415 Franklin to become the Ford's new worship and ministry center.

Since then, Knetsch, the CLT, the congregation, and the 415 building committee, led by project manager Layla Kuhl, have been praying and working diligently to discern God's vision, listen to the community, and understand Madison's values and CCDA's principles that will help identify viable, appropriate partners to join in the redevelopment of the building. "We believe that Jesus is alive! We believe in the invitation to join the kingdom of God here in this neighborhood, city and world," writes Knetsch. "When I close my eyes and imagine the 415 Franklin Chapel, I can see Jeremiah 29:7 painted on the wall of the sanctuary: 'Seek the peace and prosperity of the city . . . because if it prospers, you too will prosper.' Join us as we live out the Gospel for the glory of God for this generation and the generations to come!"[27]

Jesus and Me—JAM

Hailing from New Jersey, with roots in Puerto Rico, Cisco Gonzalez started attending Madison when he was a student at Calvin College. Though he later obtained a Master of Social Work degree and moved into employment in that field, he never totally quelled a sense of call to ministry. Having joined the preaching team in 2005 and witnessed the 2008 launch of the Ford site, in January 2009 Gonzalez shared with the elders his own sense of call to serve as a campus pastor.[28] Although this rushed Madison's multisite timeline, the pastors and elders committed to a period of discernment for God's leading in regard to Gonzalez's calling as well as potential location, strategy, workers, and timing. Within the year, with the blessing of the elders and the support of a few faithful folks from Madison, Gonzalez was commissioned as Madison's second campus pastor.

In fall 2009, while still employed as the dean of students at Kuyper

27. "Madison Ministry Plan: 2015–2016," 20.

28. "Madison Elder Minutes," January 20, 2009.

Pastor Cisco Gonzalez

College, Gonzalez launched an urban-flavored ministry to mostly young adults. He called it JAM, Jesus and Me! For about a year JAM met in the YMCA facility in downtown Grand Rapids. While waiting on God for a more permanent facility, JAM then continued regular gatherings at Kuyper College.

In 2012, One Wyoming came into being: a joint church-planting initiative of the Reformed Church in America (RCA) and the CRC. With Wyoming, Michigan selected as one of four initial pilot areas, the JAM multisite was approved as a church plant of One Wyoming. Gonzalez ended his employment with Kuyper College and relaunched JAM as "a multiethnic movement of reproducing worshiping communities who share and live the Good News of Jesus together."[29] Meeting locations included Ideal Park CRC ministry center, Gethsemane Lutheran fellowship hall, Roadside Ministries, and the Spartan Stores YMCA.

Early in 2014, Gonzalez was invited to begin holding Sunday gatherings at Calvary CRC in Wyoming. By midyear, Gonzalez and Pastor Mark Van Drunen of Calvary began exploring ways to strengthen the Calvary/JAM relationship and increase JAM's ministry impact. That fall, JAM transitioned from a multisite of Madison to a church plant of Classis Grandville, and Gonzalez transitioned from JAM campus pastor under the supervision of Madison to JAM church planter with Calvary as his calling church. Both transitions were affirmed and became official on January 1, 2015.

Madison Church: North Campus

Of Madison's three commissioned pastors—Joy Bonnema, Cisco Gonzalez, and Alton Hardy—Bonnema was the first to enter a staff role at Madison (pastor of congregational life) and the third to initiate a multisite congregation, eventually founding Madison Church: North Campus.

29. *JAM News*, holiday issue, January 1, 2014.

Loving My Neighbors

By Lorilee Craker*

The same Shepherd who guided Pastor Joy as pastor of congregational life continued to direct her steps. After only a few years on Madison's preaching team, He began nudging her to consider another bold move: Planting a Madison site on the northeast side, where she lived with her family.

"As soon as I was hired in 2008, I felt we should move closer (to Madison Square)," she said. "How could I be a pastor on the southeast side with any integrity? I lived with this tension, trying to be present with my neighbors and doing ministry at Madison."

In 2011, days after Joy's daughter, Meikea, expressed concern that her neighborhood friends were lost and "falling apart" without Jesus, her good friend was killed in a shooting spree that claimed seven lives altogether. This impacted Joy deeply. "The urgency became clear: People were dying without Jesus." With the blessing of the Madison Square congregation, Pastor Joy, led again by the Shepherd, launched Madison North in October 2013. Their motto: Sharing our lives with each other through Jesus Christ across ages and cultures. In 2014 the site celebrated one year of shared lives and God's faithfulness.

"People all over the city need Him," said Pastor Joy. "But He is calling me to the northeast side; He has a plan for us there."

*This is a continuation of the Joy Bonnema story as told by author Lorilee Craker in chapter 9.

God used Gonzalez in particular to help Bonnema hear His call.

> The turning point came in April [2012] when our preaching team went away on a retreat. . . . It came through Pastor Cisco, who began to probe with questions like, "So why is it you haven't planted that church on the north end yet? What's holding you back?" Then, within a span of seven days, six different people said things to me [seemingly out of the blue and unsolicited] like: "You are called as a pastor. I see you pastoring your own church. What happened to your dream about a church on the north end?" This culminated with a comment from Joel Hogan: "I felt the Lord telling me to tell you to continue with the vision He is birthing in you."[30]

With the affirmation of the council, Bonnema followed through on an already-planned sabbatical and then embarked on transitioning from pastor of congregational life at the Square to Madison's newest campus pastor. In God's good providence and provision, Bonnema garnered the affirmation of north side CRCs, gained approval for meeting in the Kent Hills Elementary School, and gathered about one hundred total souls, children and grownups, to seed the newest multisite congregation. Madison Church: North Campus held its first worship service on October 27, 2013. They continued to organize and grow, eventually sending out

30. Joy Bonnema, personal report, October 28, 2012.

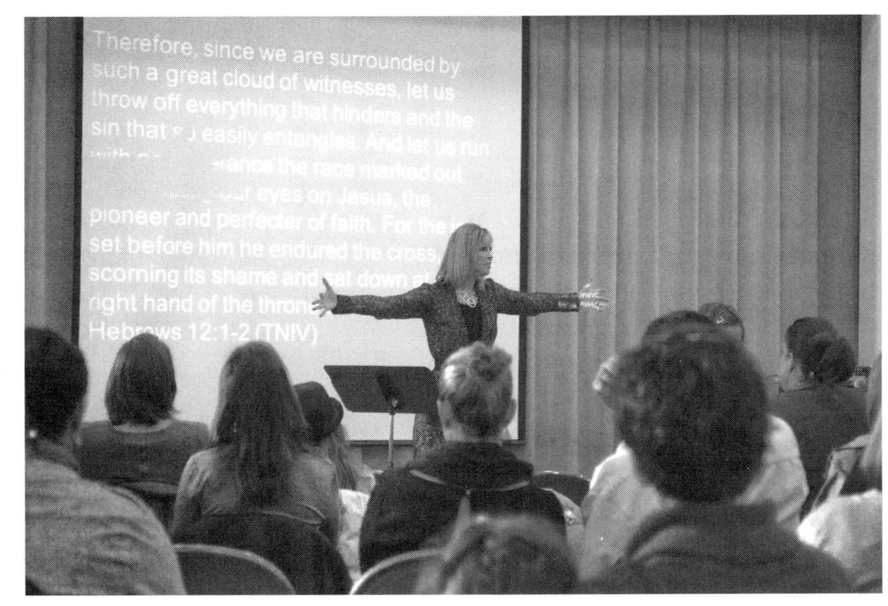

First Service at Madison Church: North Campus, October 2013

twelve teams into the immediate community on April 6, 2014 and inviting the neighbors to its public launch two weeks later on Easter Sunday.

One year later, Bonnema described the young but developing congregation: God was growing them through prayer retreats, prayer trainings, prayer walks, and Sunday morning prayer times. Their worship circle had grown, and on a typical Sunday morning their children's ministry engaged ten to thirteen workers. In the first year, they had celebrated ten baptisms and two weddings. They hired Eric Nykamp as director of worship design and Katie Proctor as office coordinator.

In May 2016, as part of Madison's annual report, Nykamp noted several things: (1) their worship team leaders were attending Madison's Antioch Worship Leadership Trainings; (2) the teams are multiethnic, multigenerational, and growing; (3) dance is a regular part of worship; and (4) one of the dancers made profession of faith and was baptized! Nykamp also observed that while North seems "to have many introverts, the depth and vulnerability of people's stories and prayer requests provides a crucial connection to one another in worship."[31] Similarly, Bonnema celebrated seeing God at work at North. Worship services were increasingly marked by vulnerability, authenticity, and dependence on God. Small groups were meeting throughout the city. Congregants had several painting, packing, and moving parties, and meals were showing up on people's doorsteps. "Our circle is

31. "Madison Annual Report: 2015–2016," 6.

The En Gedi Center

The En Gedi Center

In 2000 **Dr. Ron and Mary Van Valkenburg** had a spacious home constructed at 1441 Prospect, just west of Madison's church building at 1441 Madison. They named their new home En Gedi after an oasis in Israel; it was designed to also serve Madison with classrooms, retreat space, and guest housing. The Van Valkenburgs generously transferred their ownership to Madison in 2016 for ministry purposes still to be determined.

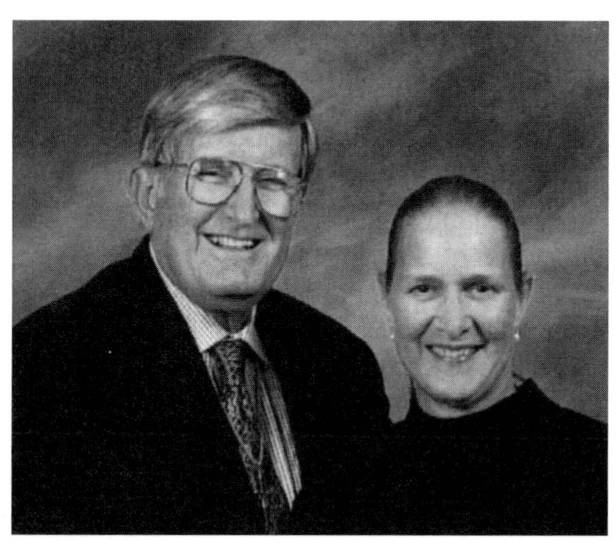
Ron and Mary Van Valkenburg

growing," Bonnema reported. "We are growing in numbers and in grace and truth."[32]

Back to Square One

Anyone who has lived for one hundred years or more has undergone a whole series of significant transitions: from toddler to teenager, to young adult, to middle age, to matriarch or patriarch. This also is true of Madison in its one-hundred-plus years: transitioning from a mission

32. Ibid., 5.

to a chapel, to a small church, to a large church, to a multisite church. And there are at least two more transitions in process.

The first ongoing transition is living more fully into Madison's new identity as a multisite church. People can no longer assume that when referring to "Madison" one is speaking of the congregation at 1441 Madison, or that "Madison's neighborhood" is necessarily south of Hall Street, or that its facilities are all located in a cluster near Madison and Oakdale. Since Pastor Darrell Delaney became campus pastor at the Square in 2014, Pastor Beelen has been preaching less often there and more at the other campuses. When the council convenes, its focus has expanded from one to three congregations.

Although the feel and flow of worship differs from one campus to the other, the foundations and forms of ministry remain similar and complementary. All sites are compelled by the same vision: *following Christ together as diverse communities.* The seeds of the disciple-making pathway are being sown in and by all the sites. Governing elders are drawn from all three congregations and serve Madison church as a whole. Pastoral care elders are from all three sites and serve their respective body of believers. All campus pastors serve with Beelen on the multisite leadership team. Each congregation has representatives on Madison's antiracism team, plus other teams and task forces of shared concern. Madison is increasingly speaking and living as one church with multiple congregations.

The second ongoing transition involves the Square Campus specifically. When the multisite concept was embraced, the motivation was "to proclaim good news to the poor" and "to bind up the brokenhearted."[33] Madison Square Church, as the originating site, began "giving itself away." In less than a decade, the Square "gave away" its apprentice preachers, its pastor of congregational life, many gifted leaders, and around two hundred members. Reflecting in 2015, Beelen observed: "Our sites are growing and challenging the originating site. . . . We at the Square want to become a church which cares for people more compassionately and effectively. . . . We want to declare a year of 'people care' which helps us disciple those whom God has led to us with greater love."[34] While united in vision and purpose with the other congregations, the Square congregation also has its own unique story and distinct call-

33. Key phrases from Psalm 61:1.
34. "Madison Ministry Plan: 2015–2016," 6.

Ken Schripsema

ing under God: its own flavor, its own creativity, its own ministry pulse, and its own ministry impact.

In 2016, Ken Schripsema, the Square's executive director of ministries, reported that there is "increased clarity on a discipleship pathway that will effectively make disciples who make disciples" and "momentum in the area of People Care, including Connection Specialists, Section Neighbors, and Caring Communities."

Campus Pastor Delaney added: "It's been exciting to see what God has been up to for the past year! God has been in the process of making us more available to the Holy Spirit. . . . Here's what God has been saying to our congregants: 'Prepare for what is coming. Get ready. Time for new wine and new wineskins. Fear not . . . I am with you.' God is preparing us and pruning us this year so that we can bear more fruit."[35]

35. Ibid., 5–6.

Summary Timeline

1968 to 2016

BY BRENDA SCHUYLER

Note: The lines in ***italics*** identify contextual events; the numbers in parentheses refer to page numbers.

1968 Rev. Vernon Geurkink is installed as pastor for Madison Square Chapel on January 14 (69)

April 4, 1968 Dr. Martin Luther King Jr. is assassinated (49, 69)

1968 Geurkink calls the CRC to a greater commitment to the needs of the neighborhood (70)

1970 Madison Square Chapel is officially organized as Madison Square CRC (71)

1971 John Toliver, Madison's first African American elder, leaves to join an all-Black church (71)

1970s Madison is served by Summer Workshop in Missions (SWIM) teams (73)

1973 "Key Contact" helps members develop many long-lasting Black/White relationships (74)

1974 Geurkink accepts a ministry position with Calvin Seminary (74)

Madison calls Rev. Virgil Patterson as the first Black CRC pastor in Grand Rapids (74)

1975 Tom Raysor, an African American, is hired as Madison's Youth Leader (75)

1977 Patterson resigns; Madison calls Rev. David Sieplinga, a White pastor with urban ministry experience and a vision for racial reconciliation (77–79)

1978 Raysor resigns; Madison calls Dante Venegas to become its Minister of Evangelism (80, 87–89, 110)

Jackie Venegas begins to enhance and expand Madison's ministry of music (90, 110)

Marian Takens is elected as Madison's first female deacon (162)

1979 Madison marches from the Chapel to its new church home at 1441 Madison (112)

1981 Madison votes that all professing members are eligible for all church offices (163)

Dante Venegas is ordained as a Minister of the Word in the CRC (92)

1982 Sieplinga moves to Garfield CRC, Chicago; David Beelen becomes co-pastor with Venegas (97–98)

Ruth Apol Zoodsma begins as long-term volunteer, later becomes secretary/administrator (97)

1983 Founding of John M. Perkins Foundation for Reconciliation and Development (192)

1984 Sunday morning attendance exceeds the 400 mark (98)

1986 The council issues prayer and healing ministry guidelines for elders and prayer servants (131)

1987 Sunday worship attendance surpasses the 500 mark (100)

Madison changes from two to three morning services (100)

1988 George Davis is hired to lead the Gospel Choir and one of the morning services (101)

Elaine Smeelink is elected as Madison's first female elder (164)

1989 Christian Community Development Association (CCDA) is formed (192)

1990 Madison establishes a building committee and starts construction of a new sanctuary (101)

The Tabernacle Progression model of worship is introduced (121)

1992 New sanctuary is dedicated in January and Madison returns to two morning services (101)

1993 Greg Cumberland is hired as youth minister, ushering in a very painful period (103, 178–180)

1994 Earl James is hired as first director of ministries and communications (102, 192)

Bonny (Wynia) Mulder-Behnia is hired as first director of children's ministries (102, 165)

Twenty-plus years of expanded drama ministry begins (118)

1995 Davis resigns and Ken Reynolds, Jr. becomes the new music director (123)

Madison launches CentrePointe Church with Glandion Carney as its first pastor (196–197)

1996 Pastor Greg Cumberland resigns after a leave of absence (103)

Pastor Dante seeks the elders' permission to search for a new ministry; the Venegas's are honored at a farewell dinner (103)

Laura Carpenter Pritchard is hired as Madison's youth ministry director (175)

1996 CRC Synod adopts "Biblical and Theological Principles for the Development of a Racially and Ethnically Diverse Family of God" (182–183)

1997 Madison calls Pastor Samuel Reeves to serve as co-pastor with Pastor David Beelen (104–105)

Audrey Laninga is hired as Director of Arts and Worship (120)

Restorers, Inc. launches with Renita Reed as its first Director (194–196)

Pastor Andre Daley becomes CentrePointe's second pastor (197)

1998 Reynolds and the Madison Gospel Choir produce their first worship CD (124)

1999 Madison adopts a formal partnership with Providence Baptist Church, Monrovia, Liberia (105–108)

2000 Dr. Ron and Mary Van Valkenburg construct the En Gedi Center at 1441 Prospect (210)

2001 Reynolds moves to Resurrection Life; Charsie Sawyer becomes the choir director (125)

Madison, Church of the Servant (COS), and Coit Community Church begin antiracism training (183)

2002 Madison's Antiracism Team (MART) is commissioned (184)

2003 Pastor Mark Mayor is called as CentrePointe's third and final pastor (197)

2003 Christy Carlin Knetsch becomes Madison's director of youth ministry (153)

2004 Reeves returns to his home church, Providence Baptist Church, as its Senior Pastor (107)

2005 Beelen is joined by the preaching team of Joy Bonnema, Cisco Gonzalez, and Alton Hardy (197–198)

Sandra Hardy becomes the second director of Restorers, Inc. (196)

Madison changes from two to three morning services (127)

2006 Nick Hopkins becomes the choir director (125)

Madison, COS, and Coit form *Congregations Organizing for Racial Reconciliation* (186)

Madison Place at 1401 Madison is purchased, renovated, and dedicated (198–199)

Beelen launches the *Antioch Leadership Development Network* (148)

2007 Alton Hardy becomes campus pastor of Madison's first multisite at the Ford school (198)

April 13, 2007 Pastor Dante Venegas passes away from cancer

2008 Joy Bonnema becomes Madison's first pastor of congregational life (166–167)

2009 MART is affirmed as a "sub-team" of council (184)

Cisco Gonzalez launches "Jesus and Me" (JAM), initially meeting at the downtown YMCA (206)

2010 Leslie Montgomery becomes Madison's choir director (125)

Hardy acknowledges his reservations about women in church leadership roles (167–168)

2011 Hardy resigns as Ford's Campus Pastor (201)

2012 Brad Knetsch is affirmed by the Ford congregation as their new campus pastor (202)

Kafi Carrasco becomes the third director of Restorers, Inc. (196)

Madison is awarded a Calvin Institute grant to study tabernacle worship (121–122)

Ken and Claudie Vos become the prayer leaders (131, 133)

Victoria Gibbs and Patty Hogan are appointed as Reaching IN co-directors (158, 188)

Ricardo Tavarez becomes the director of outreach and community partnerships (158)

Darrell Delaney becomes middle school youth ministry coordinator (158)

2013 James Abney becomes Madison's Gospel choir director (125)

Madison North launches at Kent Hills Elementary with Bonnema as campus pastor (208–209)

2014 Kristen Buurma Lewis is ordained as children's ministries pastor at the Square (171)

Darrell Delaney called and ordained as pastor at the Square Campus (133, 210, 216)

Madison and St. Francis Xavier jointly celebrate their Centennial (28)

Madison's Centennial culminates with special celebration activities in August (227–230)

Gonzalez and JAM transitions to a church plant with Calvary CRC, Wyoming, MI (207)

2015 The 415 Franklin building is donated to Madison as Ford's "future and permanent campus" (205–206)

2016 The Van Valkenburgs donate the En Gedi Center to Madison Square Church (210)

Epilogue

"Leaning on the Lord"

BY DARRELL DELANEY

> In all my prayers for all of you, I always pray with joy
> because of your partnership in the gospel
> from the first day until now,
> being confident of this,
> that he who began a good work in you
> will carry it on to completion
> until the day of Christ Jesus.
>
> Philippians 1:6

God Is on the Move

God is on the move at Madison Square Church. God has used this past century to log a dramatic history of His story through this church. He has dipped His pen into the river of history and chronicled what has been nothing short of amazing. What you have read in each chapter can only be regarded as a miraculous faith journey. We have truly come this far by faith—a faith journey by people whose trust in God enabled them to take chances, make sacrifices, and follow the Lord in ways that have made an eternal difference for many people. I have met up with people who used to attend Madison and who, once they learn I am a pastor here, are eager to share their faith stories. They have fond memories of deep encounters with God or of people of God blessing them in a special way while they were here. I am honored to be a person whom God has chosen to be a part of this wonderful journey.

And God is not done yet. Even though the ink has dried on past decades, God is dipping the pen again, but this time to chronicle the future. I would be lying if I said I knew what God is going to do with his Bride at Madison. But every now and then God gives me glimpses, mini-previews of what He is up to. When the Spirit of God moves during worship services, I see a glimpse of the past and the future at the same time. When I listen to people

The Delaney Family

Pastor **Darrell** and **Kia** were married in 2004 and have three children: Christopher, Tristan, and Acacia. Delaney obtained a Master of Divinity degree and Grad. Cert. of Urban Pastoral Theology from Western Seminary in 2012; he was awarded a Masters in Theology from Calvin Seminary in 2014. Serving as pastor for Madison's Square Campus, his sweet spots in ministry are shepherding, teaching, evangelism, and mentoring. He enjoys walking, blogging, family time, and chess. His life verse is John 15:16.

For we are God's handiwork, created in Christ Jesus to do good works, which God prepared in advance for us to do. (Ephesians 2:10)

and walk with them through difficult times, I recognize I am standing on holy ground. When people are led to the Lord, when people walk through the community spreading love and hope, and when people are prayed for, I see God moving in those places as well. Again, I am excited and humbled to be a part of what God is doing.

Learning to Follow

Madison's vision is often summarized this way: *Following Christ together as diverse communities.* My sincere prayer is that God will empower us at Madison to follow Christ more closely in several important ways.

Making New Disciples

As we follow Christ more closely into the future, I believe He will deepen the ways in which we walk alongside one another in discipleship. In walking the way of repentance, we will see new paths open before us. We will discover tools that help us understand where we are along the way. We will use these tools to grow one another for higher levels of discipleship in Christ. This is key: Building one another up as disciples and disciplemakers. Walking as Jesus walked will lead us to greater unity, justice, and shalom.

Embracing New Partners

As one small part of God's church family, I believe God is calling Madison to embrace new and expanded ministry partnerships in the greater Grand Rapids area and around the world. This may mean cooperating with service organizations that engage our communities for the common good. This may involve launching new sites and planting new churches for drawing more neighbors to fall in love with God and one another. This may include partnering with missionaries in other lands for making more and better disciples of Jesus everywhere.

Enlarging the Circle

In His providence, God has been leading Madison on an already long and tedious antiracism journey. In past decades this journey has been a predominantly Black/White conversation. As God guides us in the twenty-first century, He is expanding our table to include other people groups. Asians, Latinos, Native Americans, biracial folks, and others are already gathering around the table. And through God's transforming work of reconciliation, He will convict us of our past failures in acknowledging and valuing one another and will empower us to more fully love and embrace each other as equally precious image bearers of God.

> **"Lord, stir up within us a 'divine discontent'"—a feeling of dis-ease with the status quo accompanied by a hunger for something more.***
>
> *David Sieplinga's 2009 recollection of a frequent prayer by Pastor Dante Venegas

Grateful Being and Doing

In keeping with God's call upon Madison in years past, I see God raising up leaders in each new generation. God calls us as His people to grow up into Him and empowers us to make life-giving differences in our homes, our schools, our work, our extracurricular activities, and our social networks. Also, God has already been showing us that *being* the church is more important than *doing* church. As we dig down to what lies beneath the surface of our lives, God shows us that when we allow His truth to reign—the truth that we are already loved and valued by Him, and that we have done nothing to earn His love—who we *are* in Him supersedes what we *do* for Him. It is out of gratitude that we serve. It's the least we can do.

God gives us these glimpses of His vision—a vision too big for any one person or even a whole congregation to accomplish! But that is just the way God likes it. He sovereignly casts a world-changing vision that overwhelms all human effort. And then He challenges us to shed the cocoon of the status quo and take on the metamorphosis of spiritual boldness at a level that Madison has yet to experience.

Deep trusting and bold following will cost us. There will be sacrifice! But we know that the future is also His story, and by His grace we are privileged to participate in it.

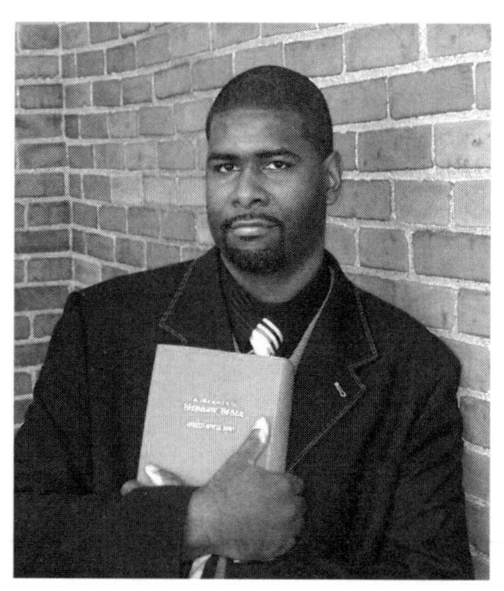
Pastor Darrell Delaney

Learning to Lean

So, what is God up to next? Yes, Madison has come this far by faith. Madison has done its best, and in God's surprising grace it has been blessed richly. As Madison leans into the future, if God is to be glorified in His own way, and if the Lord is to have free rein in all our comings and goings, we need to lean on the Lord as we never have done before. "Whoever has ears, let them hear what the Spirit says to the churches" (Rev. 3:6).

> **Therefore, I urge you, brothers and sisters, in view of God's mercy, to offer your bodies as a living sacrifice, holy and pleasing to God—this is your true and proper worship. (Romans 12:1)**

As we follow our Lord with abandon, we will move the ball forward incrementally. We will follow Christ together as part of the Church universal, which includes believers already with the Lord—that great cloud of witnesses—cheering us on. With the Spirit of God blowing fresh wind upon us, with our resurrected Lord interceding for us and empowering us, and with the Father tenderly caring for us, leaning on our Triune God will carry us boldly into His future.

Undoubtedly we will face uncertain days; at times we may even feel compelled to make decisions when we are unclear about the Lord's purposes. But even when we cannot trace Him, we will trust Him; we will lean on Him, knowing that He's never failed us yet!

He is able to do this because He
is almighty God,
He desires to do this because
he is a faithful Father.[1]

1. "Lord's Day 9," *The Heidelberg Catechism.*

Acknowledgments

With gratitude to the One Great Author and Finisher, the editorial team thanks all those who assisted in the composition of this book. We thank the Calvin College Heritage Hall, the Grand Rapids Public Library, and Madison Square Church—its staff persons and individual members. We especially acknowledge those persons listed below for helping to make *This Far by Faith* become a reality.

Centennial Celebration Committee and Centennial Book Committee

Pastor David Beelen
Ardie Burger
Don Bryant
Victoria Gibbs, co-chair
Don Huizinga, co-chair
Joel Niewenhuis
Marisol Rosser
Bob Schuyler
Brenda Schuyler
Jackie Venegas
Claudie Vos
Ken Vos
William A. Wiarda

Editorial Team

Don Bryant
Victoria Gibbs
Al Mulder
Jackie Venegas
William A. Wiarda

Lead Writers

Pastor David Beelen
Andrea Bult
Pastor Darrell Delaney
Donald J. Griffioen
Audrey Laninga
Lois Meyne
Al Mulder
Richard Rockwood
Bob Schuyler
Reginald Smith

Contributors

Kathleen Ammons
Betsy Bascom
Lorilee Craker
Christy Carlin Knetsch
Earl James
Pastor Sam Reeves
Brenda Schuyler
Bill Zeilstra

Photography

Don Bryant
Shelli Fynewever
Alfield Reeves
William A. Wiarda

Special Helps

Rudy Carrasco
Denise Fase
Pastor Emmett Harrison
Ben McKnight, council chair
Carla Mockabee
Linda Naranjo-Huebl
Joel Niewenhuis
Lori Robbins
Ann Spangler
Steve Timmermans

Publishing

Pierre Camy, Chapbook Press
Dan Malda, format and design
Ed Van Poolen, book cover
Lindsey Spoolstra, copyediting

Appendix A

"I Remember When. . . ."

COMPILED BY VICTORIA GIBBS

Along the way to creating *This Far by Faith*, members of the editorial team interviewed a special group of long-time Madison members. These faithful folks included Ardie Burger, Bruce Cancler, Lee Coy Cancler, Rodney Cancler, Karen Coger, Don and Dorothy Huizinga, Ron Joseph, Marty and Lois Meyne, Lu Mulder, and Marian Takens. Their treasured reflections—from the 1940s into the 1980s—are organized under a series of leading questions, with each response identified by the member's first name.

Why did you decide to join Madison?

Karen: I first came when it was Madison Square Gospel Center in a storefront on Madison and Crawford; I came because it was the closest CRC in the area.

Ardie: I was assured that a suit and tie wasn't necessary to come into the church, so I came in. I started getting to know people, appreciated the music, and accepted that God was working in mysterious ways. I've always felt like this is where I'm supposed to be.

Bruce: Madison was Baptist, Pentecostal, and Reformed all mixed into one. I was attracted to this diversity since I was ten years old. I also like it that Madison is a Bible-believing church.

Don: When we started coming in 1969, there was a group called People Against Racism (PAR). This was a very powerful experience, so we decided to stay and have been here ever since.

Dorothy: The fact that Madison was integrated was the biggest attraction for us; churches we attended before were not willing to have integration.

Marian: I needed to find a place where singles fit in because a lot of churches typically were family-oriented. Also, I wanted a church that stayed true to God's Word and was moving toward multiculturalism.

Long term members, from left to right. Back row: Marty Meyne, Lee Coy Cancler, Bruce Cancler, Ardie Burger, Rodney Cancler, Don Huizinga, Ron Joseph. Front row: Lois Meyne, Karen Coger, Marian Takens, Dorothy Huizinga. Not pictured: Lu Mulder

What were some defining moments for you in Madison's history?

Karen: My husband died while I was expecting a baby and that was tough. Pastor Geurkink promised to visit me in the hospital and he did what he said he would do. He also worked to make sure I was connected to a small group of people for support.

Don: Pastor Patterson went to South Africa with denominational leaders to help convince South African Whites to turn from apartheid. While he was there he had to wear a badge that made him an "honorary white man" and allowed him to be in places where African "coloreds" were not allowed to go. This was extremely painful for him and changed him.

Lee Coy: The trip to South Africa was the last straw. It kind of hit him in the gut.

Lois: Patterson was the "token Black" and was used by the denomination; this also drew his energy away from Madison.

Bruce: Patterson started the movement of the Spirit, and this has stayed with Madison.

Dorothy: At the time Patterson began emphasizing the outward leading of the Spirit, there was resistance from many of the congregants.

Lu: Patterson really pushed the congregation to grow and lean into the prompting of the Holy Spirit at a time when no one was accustomed to this type of leading. In essence he wanted us to "grow up."

Lee Coy: Even though I was just a teenager, I told my mom that Patterson's change in preaching style would cause him to not be around very long.

Marty: He talked to me a lot because I went to deliver his check to him, and we would have deep conversations. He confided to me that two things caused him to leave: the doctrine of the Holy Spirit and the racial issues.

Ron: Although Patterson started the move of the Spirit, Pastor Dante enhanced the free worship and move of the Spirit.

Don: It took a while for us to stop sitting in the pews like a bunch of rocks; we were really slow to engage in "call and response" style of preaching.

Marian: Using the entire body for worship was so different for me; when I was a child my dad would pull my ears for moving at all.

Ardie: With the arrival of Pastor Dante and Jackie, there were changes in musical style. Many believe this is what was at the heart of our sudden new growth.

Ron: Pastor Dante encouraged greater freedom in worship and the movement of the Holy Spirit, and Jackie played the piano just like a homey.

Lu: We could choose songs from the *Red Book* versus the preselected songs on the board.

Marian: You didn't even have to see if it was Jackie playing; you just knew it was her.

Don: Women in leadership.

Ardie: The decision was made and we as a church held our ground.

Marian: Yes, women being allowed in leadership. A while ago I had a surgical procedure and male leaders visited me. I realized then how having a woman visit with the authority of the church behind her would have been much more inviting. I also was the first female to serve on Madison's council.

What have you appreciated about Madison over the years?

Karen: I feel God's presence at Madison all the time and have always wanted an environment that was multicultural.

Lee Coy: All of the pastors have blended well and have made everyone feel at home.

Lois: Madison is diverse in many ways: Age, race, education, socioeconomic. The thing we share in common is Jesus. People come with a little of this tradition and a little of that, and when it all comes together we are richer.

Don: There have been a lot of young White people who were not as entrenched in tradition and keeping things the way they were. They were committed to "working their way through" to see if it would work.

Dorothy: There is this openness to see what God has in store and what God has blessed during the changes.

Don: Only God could produce and use "this motley group."

Rodney: The teaching element has always been strong; we leave every Sunday knowing something more about Jesus. What also keeps me coming back is the diversity—different pastors and different congregants.

Marian: There is no perfect church; I won't find that until God calls me home. But I do experience authenticity, and it is obvious to me that our pastors love God's word.

In what other ways have you seen God shape Madison?

Lois: Justice has always been a big issue at Madison. We did a lot of things because we were concerned about justice.

Don: If you were hurting in the CRC, you came to Madison. That's how it became the "church of the broken wing."

Ardie: A strong point for Madison is being a "sending church," preparing people for service and then sending them into the mission field.

Don: Pastor Dante brought the salt and pepper teams together that went into the neighborhood. He could get people to start talking about Jesus within thirty seconds; he was amazing. Every conversation led to Jesus.

Don: We wanted to be a multicultural church. But when we first went from two to three services, the middle service was filling up with White Calvin students. We didn't want this, but we soon recognized that we had to be the church for whoever showed up.

Lois: We emphasized playing with the children because we wanted them to know that Christians have fun.

Bruce: When we reached the kids with the Word, they would draw the parents.

Would you share an interesting or poignant anecdote?

Rodney: I remember being accused of going to a White church.

Bruce: Pastor Patterson made a marked impression on my father when he came to visit him; he told him he didn't have to hide his beer because "I'm not God; I'm just your pastor."

Lu: We took turns cleaning the church as Household Groups (Care Groups) because we could not afford to hire anyone.

Marian: One time, when I was cleaning with Pastor Sieplinga, he informed me that we couldn't clean too well or it would look like a suburban church.

Don: We wanted a pastor that was excited about urban ministry. Pastor Sieplinga was so excited about coming to Madison that he said he would be here for the rest of his pastoral life. So when he left, we let him have it.

Lois: We would go into congregational meetings and say, "Hokey Pete, there is no unity here, nothing but arguing." But everyone just had to have their say, because at the end of the meeting we were all on the same page.

To view the complete interviews, see www.madisonsquarechurch.org/history

The "100+ Happy Anniversary Madison" banner, designed by Tim Jen, graces the main entrance

Appendix B

Madison 2014 Centennial Celebration

August Centennial Thanksgiving Meals

One hundred years of faithful ministry and eighteen months of diligent planning culminated in a monthlong series of worship services and other celebratory centennial events. Granting that every ninety-minute worship service is food for the soul, August 2014 consisted of a rich and enriching menu of Thanksgiving meals.

Sunday, August 3, 9AM & 11AM

Worship leading by Shelli Fynewever and Gordon Griffin

Preaching by Pastor Emmett Harrison of Oakdale Park CRC

Hebrews 11:20–22, "The Journey of Faith"

Sunday, August 3, 1PM

Congregants gathered in nearby Garfield Park to fellowship with honored guests from Providence Baptist Church in Monrovia, Liberia. Everyone enjoyed a noon meal featuring Liberian and American dishes and then expressed fond farewells as the Liberian guests departed for their homeland.

Sunday, August 10, 9AM & 11AM

Worship leading by Laura Pritchard and Jackie Venegas

Preaching by former Madison pastor David Sieplinga, Emeritus

Isaiah 61:1–7, "100 Years of the Lord's Favor"

A Hearty Side Dish

Madison Square was one of two churches in the neighborhood celebrating one hundred years of God's faithfulness. The other was St. Francis Xavier, only a few blocks away at 250 Brown St. Early in 2014, the two congregations began celebrating their centennials by observing Ash Wednesday together (see page 28). On August 16, Madison joined St. Francis in a day-long "100+ Celebration" festival! Madison hosted a daytime booth featuring a variety of ethnic foods; St. Francis topped off the evening with a concert by famed Nicaraguan American guitarist Tony Melendez.

Also see http://www.mlive.com/living/grand-rapids/index.ssf/2014/02/charley_honey_two_century-old.html, and "Like Never Before" and "Two Centennials" at www.madisonsquare-church.org/history

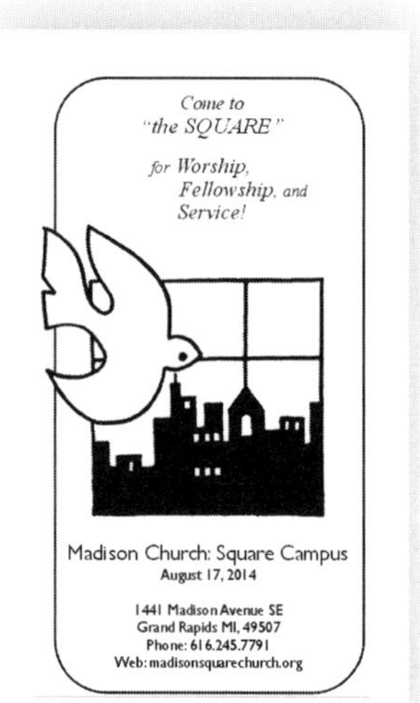

The Sunday bulletin design is a reproduction from the 1980s.

Sunday, August 17, 9AM & 11AM

Worship leading by Madison Square Gospel Choir

Preaching by former pastor Samuel Reeves from Providence Baptist Church, Liberia

Ephesians 2:10, "Shaped for Service"

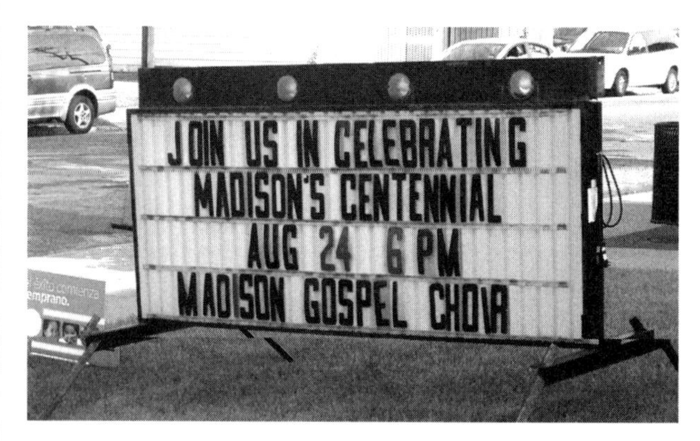

Madison's outdoor portable sign invited all passers-by to take in the August 24 Gospel Choir's centennial concert at the Square.

Sunday, August 24, 9AM & 11AM

Worship leading by Ken Reynolds Jr.

Preaching by Senior Pastor David Beelen

1 Sam. 7:1–12, "Stones of Remembrance"

An After-Dinner Centennial Concert: Madison Square Gospel Choir with former director Nick Hopkins holding the microphone and director James Abney facing the choir

Madison Square Church Centennial Concert

Sunday, August 24, 2014 at 6 p.m.

Featuring Director James L. Abney, Sr. and the Gospel Choir

"We've Come This Far by Faith"

Welcome and Opening Prayer	*Rev. David Beelen, Lead Pastor*
Gospel Choir:	
"So Glad I'm Here in Jesus' Name"	James Abney, Director and Lead
"Awesome God"	James Abney, Director and Ayana Johnson, Lead
"The Lord Is my Light"	Pastor Nick Hopkins, Director
"Total Praise"	Dr. Charsie Sawyer, Director; Trio: Stacia Hoeksema, Sharon Harris, James Abney
"I Bowed on My Knees"	James Abney, Director, Bob Schuyler, Lead
"He's Able"	Ken Reynolds, Director, Leads: Ricardo Tavarez, Ben Reynolds
Offering for *Camp Tall Turf*	*Pastor Darrell Delaney, Square Campus*
URUYANGE Rwandan Dance Group	Christine Ingabire, Instructor
100 Years - Historical Slideshow	Maurice Townsend and Worship Team

"What will be your contribution to the next 100 years?" - Video

Gospel Choir:	
"We've Come This Far by Faith"	Beth Mellema, Director, Leads: Jay Laninga, Sara Fynewever-Muyskens, Shelli Fynewever
"My All"	James Abney, Director; Herb Fynewever, Narrator
"Glorious"	Laura Pritchard, Director and Shelli Fynewever, Lead
"Sovereign God Medley"	James Abney, Director
"Every Praise" Finale Dancers	James, Nick, Ken, Charsie and Maurice with Choir and Dancers

All Glory to God!

Following the choir performance, concert-goers gathered in the community room at Madison Place for spirited fellowship and un-spirited drinks and desserts.

Centennial celebration leaders and others huddled around one hundred deliciously decorated centennial cupcakes. From left to right: (front row) Arturo Brizio from St. Francis Xavier, Claudie Vos, Pastor Emmett Harrison, Father José Luis Quintana of St. Francis Xavier, Brenda Schuyler, (back row) Bob Schuyler, Ken Vos, Don Bryant, Victoria Gibbs, Don Huizinga, Ardie Burger, (in the background) Pastor Darrell Delaney

Appendix C

Madison Missionaries 2016

BY BILL ZEILSTRA AND KATHLEEN AMMONS

Jesus said, "All authority in heaven and on earth has been given to me. Therefore go and make disciples of all nations, baptizing them in the name of the Father and of the Son and of the Holy Spirit, and teaching them to obey everything I have commanded you. And surely I am with you always, to the very end of the age."

Matthew 28:18–20

From the 1980s forward, Madison has supported many Christian missionaries both in the United States and around the world. One of the first and longest-term missionary teams was Terry and Judy Schram. Terry was a Wycliffe Bible Translator in Mexico; for a time Judy was Wycliffe's executive director.

Over the years, Madison has partially supported an estimated thirty missionaries for extended periods of time, as well as twenty short-term missionaries serving anywhere from a week to a year. Many of these partnerships have been with sons and daughters of Madison. Others were with college and seminary students who caught a vision for the mission of God while attending Madison. At one point Madison was sponsoring twenty-four missionaries and had a waiting list. In recent years, with a view to sustaining more vital relationships, Madison has limited its active missionary partners to one dozen.

The missions team is Madison's heart and hands for embracing its missionary partners. In an earlier day, team members would write letters, share cassette recordings of worship services, send Christmas gifts and greetings, and receive and distribute letters from the field. Salient points from missionary newsletters were transferred to 3 by 5 cards to assist team members with personal prayer support.

Since the mid-1980s, team members have sustained a monthly prayer time for missionaries. Communication between the congregation and missionaries has remained constant, but now is augmented with news through emails, newsletters, blogs, and videos by way of laptops and smartphones.

Troy and Faith Bierma

Troy and Faith Bierma, serving with Christian Reformed World Missions in Kathmandu, Nepal

Troy teaches at EPTS Seminary, and Troy and Faith participate in Gospel outreach with Crossway Church. They also are partners in a hydroponic farming business.

Did You Know? In Nepal people shake their heads side to side for "Yes" and nod up and down for "No."

Dave and Jessica Fick

Dave and Jessica Fick, serving with InterVarsity Christian Fellowship in Kansas City, Kansas, USA

Dave ministers to students at Kansas State University where he is starting up a chapter of InterVarsity Christian Fellowship.

Tim and Jeana Golin

Tim and Jeana Golin, serving with Youth with a Mission in Chiang Rai, Thailand

Tim teaches at the Discipleship Training School in Asia and serves the Mekong Minority Foundation. Jeana serves with the Family Learning Center, their children's school.

Did You Know? In Thailand, self-respect and respect of social hierarchy is crucial for everyone but the king. Also, visitors are called "holidaymakers."

Calvin and Jamie Hofland

Calvin and Jamie Hofland, serving with Christian Reformed World Missions in West Africa

Calvin treks to surrounding villages with the Scriptures and prayer. Jamie ministers in their village with her nursing skills.

Did You Know? At important events in West Africa, traditional storytellers sing songs about each guest, mentioning their name, physique, and personality.

Joel and Jeannie Huyser, serving with Christian Reformed World Missions, based in Dallas, Texas, USA

Joel develops and supports Transformational Networks in Central America and other countries, having previously been based in Nicaragua for eighteen years. He is also involved with Christian schools in Central America. Jeannie teaches English as a Second Language to many nationalities. Joel is also co-chairing the organizational design team for the merger of CRC World Missions and Home Missions.

Joel and Jeannie Huyser

Carlos and Becki Pinto

Renita Reed-Thomson

Carlos and Becki Pinto, serving with United World Mission (formerly Latin America Mission) in Quito, Ecuador

Carlos has a Christian radio program with Reach Beyond (formerly HCJB) and works with tribal missionaries and church leaders. Becki works with Corrientes, an organization that trains South American missionaries before they go to the field.

Did You Know? Family (nuclear and extended) is of great importance in Quito, and festivals are common.

Renita Reed-Thomson, serving as the Discipling Marketplace Leaders (DML) Director, International Christian Ministries

Renita equips pastors and church leaders to disciple members involved in the Marketplace (business, education, and government), in keeping with the Great Commandment, the Great Commission, and the Creation Mandate. DML ministry is underway in Kenya, Ghana, Guatemala, Ethiopia, and Nigeria.

Tim and Angie Sliedrecht

Tim and Angie Sliedrecht, serving with World Outreach Ministries and Christian Reformed World Missions in Uganda

Tim and Angie are involved with Team Beyond, ministering to orphans, widows, and former child soldiers, and also fostering spiritual growth in the local church.

Did You Know? More than forty languages are spoken in Uganda, a country the size of Oregon.

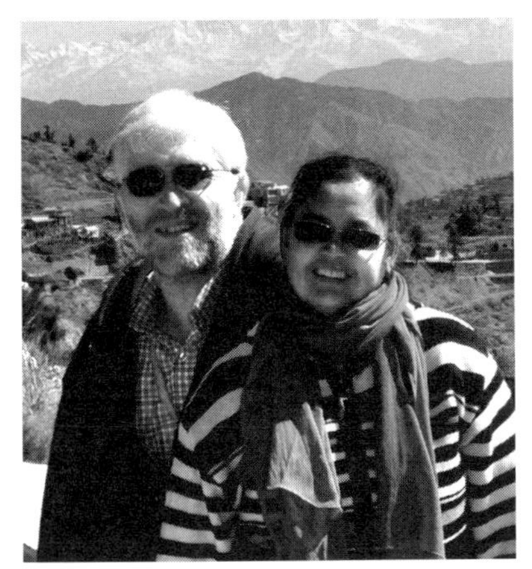

David and Daphne Smith

David and Daphne Smith, serving with Pioneers in Mussoorie, India

David and Daphne trek and camp in the small surrounding villages doing Friendship Evangelism with prayer and Bible stories. They lead a team of native missionaries. They are using Smart Dhobis (manual plunger washing machines) in their evangelization work.

Diann Takens-Cerbone

Diann Takens-Cerbone, serving with Peace of the City in Buffalo, New York, USA

Diann runs an after-school homework club and teen program, including a music and drama ministry for inner city kids. The kids produce yearly Shakespeare productions.

Jodi Ross

Jodi Ross, serving with Equip Inc. in Soddo, Ethiopia

Jodi is a nurse working with Soddo Christian Hospital. She participates in helicopter mission trips with Ethiopian missionaries and conducts prenatal clinics in outlying areas.

John and Chi Chi Eigege and family

John and Chi Chi Eigege, serving with New Life Christian Reformed Church in Houston, Texas, USA

John is Community Chaplain of the Third Ward in Houston. As part of a Transformational Network, John encourages, equips, and networks faith-based ministries as well as businesses and public institutions for the social and spiritual renewal of the neighborhood.

Go and Make Disciples of All Nations

The Great Commission
leads from above and from up front
even as the world is
both smaller and larger than ever

Surely Jesus is with us Always, to the End of the Age

Appendix D

List of Photos and Illustrations

Unless otherwise acknowledged in captions or footnotes, photos and illustrations are provided by Madison Square Church and its members.

For more photos, illustrations, and other historical information regarding Madison Square Church, see **www.madisonsquarechurch.org/history**